THE DOORS

THE ILLUSTRATED HISTORY

Also by Danny Sugerman
NO ONE HERE GETS OUT ALIVE

THE DOORS
THE ILLUSTRATED HISTORY

By Danny Sugerman

Edited by Benjamin Edmonds
With a Foreword by Jerry Hopkins

WILLIAM MORROW AND COMPANY 1983

This book consists of magazine and newspaper articles, interviews, record reviews, excerpts from books, and other material related to the history of The Doors, to whose memory it is dedicated.

Design by Lesley Achitoff

Library of Congress Cataloging in Publication Data
Sugerman, Daniel.
The Doors, the illustrated history.

1. Doors (Musical group)   2. Rock groups—United
States—Pictorial works.   I. Edmonds, Benjamin.   II. Title.
ML421.D66S9   1983   784.5'4'0922   [B]   83-691
ISBN 0-688-01362-7
ISBN 0-688-01363-5 (pbk.)

Printed in the United States of America

8   9   10

Grateful acknowledgment is made for permission to quote from the following:
Chapter I: "Love and the Demonic Psyche" by Digby Diehl, *Eye* magazine, April 1968. Reprinted by permission of the author.   "Artaud Rock: The Dark Logic of the Doors" by Bill Kerby, *UCLA Daily Bruin,* May 24, 1967. Reprinted by permission of the author.   "The Doors at the Whiskey-a-Go-Go" by Pete Johnson, *Los Angeles Times,* July 18, 1966. Copyright © 1966 by *The Los Angeles Times.* Reprinted by permission.   "What Goes On," *Crawdaddy!,* Issue #7. Reprinted by permission.   "Rock Is Rock: A Discussion of a Doors Song" by Paul Williams, *Crawdaddy!,* 1967. Copyright © 1967 by Paul Williams. Reprinted by permission.   "Pop Eye" by Richard Goldstein, *The Village Voice,* January 22, 1967. Reprinted by permission of *The Village Voice* and the author.   "The Doors Open Wide" by Richard Goldstein, *New York Magazine,* March 19, 1967. Copyright © 1967 by News Group Publications, Inc. Reprinted by permission of *New York Magazine* and the author.   "Pop Eye" by Richard Goldstein, *The Village Voice,* March 23, 1967. Reprinted by permission of *The Village Voice* and the author.   "Teen Talk" by Susan Szekely, *New York Post,* April 7, 1967. Copyright © 1967, New York Post Corporation. Reprinted by permission of the *New York Post.*   "The Doors," *Hullabaloo,* October 1967. Reprinted by permission of *Circus* magazine.   "Doors Open Up" by Pete Johnson, *Los Angeles Times,* February 26, 1967. Copyright © 1967, *Los Angeles Times.* Reprinted by permission.   "The New Group" by Paul Nelson, *Hullabaloo,* May 1967. Reprinted by permission of *Circus* magazine.   "Doors Producer Paul Rothchild Speaks" by Paul Williams, *Crawdaddy!,* August 1967. Copyright © 1967 by Paul Williams. Reprinted by permission.   "What Goes On" by Paul Williams, *Crawdaddy!,* Issue #11. Copyright by Paul Williams. Reprinted by permission.   "Doors, a Way In and a Way Out" by Robert Windeler, *The New York Times,* November 20, 1967. Copyright © 1967 by The New York Times Company. Reprinted by permission.   "The Doors Seek Nirvana Vote Here" by Alfred G. Aronowitz, *The New York Times,* November 25, 1967. Copyright © 1967 by The New York Times Company. Reprinted by permission.   Caption to photo by Alexis Waldek appearing with "Love, Mysticism, and the Hippies" by Kurt von Mier, *Vogue,* 1967. Courtesy *Vogue.* Copyright © 1967 by The Condé Nast Publications, Inc.   **Chapter II:** "Four Doors to the Future: Gothic Rock Is Their Thing" by John Stickney, *Williams College News.* Reprinted by permission of *The Williams Record* and the author.   *The Way of the Shaman,* abridged from pp. ix and xii in *The Way of the Shaman: A Guide to Power and Healing* by Michael Harner. Copyright © 1980 by Michael Harner. Reprinted by permission of Harper & Row, Publishers, Inc.   "Doors and Kinks" by Sandy Pearlman, *Crawdaddy!,* Issue #12. Copyright by Paul Williams. Reprinted by permission.   "Love and the Demonic Psyche," Part II, by Digby Diehl, *Eye* magazine, April 1968. Reprinted by permission of the author.   "This Way to Egress," *Newsweek,* November 6, 1967, page 101. Copyright © 1967, by Newsweek, Inc. All Rights Reserved. Reprinted by permission.   "Pop Music: Swimming to the Moon," *Time,* January 24, 1967. Copyright © 1967 by Time Inc. All Rights Reserved. Reprinted by permission from Time.   "The Doors at the Hullabaloo" by Hank Zevallos, *Happening.* Reprinted by permission of *Happening* and the author.   "Who's Afraid of Jim Morrison?" by Judith Sims, *Teen Set,* February 1968. Reprinted by permission of the publishers, Regensteiner Press Enterprises, Inc.; the editors, Capitol Records; and the author.   "Wicked Go The Doors" by Fred Powledge, *Life* magazine, April 12, 1968. Reprinted by permission of the author.   "New Haven Police Close 'The Doors,'" *The New York Times,* December 11, 1967. Copyright © 1967 by The New York Times Company. Reprinted by permission.   "Strange Days" by Gene Youngblood, *Los Angeles Free Press,* December 1, 1967. Copyright © 1967 by New Way Enterprises, Ltd. Reprinted by permission.   Review of "Strange Days" by Eric VanLustabader, *Circus.* Reprinted by permission of *Circus* magazine.   "Pop Eye," by Richard Goldstein, *The Village Voice,* December 14, 1967. Reprinted by permission of *The Village Voice* and the author.   Lizze James Interview with Jim Morrison, Part I. Reprinted by permission of the author.   **Chapter III:** Excerpt from pages 21 through 25 of *The White Album* by Joan Didion. Copyright © 1979 by Joan Didion. Reprinted by permission of Simon & Schuster, a Division of Gulf & Western Corpora-

(continued on page 206)

CONTENTS

FOREWORD

After the plague, Jim Morrison wrote, there would be an incredible springtime, a celebration. First, though, must come the plague, and there must be death, famine, darkness, and sickness. Those then must be cured by the shaman séance. Cured by ecstasy and celebration.

Danny Sugerman, a typical teenager, was plagued. He saw The Doors and during the first half of the concert subconsciously acknowledged the sickness, the separation. By the second half of the ceremony, he was cured, or believed he was. He felt different; he felt better, stronger. Morrison and The Doors touched him through the magic of music. The brotherhood of the audience engulfed him. Where once there was confusion and nothingness, there now stood a family and a leader.

Morrison pointed; Sugerman followed. And he made it his job to get as close as possible to this band and to this man who had told him to dance on fire and break on through. Danny felt an irresistible force drawing him in, coupled with a desire to serve his new guide. You could call him a fan, a gofer, but it didn't matter. As Sugerman himself has admitted, "Hell, you could have called me Morrison's pet and I wouldn't have minded."

Of course he wasn't, although he was virtually The Doors' mascot. Easily ten years the junior of everybody in The Doors' office, he was—from the moment of that fateful concert—ready, willing, and available, cutting classes to help or merely to hang out. He was given small chores. He sorted through the weekly sack of press clippings and assembled a scrapbook. He opened the mail, searching for answers; it was almost as if Danny hoped to discover the secret of his own transformation in the writings of the fans, and he reveled in the confirmation the mail provided that, indeed, it was real—others had been touched, too. He answered the letters with Jim's blessings.

Mainly he lived for the next Doors concert. Danny got there any way he could, hitchhiking ridiculous distances for a fourteen-year-old. One weekend, he thumbed from L.A. to Bakersfield, some three hundred miles away, for one show on Friday; then after the show that same night, he went to San Diego, five hundred miles to the south, for the next concert.

The Doors traveled by bus that weekend, and there wasn't room for Danny. Morrison found out during the bus ride south, and, upon arrival in San Diego, gave Danny fifty pairs of concert tickets and a handful of backstages to give to "friends." Danny sold them, bought a case of Coors, and got drunk with Jim after the show. Jim then ordered The Doors' agent to fly him home and give him cab money.

Jim Morrison cared for Danny, and Danny idolized Jim in return—blinded by his devotion, he never judged his hero, never questioned him. And it is this exact devotion that brings Jim and The Doors to you today. It was this devotion and dedication that moved *No One Here Gets Out Alive* from my closet of unpublished manuscripts to the public eye. He created this book, went to The Doors' concerts, and, for nearly fifteen years, has talked to anyone who would listen to him about the magic and meaning of The Doors—all because of this devotion. I know The Doors are not Danny Sugerman's only purpose in life but I also know that the more he gives to The Doors' spirit, the better he feels.

It is no coincidence that Morrison convinced Sugerman to become a writer. (Morrison joked that it was the best way he knew to shut the kid up: just transfer the talk to paper.) Sugerman first wrote an interview with Jim. Morrison wrote down twenty questions and turned on a tape recorder, instructing Sugerman, "Ask them. Don't interrupt me. Never interrupt anyone you ever interview. When I'm finished, then ask me the next one, or if it fits, ask me something else." An hour later Morrison dropped the cassette on the desk of a typing service down the street. Later that week he picked it up, paying for it himself. Then at The Doors' office he called Sugerman to his side and wrote "By D. Sugerman" at the top. Thus was Danny's first article composed. Jim sent it off to a San Diego rock weekly. It was printed.

Much of the rest of the story is told in the pages of this book, for it is not an overstatement to say Danny's story is The Doors' story. Not even when Jim died—some say disappeared—under mysterious circumstances in Paris in 1971 did Danny's devotion and enthusiasm waver. If anything, they increased. At times it seemed Danny was determined to make Jim the object of a one-man cult.

Danny and I were friends by this time. I had met him when I first began researching *No One Here Gets Out Alive*, which was commissioned by Simon and Schuster, the publisher that printed my first Elvis Presley biography (which, in turn, had been suggested to me by Jim Morrison and therefore was dedicated to him). Simon and Schuster also published Jim's poetry, so it seemed appropriate that they publish his biography. But when the manuscript finally arrived in New York, after being rewritten and cut from the size of an elephant to that of an elephant's skeleton, Simon and Schuster determined that Jim

Morrison's time had come and gone. His poetry book, *The Lords and the New Creatures*, was selling poorly. Over the course of the next three years, the manuscript was submitted to and rejected by at least forty publishers, in Britain and the United States.

In 1978 I decided, the hell with it. I'd given Mr. Morrison enough of my energy for one lifetime. The manuscript was retired, shoved, literally, into my closet, into a box of other unpublished works. I told Danny what I had done. He was incredulous. "It's got to come out," he insisted. "Let *me* try!" he cried. "Let *me* find a publisher!" I shrugged, said, "Sure, why not, and if you find one, you can take ten percent off the top." In this manner, the elephant-sized manuscript again moved from office to office. More time passed.

One day about eight months later, Danny shouted the news: "I did it, I did it, I did it!" We had an offer from Warner Books. I shook my head. Warner Books had rejected the same manuscript *twice* before.

Actually, Warner Books still didn't want the biography, but the young editor Sugerman had contacted had a good track record. She had picked a number of successful books in a row and was given the go-ahead by her superiors, providing she could get the authors to agree to a piddling sum in advance ($1,500). We agreed in a flash.

Soon after that, Danny asked if he could work on the manuscript, sort of shuffle the two versions gracefully and add some content of his own, an introduction as well perhaps. He also suggested going after the poet Michael McClure, who had known Jim, to write an afterword. Danny's percentage was increased, and he became my co-author, writing me at one point:

"I saw Jimbo last night, in a dream. I never remember my dreams, but this one is very clear. It also was one of those dreams that didn't feel like a dream, it felt very real. I was walking across La-Cienega and Santa Monica Boulevards toward The Doors' office, and I saw Jim on the other side of the intersection, looking rather thin and Christ-like in blue jeans and a faded blue tee-shirt, bearded and very long-haired. And I said, 'Hey, man, I *got* to talk to you.' And he said, 'Man, you've grown up! You wanna go get a beer? Ya old enough to drink yet?' So we walked to the bar next door to Elektra and got a pitcher of beer and I told him I was rewriting the book on him and I wanted to know what kind of book he really wanted to immortalize him, as it were. And he took a swig off the beer and I was wondering how come he didn't get foam on his moustache like he used to and he gave me this real thoughtful look and then spoke: 'I don't know, man. My appearance in life was like a stamp. I just made impressions. I used people's consciousness as a sort of collective carbon paper. Write your impressions. You were close to me. The impressions are clear. Trust them. Be a journalistic mirror. In other words, write whatever you want, it can't be wrong. I gotta go now.' And he got up and disappeared! With the pitcher of beer! Weird fucking dream . . . "

What happened in the summer of 1980 seemed dreamlike, too, as *No One Here Gets Out Alive*— which took its title from one of Jim's songs—went rocketing to the top of *The New York Times* best-sellers list, then stayed on the list for nine months. A year later there were more than a million copies in print.

By this time Danny was managing the career of The Doors' keyboard player, Ray Manzarek, and doing management-publicity for The Doors. It was a dream come true. His reaction to the responsibility was simply to continue what he had been doing all along: spreading the word. He also got involved with some brash young Los Angeles bands and achieved a degree of success with several. But, really, it was Jim Morrison and The Doors who remained in full control. More and more, Danny found himself beating the drums for the man and the band through which he had been reborn. He called radio stations and wrote stories for magazines and hounded rock columnists and did interviews himself and bullied a television documentary into reality.

Simultaneously, the recordings of The Doors in Elektra's catalog sold in fantastic, unprecedented quantity: 2.5 million records sold in 1981, and even more in 1982, while *The Doors' Greatest Hits*, an album released ten years after Jim Morrison left the planet, became the band's all-time best-seller. Jim's picture and the band's logo and pictures began appearing on posters and lapel buttons again. The records were played on radios everywhere, attracting a new, young audience that thought The Doors were a new band (teenagers who were toddlers when The Doors were big in the sixties). More than a dozen national publications (including *Rolling Stone*) put Jim on their covers. As I write this, *three* major motion pictures are being planned.

Obviously, Danny's one-man cult has grown. So what follows is not the casual observer's story. It is Danny Sugerman's story, and it is his presentation of his friends, his mentor, his favorite band. I'll leave it to the sociologists and social historians and psychologists to explain why Jim Morrison is such a hero in the 1980s, and I'll leave it to the popular-music pundits to say why The Doors are such a seminal group.

And I'll leave it to Danny Sugerman to put forward the rest. True passion demands respect.

—*Jerry Hopkins*

INTRODUCTION

I spent four years watching, listening, and learning from Jim Morrison. Since then I have spent nearly eleven years talking and writing about him. I don't necessarily like that ratio, but then I can't have it any other way. Jim Morrison passed away July 3, 1971.

Repeating the experiences we shared seems to dilute rather than intensify my memories. Sometimes I fear I am losing one of my best friends. But, of course, I haven't lost a friend at all. Jim Morrison and The Doors are still with us today. I hear The Doors' music more than ever, and Jim leaps back to life in his full glory, roaring and very real. No, I haven't lost Jim Morrison, but I am called on to share him and I don't mind doing that at all. Writing about The Doors and Jim also brings him back to life in a sense, for me and for you, too.

I can still see myself fourteen years ago, sitting in Jim and Pamela's living room of their West Hollywood apartment. I am waiting, watching . . . wanting some action; wanting to go out and *do* something. After all, I reasoned, what good is it knowing Jim Morrison if I can't take him out and show him off a bit? But I sensed one of the reasons Jim tolerated my presence was because I didn't expect that sort of nonsense from him. But, of course, I did and he knew it. Bo Diddley was playing at the Whisky-a-Go-Go that night and Jim had promised me the week before that he'd take me out to see him. I was hoping he remembered and I wouldn't have to remind him. Jim meanwhile seemed oblivious to having made such a promise.

I was thinking such thoughts, sipping a Coors beer, while Jim sat in his big purple-velvet reading chair, looking very dignified in his leather pants and white Mexican wedding shirt. He was making notes in one of his notebooks, drinking Coors also. Pamela was in the kitchen making lasagna. A very domestic scene altogether. I was, however, bored shitless and it showed. So Jim picked up on it and said: "Don't you have any homework to do?" I lied: "I did it all." I wasn't about to let homework, or anything else, interfere with going out. "Don't you have any *books*? Anything to *read,* ya know, with *pages*?" "Not here, Jim." "And you have nothing left to learn, huh? You know it all?" I looked down at my feet. Jim was very good at making people feel uneasy. "Don't you have any *notes*? Something to study?" I shook my head. "Nothing to write either, I suppose." "No, Jim, nothing. I told you, I finished everything." He groaned; then he got up and lumbered slowly, like he did everything offstage slowly, over to the bookshelf, made up of boxes with their tops ripped off, turned on their sides, and stacked against and on top of each other. Jim must have saved every book he ever read. Kneeling in front of the boxes, he picked up a few books and peered at the titles. "Hmmmm, let's see what we have here that might possibly interest the inquisitive mind of a growing fourteen-year-old boy." The smirk was becoming broader. He started pulling books out and stacking them beside his knee. After gathering a significant pile, he picked them up and returned to his velvet throne. He set the books down on the little wicker table near his chair and picked up the top copy, turning it over in his hands, inspecting it. "Jack Kerouac." And he threw me *On the Road.* "I loved that when I was your age," he said. I flipped through a few pages. It seemed old to me. "Baudelaire," he said, sailing two more books my way," and if you like those, you'll love this," he continued, tossing over Rimbaud's *A Season in Hell* and *The Drunken Boat.* I became more and more uncomfortable. A copy of Edith Hamilton's Greek mythology volume then landed at my feet, followed rapidly by books by Jack London (*A Sailor on Horseback*), John Rechy (*City of Night,* which I am still shocked he gave me to read), and finally Sinclair Lewis's *Main Street.* I looked at the Hamilton mythology book, indignant. "This is the same shit they give me in school to read!" At that, Jim's smirk cracked into a smile as his satisfaction increased. "Exactly, that's right. Now shut yer hole and do your homework like a good boy. And I want you to remember what you've read because when you're finished I am going to test you."

Later that same night, during dinner, Jim and Pamela fought. Jim had poured too much wine and Pamela kept taking catnaps in her pasta. After her third or fourth dip, Jim turned to me. "So, I suppose you want to go *out* tonight, don't you?" "Well, yeah, sure, Jim, if you want to, that is . . . I'd love to . . ." He got up out of his chair and, standing, said, "Shut up and get your coat . . ." We headed toward the door, Jim slipping on his pea coat. Pamela was, by then, wide awake and livid. "Where are you going?" she screamed. "Jim Goddamn Morrison, you'd rather be with that fucking *kid* than at home . . . Goddamn you, I fix a decent meal for you . . . and *you* rather go out . . . and *pervert* some kid who's so fucked up he rather be with you than . . . at his own home . . . and *you're as bad as he is! Worse!* Fuck you, Jim! you aren't even listening to a word I've said . . . Jim!"

Pamela was still yelling as we skipped over the front lawn and up to the Sunset Strip, the Whisky-a-Go-Go, and Bo Diddley. Jim was laughing and running away, pushing and pulling me, warning, "C'mon man, before she starts throwing things; that chick has an arm you wouldn't believe!" We were thrown out of the Whisky when a drunken Jim screamed a string of obscenities at the audience and a thousand eyes moved in on us as the club manager grabbed us from behind and ushered us to safety through the fire door. "You try that shit again, Morrison, and somebody is gonna cut you."

Back home Jim insisted I climb through the window, since Pamela had dead-bolted the front door, locking us out. (It was a stunt Jim would have me later—and then consistently— perform to enter The Doors' office when he needed a place to crash.) Once back inside the apartment, Jim instructed me to go back to my reading. "You had your fun, your recreation period, I entertained you. Now you learn how to entertain yourself. That's what books are for. I'm not going to be around forever, you know. You do want to grow up and be smart, don't you? You don't want to be a loud-mouthed punk who doesn't know his asshole from his armpit for your entire life, do you? I'm tellin' ya, man, ya gotta read. You'll thank me someday, I swear."

Jim once wrote: "I won't come out, you must come in to me. Into my womb-garden where I peer out. Where I can construct a universe within the skull, to rival the real."* With Jim, the world could suddenly, without any warning, become bizarre and frightening. Sometimes he was gentle and reassuring, but occasionally his own inner terror leaped from the depths of his soul and entered into your soul. There were nights we tried to die flat on our backs, staring into space, without any sense other than that of falling and falling, having no control left, aware of nothing beyond Jim's hysterical laughter ringing in our ears, and his yelling, "Let's run . . . Run with me." "Run? Jim, I can't even get up." But he wanted to always get "inside the gates by evening"; "try to run, try to hide . . . Break on through to the other side." When you were with Jim, you went his way, or you didn't go at all.

Jim probably did die from self-indulgence, like Janis Joplin, Jimi Hendrix, Ernest Hemingway, Dylan Thomas . . . and, like them, Morrison made it look appealing, tempting. But Morrison wasn't into dope. He loved booze. "It's so sociable, and accessible . . . conventional. Besides, booze beats dope anyday for me. Soul beats money and booze beats dope. Hands down. Quote me." Morrison really drank with a flair; he was a marvelous drinker. Robby Krieger once remarked, "People would tell Jim he shouldn't drink so much and he'd take them out to talk about it and get them drunk in the process." Jim told buddy-poet Michael McClure he couldn't ever picture not drinking. He loved it. "He drank to hail and communicate with his muse," producer Paul Rothchild states. It was traditional for writers and poets to drink and so Jim justified it.

He was less honest about its effects. Drinking made life tolerable; it numbed the pain and enabled him to unlock worlds the pain otherwise overrode, blocked, and blanketed. Without the pain, Morrison would probably be alive today, but he would not have written what he did, he would not have generated a magic so powerful that it still lives today. He would be alive, yes, but we would not know him or care for him as we do now.

While Jim was alive, it was obvious to those of us who knew and loved him: We could not deal with his pain for him, we could offer no hand to help. We could only mutely wish it would go away. Between the hours of joyfully joining him down his path littered with genius and shit, we occasionally reminded ourselves that this absorbing man, for whom there was nothing we would not do, whom we loved so much and whose existence made ours so much richer, this great friend, was killing himself. Occasionally, someone told him, "I wish you wouldn't drink too much, Jim." He retorted, "I don't tell you how to live your life, why are you telling me how to live mine?" "Because we care, Jim." "Well, don't care." Jim did not care for our concern; he wanted us to listen, not care.

Jim was obsessed with discovery: finding meaning, understanding why we are and where we are going. He searched compulsively for the pulse of the world. As has been said of Rimbaud, Jim wanted also to "see all, feel all, exhaust everything, explore everything, say everything." He traveled as quickly as possible, always forward, purposeful, and confident.

He and The Doors had a purpose: They proposed to set us free and that didn't sit at all well with the authorities. The government was ahead of Jim, with its restrictions, its shackles, courts, and laws. Time and time again they beat Jim down. In New Haven, Connecticut, breach of peace was among the charges. How does a truth seeker breach peace? And he was arrested in Phoenix, Arizona—for inciting a riot; on the streets of L.A.—for drunk and disorderly behavior; and finally in Miami, Florida—the list of charges would take up an entire paragraph.

The only law Jim abided by was "be true to your own nature." And his law was the law of nonconformity. He found that for practicing what he spoke, he was regarded by writers as a fool. For trying to take his audience to Paradise now (rather than later), he was ridiculed. And this by the same writers who licked their lips and sharpened their pencils and dished out such delicious adjectives that meant (if you chose to take them literally) that Jim was a new messiah; The Doors were messengers from a strange, new, wonderful world; they were the greatest show on earth; and so on. Then, The Doors were told no one appreciated them . . . that Jim's efforts were in vain, no one was listening to them anymore, time had passed them by, that Jim was finally a cheerleader with no game going on, except the game his ego was playing inside his own head.

Jim had the choice of fighting his detractors. I asked him once how he dealt with them. "Detractors," he said, with a mischievous grin on his mug. "I either fight or run." Jim could have easily spent the rest of his life fighting, or running. But he could not and he would not compromise because compromise was not a word in his vocabulary. He was a fanatic. A person who went whole hog or died. In this lies much of Jim's purity, his innocence. For him to limit his self-destruction, curb his cruelty, or alter his behavior in any way would have meant compromise. That was a cop-out and that was unthinkable.

Jim could be tremendously kind; he was often charitable and hospitable. But Jim did not cultivate these traits; they were not his goals. They had nothing to do with his search, his attempt to merge with everybody and everything at once. That was Jim's concern. He wanted to get us off and get himself off in the process. (And I can picture him nodding his head in all earnestness: "Yeah, that would feel good. I could dig that.")

His charm and generosity were so extreme, however, they were self-destructive (as well as totally self-less). He gave himself away. Money, he lent, spent, and gave away. The man could not say no. When Jim Morrison drank, the room got drunk. He spent little directly on himself, but hosted his friends to rooms, food, drink, and women. Eventually, he fled L.A. to go to Paris, not to hide from any enemies, but to escape his friends and admirers. In Paris he found new friends, more bars, more fans, and, without a focus for his enormous talents and his rebellion, without any satisfying results from his strident search, he became bored, depressed, and confused. And he drank.

The pain of the mission became the pain of no mission at all. Simply because he had already done it all. But he wouldn't accept that. He still wanted more. Yet he had done all he was supposed to do, was born to do, all he could do. Jim died for the simplest of reasons. Like a retired career man who has a sudden heart attack after a lifetime of health, just when his life no longer has a purpose, Jim Morrison died because he had nothing else left to do.

Officially, Jim was in Paris with Pamela on vacation. The Doors had completed their album obligation to Elektra Records. They had been working hard, going at it for six long years. It was time for a break. They all needed and deserved one and, collectively, Jim Morrison, Robby Krieger, John Densmore, and Ray Manzarek agreed the time was right for some time off. (Jim called his sojourn "a sabbatical.")

Morrison went to Paris with a gleam in his eye and high hopes of starting a new life. In due time, he'd think about resuming the controversial life as a Door. In the meantime, he wanted to write some poetry, perhaps assemble notes taken during the Miami trial for a possible book, and do some sightseeing, all at a relaxed pace.

But Jim was not born into this world to take life easily. And the world was not willing to let him be anything other than The Doors' lead singer. His very nature defied tranquil existence, regardless of his needs; every fiber of his body was too taut for him to relax. His thirst for experience, sensation, and excitement was insatiable and, unfortunately, much greater than his need for rest. He could not slow down and he certainly could not stop.

It is plausible, though not likely, that Jim continued to run and to fight the image he'd been uncomfortably shouldering for the last years of his career. It is only true that, if there were a man alive who had the ability, the means, and the nerve to dive into anonymity, it was Jim. He did go to Paris to escape, and Paris was no escape at all. But the *reason*—Jim did not have a good enough reason to stage his own death. Sure he was sick of being Jim Morrison, especially the Jim Morrison people expected him to be, a personality he wasn't any longer. He could not escape this and, ultimately a realist, Jim knew and saw the truth. What he was looking for was not outside, it was inside: running would do no good. And he was sick of fighting. So he continued doing what he had been doing all along, what he knew how to do well, one of the few things left in life he really still enjoyed doing . . . to relieve the frustration, and the suffering, he got drunk.

Jim stared at death and evil to vanquish them. He contradicted William Blake who claimed "wallowing in the muck is not the best way of cleansing oneself." "Bullshit!" screamed Morrison. Jim was also inclined to believe that if you pulled hard enough on midnight you could unroll the dawn. Though Jim was not evil, his behavior often was. He did not advocate negativity. He certainly did not worship hell. But he did want to dynamite it so he could storm its gates and reveal it, exposing the domain of evil, until not a shred of mystery was left. "The evil is in the mind," Jim said, quoting and believing Nietzsche.

Jim Morrison insisted that his audience (specifically) and people (in general) find answers for themselves. Forget what you've been told, forget what you've been taught. Find out for yourselves. Read. Listen. Listen to the space between the words. Listen to the silence, to yourselves, and to your heart. Question all answers. Find out as much as possible, always seek and question, he encouraged. Otherwise the mind becomes stagnant. Morrison was big on learning, taking it all in, hearing everything, distilling the information, digesting the input, and arriving at his own conclusion, discovering the answer as it related to him. He expected the same of everyone.

That's what Jim did, what he encouraged me to do, and I believe it is exactly how he would want his fans to approach The Doors. It is with this philosophy in mind that I have assembled this book. It is not my history of The Doors, nor is it the history of The Doors as any one man could or would have it. It is not even The Doors' story as they perhaps would have it themselves. But it is The Doors as they were, and as they happened, lit and colored by a variety of different consciousnesses. It is told and photographed by those who were there, by those who understood what was happening, as well as those who often did not.

The Doors made people think. "Love us or hate us," they said, "but don't be indifferent." Jim once joked with an interviewer that the later press (circa *The Soft Parade*, their fourth studio album) was so negative because "The Doors are the band everybody loves to hate." Why? "Because we're so damn good."

One of my jobs when I worked for The Doors was to keep their official scrapbook. I'd go to every Doors concert I could and spend nearly every day at The Doors' office, ditching school to be near the action and the people I felt most drawn to and appreciated by. My fondest memories of that time are of being sprawled out on their brown carpet, piecing together envelopes of material a clipping service had sent in (and sent in, without fail, once a month), keeping and placing the clippings in sequential order. It was my way of trying to make some sense out of what was happening with such dizzying speed all around me. It was history in the making. I was in the midst of it, and it was my job to document the written glimpses of it and preserve it forever and for everybody. I felt it was an immensely important job and I took it very seriously.

One of my last memories in The Doors' office (corner of LaCienega and Santa Monica boulevards) involves Jim. One afternoon he was standing over me as I sat cross-legged in the middle of the office floor working on the scrapbook (I was constantly revising, editing, and expanding it). The book was about filled up. Only a few pages were left vacant and I was saving those for the soon-to-be-released *L.A. Woman* album reviews. With great satisfaction I lifted the pages back to the front of the book, trying to ignore Jim's presence standing a foot or so behind me. As I began turning the pages forward, Jim knelt down over my shoulder. I stopped. "Go ahead," he said. "You know, you're always working on this so I've never gotten a chance to really look at it. Go ahead, turn the page." Silently, we both scanned the pages. I used to marvel how little Jim resembled the photos I saw of him. The man I knew had always managed to be physically different by the time the coverage arrived in the mail. This afternoon, the man to my right did not at all resemble the photos we were looking at together. "This is amazing," he said. I was thinking the same thing.

We passed the outstanding press for the first album; the controversy beginning with *Strange Days* came next. "Christ, what did they expect?" he remarked, then sarcastically read the copy: " 'The Doors' second album fails to live up to the promise the band made on its brilliant debut.' What the fuck does that mean? 'Promise'? What promise? I could never figure that one out . . . what did they expect?" We moved into the New Haven bust coverage, *The Soft Parade*, Miami, *Morrison Hotel,* and so on through the book. Jim was leaving for Paris in just a few days, and he seemed to be taking his time to leave the office on good terms. We continued for a few pages and then it ended, abruptly it seemed. At that point it didn't so much end as simply stop. "What a trip. Jesus, I wonder how it's gonna end. This is really fantastic! Do you have any clues how you're going to finish it?" I wanted to tell him I really didn't want it ever to end. I had assumed *L.A. Woman* record reviews would fill up the remaining pages and then I'd begin another book. Then I thought, *why should it end*? Weren't The Doors going on forever? Why should they stop now? Or ever? When Jim returned from Paris, weren't The Doors going to pick up and tour the new album? It was only the last question I asked, and I didn't like the answer I received at all. Today it makes much more sense.

"Listen to me . . . you know that fall I took out the window of the Chateau Marmont last week? That one really hurt me . . . Usually I just kinda bounce . . . and continue on unscarred. I must be getting old . . . brittle or something . . . that one really hurt me. Anyway, the way I calculate it, that was the eighth time I've had a serious accident and come out of it relatively unscathed. What I'm saying is that I'm like a cat, you know, the nine-lives trip? That's me, I swear. Falling out that window onto the awning was the eighth time I've been saved, or maybe only the seventh, I don't know. But the point I'm trying to make is, I might not ever come back from Paris. And you gotta be prepared for that, man. And if I don't, then you'll know the cat's run outta lives."

I didn't know if he was putting me on. He had been especially sincere all afternoon, so I decided he was serious. He didn't seem sad or scared, only resigned. And very tired. But I believed a vacation was just the thing he needed. He'd lose twenty pounds, write a notebook of new songs and poems, shave his beard, then come home early with a passion to get back on the road. That was my fantasy. "At any rate," he cut into my thoughts, "it sure would make a helluva ending for your book here." Of course, he was right, as usual. The last segment, Jim's obituary, does make the perfect and logical ending for the amazing story of The Doors.

Over the years the scrapbook has proved to be an endless source of delight to fellow Doors aficionados; amusement and reference for those of us who worked and/or still work with the band; and a shocking reminder to the band members themselves. However, in the process of providing crash refresher courses for all of us, it has become dogeared and scarred. But the story of a wonderful, controversial career remains. It begins with the early UCLA Bruin and L.A. *Times* coverage of The Doors on the Sunset Strip, and it ends with Paris. This book is my attempt to enlarge, make definitive, expand, and perfect the original concept.

I hope you like it.

DANNY SUGERMAN
Los Angeles, California

1

THE DOORS

January, 1967

The first music I heard that I liked was *Peter and the Wolf*. I accidentally sat and broke the record (I was about seven). Then I listened to rock 'n' roll—I listened to the radio a lot—Fats Domino, Elvis, The Platters . . .

I started surfing at fourteen. There was lots of classical music in my house. My father liked march music. There was a piano at home. I studied trumpet at ten, but nothing came of it. Then I started playing blues on the piano—no lessons though. When I was seventeen, I started playing guitar. I used my friend's guitar. I didn't get my own until I was eighteen. It was a Mexican flamenco guitar. I took flamenco lessons for a few months. I switched around from folk to flamenco to blues to rock 'n' roll.

Records got me into the blues. Some of the newer rock 'n' roll, such as the Paul Butterfield Blues Band. If it hadn't been for Butterfield going electric, I probably wouldn't have gone rock 'n' roll.

I didn't plan on rock 'n' roll. I wanted to learn jazz; I got to know some people doing rock 'n' roll with jazz, and I thought I could make money playing music.

In rock 'n' roll you can realize anything that you can in jazz or anything. There's no limitation other than the beat. You have more freedom than you do in anything except jazz—which is dying—as far as making any money is concerned.

In The Doors we have both musicians and poets, and both know of each other's art, so we can effect a synthesis. In the case of Tim Buckley or Dylan you have one man's ideas. Most groups today aren't groups. In a true group all the members create the arrangements among themselves.

FULL REAL NAME: Robert Alan Krieger

BIRTH DATE & PLACE: January 8, 1946, in Los Angeles

PERSONAL DATA (*height, weight, and coloring*): 5'9", 135 lbs., brown hair, green eyes

FAMILY INFO (*names of parents, brothers, and sisters*): Stu, Marylin, Ron

HOME INFO (*where located and description*): Laurel Canyon—groovy

SCHOOLS ATTENDED: Uni High, Menlo UCLA, Cal at Santa Barbara

MARRIAGE INFO: no

INSTRUMENTS PLAYED/PART SUNG: guitar

    FAVORITE SINGING GROUPS:

        INDIVIDUAL SINGERS: Van Morrison, Jimmy Reed, James Brown

        ACTOR & ACTRESS: Brando, W. C. Fields

        TV SHOWS:

        COLORS: all

        FOODS: peanuts

        HOBBIES: music

        SPORTS: surfing

WHAT LOOKED FOR IN A GIRL: soul

WHAT DO YOU LIKE TO DO ON A DATE?: do as much as possible

PLANS/AMBITIONS: produce

I've been playing for six years. I don't really have too much to say about all of this. I took piano lessons when I was ten. They tried to get me to play Bach. They tried for two years. When I was in junior high I got my first set of drums. I played symphonic music in high school (tympani snare), then I played jazz for three years. I used to play sessions in Compton and Topanga Canyon. Since last year it's been rock 'n' roll and these creeps.

FULL REAL NAME: John Paul Densmore

BIRTH DATE & PLACE: December 1, 1944, in Santa Monica, California

PERSONAL DATA (height, weight, and coloring): 5'9½", 135 lbs., white-light?

FAMILY INFO (names of parents, brothers, and sisters): Ray Densmore, Margaret Densmore, Ann Densmore, Jim Densmore

HOME INFO (where located and description): 10610 Wilkins Avenue, Los Angeles, California—baroque

SCHOOLS ATTENDED: University High, Santa Monica City College, Los Angeles City College, San Fernando Valley State

MARRIAGE INFO: not married!!

INSTRUMENTS PLAYED/PART SUNG: drums, piano, tympani, vibes

  FAVORITE SINGING GROUPS: none in particular—Beatles are the best

    INDIVIDUAL SINGERS: Van Morrison, Jimmy Reed

    ACTOR & ACTRESS: Charles Bronson, Peter Sellers, & Claudia Cardinale

    TV SHOWS: old movies, rock 'n' roll shows

    COLORS: blue

    FOODS: vegetables, Chinese food, Zen macrobiotics, meat, fish

    HOBBIES: listening to all kinds of music

    SPORTS: tennis, basketball

WHAT LOOKED FOR IN A GIRL: sensitive

WHAT DO YOU LIKE TO DO ON A DATE?: communicate in one way or another

PLANS/AMBITIONS: musical production or engineering (musical) or management or something

I grew up in Chicago and left when I was 21 for Los Angeles. My parents gave me piano lessons when I was around nine or ten. I hated it for the first four years—until I learned how to do it—then it became fun, which is about the same time I first heard Negro music. I was about 12 or 13, playing baseball in a playground; someone had a radio tuned into a Negro station. From then on I was hooked. I used to listen to Al Benson and Big Bill Hill—they were disk jockeys in Chicago. From then on all the music I listened to was on the radio. My piano playing changed; I became influenced by jazz. I learned how to play that stride piano with my left hand, and I knew that was it: stuff with a beat—jazz, blues, rock.

At school I was primarily interested in film. It seemed to combine my interests in drama, visual art, music, and the profit motive. Before I left Chicago I was interested in theater. These days, I think we want our theater, our entertainment to be larger than life. I think the total environmental thing will come in. Probably Cinerama will develop further.

I think The Doors is a representative American group. America is a melting pot and so are we. Our influences spring from a myriad of sources which we have amalgamated, blending divergent styles into our own thing. We're like the country itself. America must seem to be a ridiculous hodgepodge to an outsider. It's like The Doors. We come from different areas, different musical areas. We're put together with a lot of sweat, a lot of fighting. All of the things people say about America can be said about The Doors.

All of us have the freedom to explore and improvise within a framework. Jim is an improviser with words.

FULL REAL NAME: Raymond Daniel Manzarek

BIRTH DATE & PLACE: February 12, 1939, in Chicago

PERSONAL DATA (height, weight, and coloring): 6', 160 lbs., blond, blue

FAMILY INFO (names of parents, brothers, and sisters): Raymond, Helen, Rick, Jim

HOME INFO (where located and description): Hollywood

SCHOOLS ATTENDED: UCLA

MARRIAGE INFO: married

INSTRUMENTS PLAYED/PART SUNG: organ, piano, bass

FAVORITE SINGING GROUPS: no good new groups at this date

INDIVIDUAL SINGERS: Muddy Waters, Jacques Brel

ACTOR & ACTRESS: Marlene Dietrich, Orson Welles

TV SHOWS: documentaries, news, sports

COLORS: blue

FOODS: oysters, snails, prime ribs

HOBBIES: projecting the feel of the future

SPORTS: tennis, swimming

WHAT LOOKED FOR IN A GIRL: compatibility, reality

WHAT DO YOU LIKE TO DO ON A DATE?: dinner, movies, walk, ice cream, drive to beach

PLANS/AMBITIONS: films

Original Elektra Records bio, 1967

You could say it's an accident that I was ideally suited for the work I am doing. It's the feeling of a bowstring being pulled back for 22 years and suddenly being let go. I am primarily an American, second, a Californian, third, a Los Angeles resident. I've always been attracted to ideas that were about revolt against authority. I like ideas about the breaking away or over-throwing of established order. I am interested in anything about revolt, disorder, chaos—especially activity that seems to have no meaning. It seems to me to be the road toward freedom—external revolt is a way to bring about internal freedom. Rather than starting inside, I start outside—reach the mental through the physical.

   I am a Sagittarian—if astrology has anything to do with it—the Centaur—the Archer—the Hunt—But the main thing is that we are The Doors.

   We are from the West/The whole thing is like an invitation to the West
                    The sunset   This is the end
                    The night
                    The sea
The world we suggest is of a new wild west.   A sensuous evil world.
Strange and haunting, the path of the sun, you know?
Toward the end.   At least for our first album
We're all centered around the end of the zodiac.
The Pacific/violence and peace/the way between young and the old.

FULL REAL NAME: James Douglas Morrison

BIRTH DATE & PLACE: December 8, 1943, Melbourne, Florida

PERSONAL DATA (height, weight, and coloring): 5'11", 145 lbs., brown hair, blue-gray eyes

FAMILY INFO (names of parents, brothers, and sisters): dead

HOME INFO (where located and description): Laurel Canyon, L.A.—nice at night

SCHOOLS ATTENDED: St. Petersburg Junior College, Florida State U., UCLA

MARRIAGE INFO: single

INSTRUMENTS PLAYED/PART SUNG: lead voice

FAVORITE SINGING GROUPS: Beach Boys, Kinks, Love

   INDIVIDUAL SINGERS: Sinatra, Presley

   ACTOR & ACTRESS: Jack Palance, Sarah Miles

   TV SHOWS: news

   COLORS: turquoise

   FOODS: meat

   HOBBIES: horse races

   SPORTS: swimming

WHAT LOOKED FOR IN A GIRL: hair, eyes, voice, walk

WHAT DO YOU LIKE TO DO ON A DATE?: talk

PLANS/AMBITIONS: make films

EYE
THE DOORS' STORY · *by Digby Diehl*

In the pristine warmth of a sandy beach and a sunny day, The Doors were conceived. Their "parent group" was a band called Rick and the Ravens which featured Ray Daniels ("the bearded blues shouter"), and they played at a bar on Second Street and Broadway in Santa Monica, improbably called The Turkey Joint West. In the spring of 1965, Rick and the Ravens had a nucleus of the three Manzarek brothers: Ray singing, Rick on piano, and Jim on guitar. They had played together in Chicago, and when the family moved to Redondo Beach, the blues band was formed for weekend gigs. A college crowd, often from the UCLA film school, frequented the bar to hear Ray belt out material like "Money," "Louie, Louie," "Hootchie-Coochie Man," and "I'm Your Doctor, I

Know What You Need" in simulated Chicago style. "I would switch from film-school grubby to a blue jacket with velvet collar and a frilly shirt to be the bearded blues shouter," recalls Manzarek. "Immediately afterward, I would put my sweat shirt and corduroy jacket back on and return to being a film student."

Manzarek never liked his piano lessons back home in Chicago, until he learned to play boogie-woogie at the age of twelve. He studied Bach, Rachmaninoff, and Tchaikovsky at the Chicago Conservatory, "but I didn't really enjoy playing other people's stuff. I dug blues." He hung around the clubs on Chicago's South Side to hear the great blues singers like Muddy Waters, not yet discovered by the white world. "I used to listen to Negro disk jockeys—Al Benson and Big Bill Hill—at home, and developed a stride-piano style." Majoring in economics as an undergraduate at DePaul University, he went to UCLA to become a lawyer. "I actually did go to law school out here for about two weeks. I couldn't believe all the nonsense. I figured those guys must be kidding and went into the cinema department." There, Manzarek completed three short films: *Evergreen, Induction,* and a design film, *Who and Where I Live*—all autobiographical segments considered very promising work by the faculty. Last December he married his longtime girlfriend, Dorothy Fujikawa, a lovely Oriental native of L.A.

During that summer of '65, Manzarek was living in Venice, an early cradle of hippiedom on the oceanfront south of Santa Monica. By accident, he ran into Jim Morrison. "I had been friendly with Jim at UCLA, and we had talked about rock 'n' roll even then. After we graduated, he said he was going to New York. Then, two months later, in July, I met him on the beach in Venice. He said he had been writing some songs, so we sat on the beach and I asked him to sing some of them. He did, and the first thing he tried was 'Moonlight Drive.' When he sang those first lines—'Let's swim to the moon/ Let's climb through the tide/ Penetrate the evening/ That the city sleeps to hide'—I said: 'That's it.' I'd never heard lyrics to a rock song like that before. We talked a while before we decided to get a group together and make a million dollars."

One of the first meditation centers of the Maharishi, in which UCLA students were particularly involved, was opening at this time, and Ray Manzarek met John Densmore, a drummer, in his meditation class. Densmore, who had played jazz drums almost exclusively until a short stint with a group called the Psychedelic Rangers, joined The Doors.

In September of 1965, six Morrison originals including "Moonlight Drive," "Summer's Almost Gone," "End of the Night," and "Break on Through," were recorded on a demonstration transcription at World-Pacific Jazz studios on the Aura label. This recording session (the only copies of which are owned by World-Pacific, John Densmore, and Billy James) was Morrison's first appearance at a microphone, and the instrumentalists included Jim and Rick Manzarek on guitars, Ray Manzarek on piano, Densmore on drums, and an unidentified girl bass player. Shortly after the recording session, Jim, Rick, and the mysterious girl bass player decided they didn't like Morrison's songs. They split for Redondo Beach, and are still presumably playing "Louie, Louie."

Robbie Krieger, who got to know Densmore and Manzarek at the Maharishi's Third Street Meditation Center, arrived with some hard-driving bottleneck guitar, and the unit was complete.

The Doors continued to audition several bass players, but were never able to find a satisfactory musician. One day, Manzarek saw a Fender piano bass and the problem was solved. He now plays the bass keyboard with his left hand and the organ with his foot and right hand. The quartet rehearsed for four or five months and played at a few private parties, including one given by Krieger's parents.

After practicing daily in a friend's house behind the Santa Monica Greyhound Bus Depot, The Doors made a humorously premature debut on the stage of UCLA's Royce Hall, providing "live sound track" to a screening of Manzarek's design film, *Who and Where I Live.* Krieger played guitar, Manzarek played flute, and Densmore, Morrison, and sundry girlfriends pounded on drums, rattles, claves, and tambourines.

A small, now defunct club called the London Fog, located between the Hamburger Hamlet and

the Galaxy on the Sunset Strip, was the first real club date for The Doors. They played for five dollars apiece on weeknights, double on weekends, seven nights a week, four sets per night. Because at that time they didn't have sufficient original material for such a long job, over half their repertory consisted of blues and rock 'n' roll classics, such as "Gloria," "Red Rooster," and "Who Do You Love?" Once again, a faithful core of fans from the UCLA film school followed them, but on the Strip a cross-section of other listeners joined. More than anything else, the London Fog job provided the opportunity to play together steadily, experiment with their songs, and to develop as a working group. Jim Morrison in particular changed, progressing from a reserved stage style to his presently flamboyant manner. Their music was ardently defended by a growing segment of the Strip population; but it also just plain scared a lot of people. Eventually, they were fired. No one in the group can quite recall the reason why.

It may seem hard to believe, but at this juncture The Doors could easily have sunk into small-time oblivion (they were turned down after four auditions at Bido Lito's and had played at the Brave New World in Hollywood for only a few nights), or disbanded, or at least could have starved a while longer

waiting for discovery. But on the very last night of their four months at the London Fog, Ronnie Haran, the chic chick who books talent for the Whiskey-a-Go-Go, came in to hear them. "I knew that Jim Morrison had star quality the minute he started singing," says Miss Haran. "They needed more polish, but the sound was there. Unfortunately, none of them had telephones (Morrison was then sleeping on the beach) and all they could give me was a number where John 'sometimes' could be reached. It took a month to contact them again, but I finally booked them into the Whiskey." Miss Haran also helped The Doors join the musicians' union, get new clothes, and organize the business side of their lives. Her tenacious insistence upon using them as more or less the Whiskey house-band, despite management objections, was the important break The Doors needed.

They played second billing to *everybody*, including groups such as Love, Them, the Turtles, the Seeds, and the number one band in Mexico, the Locos. ("The Locos were a real low point in our careers," recalls Manzarek. "They were terrible, the kids hated them, and we were caught in the cross fire.") Exposed to a wide-ranging audience—hardened groupies to Iowa tourists—The Doors began to intensify their musical Götterdämmerung and to experiment daringly. Allegedly, the experiments often took the form of drug trips, and weekly tales of The Doors' freaked-out adventures flew: "Morrison was so stoned last night he fell off the stage *again*"; "Ray sniffed an amyl nitrate cap and played so long he had to be dragged away from the organ"; "They all arrived stoned and started improvising at random—I don't know what it was, but it was great!" According to one friend of the group, Morrison was so consistently high on acid during this period that he could eat sugar cubes like candy without visible effect. But, inexplicably, the music kept getting better.

In the most important rock club in Los Angeles, The Doors began to enjoy a celebrity audience from the recording industry and the attentions of several record companies. One evening, Miss Haran brought Jac Holzman, president of Elektra Records, to hear the group. Holzman was unimpressed. However, he was more enthusiastic on a second visit. Urged on by Billy James, at that time Elektra's West Coast man, they signed The Doors in late 1966. The arrangement was, and still is, amiable on both sides, for The Doors, according to Manzarek, have been permitted freedom to work in the studio and Elektra has a top group that has enhanced its financial picture greatly. In January, 1967, their first album came out with a cut called "Light My Fire."

Before then, however, The Doors and the Whiskey had had a parting of the ways, mostly caused by "The End." "It started as a simple 'goodbye song'—just the first verse and a chorus," says Morrison. "As we did it each night, we discovered a peculiar feeling: a long, flowing, easy beat; that strange guitar tuning that sounds vaguely Eastern or American Indian. It was a form that everyone brought something to. Our last night at the Whiskey, I invented that climactic part about 'Father, I want to kill you. . . .' That's what the song had been leading up to." According to Manzarek, Morrison had missed the first set of the evening and the second set went without incident. "The place was packed for the third set. Saturday night at the Whiskey with all the tourists and everything else. Jim sang 'The End' and the place was mesmerized by it. Then he did the 'Killer awoke before dawn' sequence. Everything just sort of stopped. It was really weird. When we finished, no one applauded or even talked. Mario (the manager) just said, 'Those guys are nuts—get them out of here,' and we were fired."

No matter. By that time, The Doors were headed for the San Francisco ballrooms and a national tour.

UCLA DAILY BRUIN
ARTAUD ROCK: DARK LOGIC OF THE DOORS · *by Bill Kerby*

Ray sat at his electric organ, head bowed, just looking at the keys, John made a last-minute adjustment on his snare drum, and Robbie, looking like Robert Mitchum's electric son, twisted dials on his amp and tuned softly. Finally, after an unbearable wait, Robbie began, then John, and finally Ray. The introduction over and over, evolving complex, swelling.

Kaleidoscope was sold out. Ciro's was packed and all the people in the Western Hemisphere were wedged around the stage, waiting, craning around anxiously, recognizing the introduction.

And there he was; a gaunt, hollow Ariel from hell, stumbling in slow motion through the drums. Robbie turned to look with mild disgust but Jim Morrison was oblivious. Drifting, still you could have lit matches off the look he gave the audience. There was a mild tremor of excited disbelief as he dreamed that he went to his microphone. Morrison's clothes looked like he had slept in them since he was twelve and he just hung there on the microphone, slack. Just for a flash, his beautiful child's face said it was all a lie. All the terror, all the drugs, all the evil. Gone! The unhuman sound he made into the microphone turned the carping groupies to stone. And in the tombed silence he began to sing; alternately caressing, screaming, terraced flights of poetry and music, beyond visceral.

For an hour on that Friday night, a modern American pop group called The Doors got right out on the edge and stayed there. And because they are great and because the edge is where artists produce the best, there occurred a major black miracle.

The founder of the Theater-of-Cruelty, Antonin Artaud, poet-actor, described one of his infrequent scenarios thus: "eroticism, savagery, bloodlust, a thirst for violence, an obsession with horror, collapse of moral values, social hypocrisy, lies, sadism, perjury, depravity, etc." To anyone who has ever listened to The Doors at any length, this will appear to be a catalog of their material, but that's just a part of the whole. This context of Artaud is more than their ornamental design, more than a convenient rubric into which they stuff their music. Among their contemporaries, The Doors are going somewhere different.

Vaguely (pleased, disappointed: choose one) at his survival, Western man has begun to look inside to see what went wrong, what went right, and to see if they were ever the same thing. Order and chaos have new levels of meaning so that today a flogging can have as much validity in art as an act of amative love. And The Doors know it. This kind of irrationality is beyond dreams or madness and their songs shock and do not tell logical stories. At the end of a good set, the evil magic is out, and Morrison holds the only match in the Stygian darkness. Helplessly, you hope he won't decide to blow it out.

It is possible to go through so many changes when listening to The Doors, that a beautiful, exhilarating dream and a nightmare can be the same. "I would not try to excuse obvious incoherence by mitigating it with dreams. Dreams have something more than their own logic. They have their own existence, in which nothing but dark and intelligent truths appear." (Artaud, Morrison: choose one.)

The Doors are four men who are together; their vision is realized by all of them. But it is Morrison whom the audience watches. They are attracted to him with the same ambivalence that drives us to feast on calamity. Our perverse nature is undeniable when we look upon things we fear the most. We cringe and die a little inside, unable to take our eyes away while evil and death dance nearer and nearer to our petty conception of immortality. But James Douglas Morrison, b. Melbourne, Florida, 1943, whose parents are rumor, film-maker, star, bathes luxuriously in it. He moves on stage, dancing with an indifferent, expressionless attitude or seized with paroxysmal anger, his face convulsed with a splendid fury. He has more natural disdain, more utter contempt for his surroundings than anyone I have ever known. But when he stands, throttling his microphone, staggering blindly across the stage, electric, on fire, screaming, his is all there, waiting, daring, terrified, and alone.

And digging it.

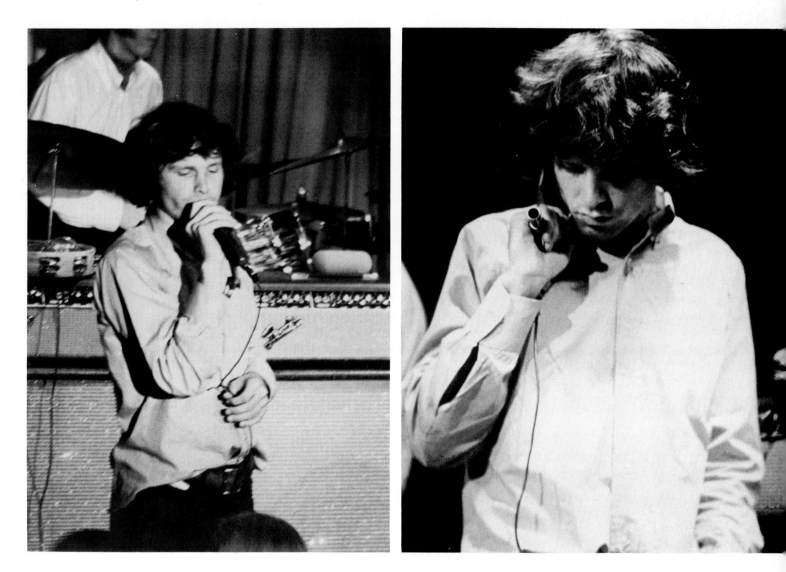

LOS ANGELES TIMES
THE DOORS AT THE WHISKEY-A-GO-GO • *by Pete Johnson*

The Doors are a hungry-looking quartet with an interesting original sound but with what is possibly the worst stage appearance of any rock 'n' roll group in captivity. Their lead singer emotes with his eyes closed, the electric pianist hunches over his instrument as if reading mysteries from the keyboard, the guitarist drifts about the stage randomly, and the drummer seems lost in a separate world.

LOS ANGELES TIMES
VIBRANT JAZZ-ROCK GROUP AT GAZZARRI'S • by Francine Grace

The Doors, a young jazz-rock group, opened last week to an enthusiastic capacity crowd in the dim ruby lights of Gazzarri's on the Sunset Strip. They close Thursday night.

The group, four long-haired Venice boys in their early twenties were at UCLA when they banded together just over a year ago.

They resist labeling their sound and forsake fancy costumes for the shirts and jeans they wear all day. "No one's ever going to put us in uniform," they say.

The Doors weld a rock 'n' roll beat with continuous jazz improvisation to produce an intense, highly emotional sound. They call their music "primitive and personal" and find it hard to work without audience reaction. Their numbers change constantly at live shows and new ones are written as they perform.

"We play and it just kinda happens," said one of the group.

Numbers start with the unhurried loud wail of an electric organ, joined by a low, groaning electric guitar and backed up by a steady drum. The words build with the music into an accelerating crescendo of frenzied sound.

Trying to avoid the "hard straight sound" of many rock groups, The Doors aim for "dramatic impact" in their music.

Gazzarri's crowded dance floor proves that The Doors' lyrical freedom hasn't hurt their strong rock 'n' roll dance tempo.

CRAWDADDY!
WHAT GOES ON?

There's a group you have to hear. They're called The Doors, and they're the best new band I've heard this year. They've been playing at Ondine's in New York, and may still be there as you read this. They have a single on Elektra ("Break on Through to the Other Side") and an album which should be out in February. The album is a great experience: from "Break on Through" ("I found an island in your arms, a country in your eyes . . . arms that chain, eyes that lie— break on through to the other side!") to "She's a Twentieth Century Fox" to a perfect rock recording of "Alabama Song" from Weill's *Mahagonny* to (unbelievably) "The End," a song which represents rock-performing and audience-reaching and communication as it must be and never has been before. I kid you not: The Doors. They come from Los Angeles. Jim Morrison sings lead and writes most of their material; Ray Manzarek plays organ, piano, and celeste; Robbie Krieger plays guitar and occasional bass; John Densmore plays drums. I recommend their music unreservedly.

CRAWDADDY!
ROCK IS ROCK: A DISCUSSION OF A DOORS SONG · by Paul Williams

Very few people have the balls to talk about "rock 'n' roll" anymore. *Revolver* made it difficult. *Between the Buttons, Smile,* and *The Doors* LP are making it impossible. "Pop music" is definable only by pointing at a current chart; The Doors are not "pop," they are simply "modern music." The term applied not because rock has achieved the high standards of mainstream music, but conversely because rock has *absorbed* mainstream music, has become the leader, the arbiter of quality, the music of today. The Doors, Brian Wilson, the Stones *are* modern music, and contemporary "jazz" and "classical" composers must try to measure up.

The Doors is an album of magnitude. Thanks to the calm surefootedness of the group, the producer, the record company, there are no flaws; The Doors have been delivered to the public full-grown (by current standards) and are still growing (standards change). Gestation may have been long and painful;

no one cares. The birth of the group is in this album, and it's as good as anything in rock. The awesome fact about The Doors is that they will improve.

This album is too good to be "explained," note by note, song by song; that sort of thing could only be boring, since the sophomoric cognitive "review" must be immediately compared to the far-more-than-mere-communicative level of the work of art itself, the album. Knowing that my reader is able to stop after any word I write and listen to all of "Light My Fire" before he reads the next word, I should feel pretty foolish offering him a merely textual description of the buildup of erotic pressure in the performance. Is there really any point in saying something like "The instrumental in 'Light My Fire' builds at the end into a truly visual orgasm in sound" when the reader can at any time put the album onto even the crummiest phonograph and experience the orgasm himself?

THE VILLAGE VOICE

POP EYE · *by Richard Goldstein*

First New York opening in a while. The Doors—fresh from Los Angeles with an underground album-of-the-hour—return. This time, they are worshiped, envied, bandied about like the Real Thing. Ultimate proof that rock is an art form is watching the pop aristocracy at play. The great danger is no longer blatant ignorance by the press—we've come too far for that—or corruption from The Men in Charge—everyone takes that for granted—but the carping, eroding adulation an emerging creator receives from the scene.

A typical East Side opening—with this difference. The Doors are a vital new group, with a major album and a sound that grips. Would they make it live?

The four musicians mounted their instruments. The organist lit a stick of incense. Vocalist and writer Jim Morrison closed his eyes to all that Arnel elegance, and The Doors opened up.

Morrison twitched and pouted and a cluster of girls gathered to watch every nuance in his lips. Humiliating your audience is an old game in rock 'n' roll, but Morrison pitches spastic love with a raging insolence you can't ignore. His material—almost all original—is literate, concise, and terrifying. The Doors have the habit of improvising, so a song about being strange which I heard for the first time at Ondine may be a completely different composition by now. Whatever the words, you will discern a deep streak of violent—sometimes Oedipal—sexuality. And since sex is what hard rock is all about, The Doors are a stunning success.

You should brave all the go-go gymnastics, bring a select circle of friends for a buffer, and make it up to Ondine to find out what the literature of pop is all about.

The Doors are mean; and their skin is green.

NEW YORK MAGAZINE
THE DOORS OPEN WIDE · *by Richard Goldstein*

"We are from the West. The world we suggest should be of a new Wild West. A sensuous evil world. Strange and haunting. . . . The path of the sun, you know."

That's what Jim Morrison, vocalist and writer-in-residence of The Doors, has to say about his music and his hometown. As part of the new wave in Los Angeles rock, he should know where things are at. Since a pop generation happens every two years or sooner, The Doors have the proximity to revere their elders, and the distance to be original.

Their initial album, on Elektra, is a cogent, tense, and powerful excursion. I suggest you buy it, slip it on your phonograph, and travel on the vehicle of your choice. The Doors are slickly, smoothly dissonant. With the schism between folk and rock long since healed, they can leap from pop to poetry without the fear of violating some mysterious sense of form. But this freedom to stretch and shatter boundaries makes pretension as much a part of the new scene as mediocrity was the scourge of the old. It takes a special kind of genius to bridge gaps in form.

Their music works because its blues roots are always visible. The Doors are never far from the musical humus of America—rural, gut simplicity.

The most important work on this album is an "extended pop song" called "The End." When Dylan broke the three-minute mold with "Like a Rolling Stone," pop composers realized that the form-follows-function dictum which has always guided folk-rock applies to time as well. A song should take as long as it takes.

"The End" is eleven and one-half minutes of solid song. Its hints of sitar and tabla and its faint aroma of raga counterpoint are balanced by a sturdy blues foundation. Anyone who disputes the concept of rock literature had better listen long and hard to this song. This is Joycean pop, with a stream-of-consciousness lyric in which images are strung together by association. "The End" builds to a realization of mood rather than a sequence of events. It is also the first pop song in my memory to deal directly with the Oedipus complex. "The End" begins with visions of collapsing peace and harmony, and ends with violent death.

The entire song revolves around a theme of travel, but this journey is both physical and spiritual. It leads to the brass-tacks fantasy of incest and patricide:

> The killer awoke before dawn
> He put his boots on
> He took a face from the ancient gallery
> And he walked on down the hall . . .

> He came to a door
> And he looked inside
> "Father?"
> "Yes, son"
> "I want to kill you . . . Mother . . . "

Morrison provides us with a series of womblike halls and doors and a reference to Greek tragedy in the ancient gallery of masks. And he juxtaposes this root fantasy with a bluesy refrain which begins: "Come on baby, take a chance with us" and ends with the proposition: "Meet me in the back of the blue bus."

There is, of course, a danger in so academic an interpretation of a song like "The End." Its whole value is its freedom to imply. Morrison's delivery (during the murder fantasy it approaches gospel wailing) tells us to absorb first, and search later.

The Doors are a major event for Los Angeles. Their emergence indicates that the city of Formica fantasy is building a music without neon, that glows anyway.

THE VILLAGE VOICE
POP EYE · *by Richard Goldstein*

When The Doors appeared, backed by a skyscraper of amplifiers, the crowd sat through some stunning improvisation, and someone actually shouted, "Bravo"—when it was over.

The Doors begin where the Rolling Stones leave off. Lead singer Jim Morrison is never far from the sexual shaman Mick Jagger represents, but his is a darker, bleaker war dance. His hand cupped pillowlike over his ear, Morrison's pudgy cherub face curls into a bristling lip. He stands like a creature out of Kenneth Anger, then sidles up to the mike, curls around its head, and belts—what he says has been called "Artaud Rock" by the *UCLA Bruin*, and I think the definition fits. It is cruel cool. The organ and guitar chatter in the background, and when they race through a bridge together, the urgent harmony between them is stunning. When the PA system begins to fight back, Morrison twists the neck of the microphone until the feedback itself becomes percussion.

And so naturally, the only thing to say is "Bravo."

NEW YORK POST
TEEN TALK · *by Susan Szekely*

If velvet came an inch deep, if endless bites of baklava never began to cloy, they'd arouse sensations like those that invade you when you listen to The Doors. You mingle in the sweet, rich sensuousness of the music; the music mingles in you. Listeners close their eyes and smile beatifically. It is as if The Doors play on some secret frequency that directly affects the smile center of the brain.

The Doors are four: organist Ray Manzarek, guitarist Robby Krieger, drummer John Densmore, and singer Jim Morrison. They say they aren't more because four people trying to get together is enough. But because they are only four, "everybody has to play much more music," says Robby. "The organ is not just a fill-in instrument like in other groups." And there is no one who just plays plunkey-plunk in the background.

The Doors also have no leader. "We're a communist group," says Ray. "No, an anarchist group," says Robby. Each contributes equally and richly. Each note has meaning, there is not a decibel of irrelevant noise. None of the noise that only shatters.

"We've all shattered ourselves a long time ago," says Ray. "That was what early rock was about—an attempt to shatter 2,000 years of culture . . . now we're working on what happens after you've shattered . . ."

"If the theatre is not just play, if it is a genuine reality, by what means can we give it that status of reality, make each performance a kind of event? That is the problem we have to solve. This is what we want to arrive at: that each performance we take a grave risk, that the whole interest of our effort lies in its seriousness. It is not to the mind or the senses of our audience that we address ourselves, but to their whole existence. Theirs and ours. So that ultimately the audience will go to the theatre as they go to the surgeon or the dentist; with a sense of dread but also of necessity. A real theatrical experience shakes the calm of the senses, liberates the compressed unconscious and drives towards a kind of potential revolt, which cannot realise its full value, unless it remains potential and imposes on the assembled crowd a difficult and heroic attitude."

—ANTONIN ARTAUD

HULLABALOO • *The Doors*
by Paul Nelson

If the Stones offer the experience of a great and established group performing up to complete expectations, a new group, The Doors, bursts into quick and deserved prominence like a sudden, unexpected bolt of lightning. *The Doors* (Elektra), superbly produced by Paul A. Rothchild, is a record which balances a lot of seeming paradoxes: expert, controlled, and precise in attack, the group nonetheless excels in performances which grow from pregnant understatement to exhilarating incandescence in a matter of seconds.

Judging from their premier effort, The Doors are *the* new group by which all other new groups must, for a time at least, be measured.

LOS ANGELES TIMES • *The Doors*
by Pete Johnson

The Doors, a quartet who have been playing in the Los Angeles area for some time, have come up with their first album, which is named after them.

This Elektra album has a strange, new sound, but it is not strange in the fascinating directions pursued by the Rolling Stones, Dylan, Donovan or the Beatles.

Jim Morrison, lead vocalist, has a voice similar to that of Eric Burdon, the Animals' singer, but he is somewhat overmannered, murky, and dull.

The best example of his faults is "The End," an eleven-minute thirty-five-second exploration of how bored he can sound as he recites singularly simple, overelaborated psychedelic non sequiturs and fallacies.

Many of the numbers drag and there is an abundance of banal lyrics, but The Doors do sound fairly good on "Break on Through," their current single, "Twentieth Century Fox," and "Alabama Song," which has a good rhythm backing and passable harmony.

HULLABALOO
THE DOORS IN NEW YORK

The Doors were in New York for the third time for some concerts and a three-week gig at Steve Paul's The Scene. It was not quite the same as their two previous trips to New York. Last fall, when they were playing here for the first time, they were virtually unknown except to the innermost circles of hippies and groupies. Early in the spring, when they returned, their album had been released and was a big underground item—big enough to keep it in the national charts around number 100 and big enough to keep the club in which they were playing chock-full of the in-crowd every night.

But now we were in the midst of a Doors boom. Their album and single were number one on the West Coast, and the week prior to their arrival in New York, both had jumped about thirty points (which is *very* fantastic) on the national charts. In three weeks, they would be Top 10, album and single, and no new group since The Monkees had seen their first album go Top 10. We were transporting, in our limousine from Newark, daisies and superstars—and we all knew it.

Even while they were here, the phenomenon was growing bigger. Everyone came to see them, and I arrived at The Scene one night to find Jim Morrison and Paul Newman talking about the title song for a movie which Newman was planning to produce. And when I called the directors of the Central Park Music Festival to arrange for passes for The Doors to the Paul Butterfield concert, I was told to have them enter

the theater one at a time or they would be in danger of being rushed. Which I told them—but they came in together anyhow and *were* rushed and loved it. If they had stayed another week, they would have needed bodyguards. Their exit was well timed; the day after they left, we had a request to use The Doors in a singing deodorant commercial, and I think everyone was relieved *not* to have to make a decision about that offer.

The Doors played their last set at The Scene on a Saturday night. At 3 A.M., when all the paying customers had left, Steve Paul locked us all in and gave a party for the boys, who had been the biggest draw in the history of his club. And on his part, Steve had been a good and groovy employer; I remember John asking Jim why he (Jim) would get to The Scene so well in advance of the time they had to perform, and Jim's answering, "Well, I like to hang around Steve Paul and listen to him rap. He's funny." Anyhow, there was a case of champagne for the closing night party, and it didn't matter that it wasn't quite chilled because everyone was happy, sloppy, and tired, and it was a beautiful party. Robbie did his imitation of a shrimp, and Jim found something lying on the floor which looked like a balloon but wasn't, so he blew it up and let it go, whereupon it landed in Ingrid Superstar's champagne glass, which made Jim laugh, and everyone loved each other without any uptightness. It would be good if everything The Doors ever have to do ends so nicely.

CRAWDADDY!
DOORS PRODUCER PAUL ROTHCHILD SPEAKS

Paul Williams (Crawdaddy! editor): How was it, recording "The End"?

Paul Rothchild: It was beautiful, it was one of the most beautiful moments I've ever had in a recording studio, that half hour when "The End" was recorded. I was emotionally wrung. Usually as a producer you sit there listening for all of the things that are right and all of the things that are about to go wrong. You're following every instrument simultaneously, you're following the feeling, the mood all the way through. In this take, I was completely, I was absolutely audience. I had done my job, there was nothing actually for me to do once the machines were rolling, I had made sure the sound was right on each instrument, you know when we did our setup, Bruce Botnick, the engineer, had been cued by me on everything that I wanted to do, and at the beginning of the take I was sitting there—producer—listening to take. Midway through I was no longer producer, I was just completely sucked up into it, and when we recorded it the studio was completely darkened, the only lights visible were a candle burning in the recording studio right next to Jim whose back was to the control room, singing into his microphone, and the lights on the VU meters in the control room. All other lights were off . . . it was . . . very dark . . .

It was a magic moment . . . Jim was doing "The End," he was just doing it, for all time, and I was pulled off, right on down his road, he said come with me and I did. It was almost a shock when the song was over, you know when Robbie plays those last little tinkling notes on the guitar. It felt like, yea, you know, like, yes, it's the end, *that's* the end, it cannot go any further, that's the statement. I felt emotionally washed. There were four other people in the control room at that time, when the take was over and we realized the tape was still going. Bruce, the engineer, was completely sucked along into it and instead of sitting there at attention the way engineers are wont to do, his head was on the console and he was just—immersed. Just absolutely immersed in this take. And he'd done it all, and he'd made all the moves right, because Bruce and I had established a kind of rapport, he knew where I wanted things done and when, and when his work was done he did exactly the same thing, involuntarily, without volition, he didn't know he was going to do it, but he became audience, too. So the muse *did* visit the studio that time. And, all of us were audience, there was nothing left, the machines knew what to do!

CRAWDADDY!
WHAT GOES ON? · *by Paul Williams*

The Doors, in person, have become the best the West has to offer. In concert at the Village Theater several weeks ago, they were frightening and beautiful beyond my ability to describe. In the audience, young men with thoughtfully groomed beards contorted like Beatles fans in the days of Shea Stadium. Robbie, Ray, and John excelled in musicianship, constantly adding to the perfection of their album (now number two in the country—!—and certainly indelible in the minds of the audience) and leaving no note unturned in their desire to communicate. And as it was meant to be, Jim stole the show. "I tell you, I tell you, I tell you we must die!" "Hope not," he added. Our hearts stopped. "The men don't know, but the little girls, they understand . . . Don't 'cha?" The audience gasped. The first show was the unexpected by way of the familiar, anticlimaxing nicely with "Light My Fire." The difference between "records" and "live," the subtleties of "new" and "old-as-new" were illustrated with utter clarity. Jim brilliantly carried the audience from anticipation to excitement to over-the-edge fright and joy. And the second show, opening with "When the Music's Over," made the first an introduction. If "Horse Latitudes" had shaken us stem to stern, still we didn't know how lost we were till Jim spoke, without accompaniment, the Sophocles section of "The End." And then fell, worshiping some young lady who knelt before the stage. And suddenly flew into the air, a leap to make Nureyev proud. And finally swung his microphone on its cord, around his head, toward the audience, more and more violent, prepared to release—everything; and we knew he'd do it. One of us would die. "This is the end," he sang into the now frustrated, unviolent microphone, "my only friend," and Jim was wonderful, shrugging his shoulders and letting the boys carry on in "Light My Fire." The Doors are now the best performers in the country, and if the albums are poetry as well as music, then the stage show is most of all drama, brilliant theater in any sense of the word. Artistic expression transcending all form, because you knew as Jim died there for you on stage that that wasn't mere acting—but it *was* all for art. Christ, they say, became the perfect criminal, negating all crimes in his own most heinous one. Absolving the world by absorbing all sins. And Jim dies a little more each day, pulling toward him all the violence around him, frightening and beautiful as he strains to perfect his art. And every day more of a pop star, pied piper of mice and the flower kids, and when the music's over. . . . When I first heard a dub of *Strange Days*, I thought of Rap Brown's troubles and suggested that

in six months everyone connected with this album might be in jail. But I wasn't kidding. Cancel my subscription. . .

THE NEW YORK TIMES
DOORS, A WAY IN AND A WAY OUT, ROCK ON COAST · by Robert Windeler

The Doors is one pop music group that may make it to the end of this rock generation, which is to say it may last another five years.

An audience of 4,500 packed Winterland, an abandoned ice-skating rink in a run-down section of San Francisco, last night and Friday night to find out why or to pay tribute.

When The Doors came on to do their thing, there was sudden silence and the crowd sat as if it were about to hear a chamber music concert.

And they did hear everything from Bach chord changes to a Brecht-Weill song and The Doors' Top 40 hit "Light My Fire." But more important, they sat in rapt attention to every visual and vocal gyration of The Doors' lead singer, Jim Morrison, as if in homage to some primitive ritual.

It is precisely this total attention that The Doors' audiences seek and The Doors exploit. "For me it's a religious involvement," said Ray Manzarek, the group's organist. "For the public it's a total submersion into our music."

Consequently, public performances are what The Doors do most, although they have all the requisites of a top pop group.

On stage the twenty-three-year-old Mr. Morrison, dressed in skintight black vinyl, mouths each lyric—sung or spoken—as if it were poetry, which it sometimes is, albeit punctuated by ear-piercing blasts by organ, guitar, and drums. The other members of the group, Mr. Manzarek, twenty-five, Robbie Krieger, twenty-one, and John Densmore, twenty-two, are essentially instrumentalists.

The best definition of pop is the one that counts at the box office, but lion-maned Jim Morrison considers The Doors as something more than a hit rock 'n' roll group. "Think of us," he likes to say, "as erotic politicians."

Mr. Morrison is the twenty-three-year-old lead singer of The Doors, and the campaign for whatever it is he's running for is directed at the same constituency as The Monkees': those fourteen-year-old girls of America's suburbs.

At the Hunter College auditorium last night, he came out in skintight black vinyl pants. He walked languidly to the microphone, the way Marlon Brando might have if he had started out in rock 'n' roll.

He grabbed the microphone with both hands and put one boot on the base. He closed his eyes and tugged on the microphone. First it was too high. Then it was too low. Then he opened his mouth as if he was about to sing. Then he changed his mind and closed his mouth again.

On his face, there was the look of suffering of someone who knows he is too beautiful to ever enjoy true love. Jim Morrison is a pop star with a vision. The vision is packaged in sex. His campaign motto is "Nirvana now."

At Hunter College, they filled every seat in the house.

The program started out with The Nitty Gritty Dirt Band, who, like The Doors, are from California but who play sweet old-time music with acoustical instruments. The Doors, of course, are electric, with twenty-five-year-old Ray Manzarek providing the musical genius from his command post at the organ.

Mr. Morrison writes the lyrics, and they are filled with the tension of his impatience. "Cancel my subscription to the Resurrection. . . . We want the world and we want it now. . . . Deliver me from reason, I'd rather fly. . . ."

At last night's concert Mr. Morrison introduced some new material. "Wait until the war is over," he sang, "and we'll both be a little older . . . Make a grave for the unknown soldier . . ."

Mr. Krieger played a siren on his amplifier and then aimed his guitar at Mr. Morrison while Mr. Densmore rat-tat-tatted a machine-gun staccato. At the other end of the stage, Mr. Manzarek issued a blast from his amplifier and Mr. Morrison shuddered, languidly.

Have The Doors become successful enough to start taking themselves seriously?

LOVE, MYSTICISM, AND THE HIPPIES · by Kurt Von Meier

Jim Morrison, the lead singer and songwriter of The Doors, is at twenty-two one of the most shaken loose, mind-shaking, and subtle agents of the new music of the new, mysticism-oriented young. His voice, weak on high notes, lacks stamina and belt, but it couldn't matter less. He gets people. His songs are eerie, loaded with somewhat Freudian symbolism, poetic but not pretty, filled with suggestions of sex, death, transcendence. Part of his swamping magnetism is an elusiveness as if he were singing for himself. Four young men who met as university students in Los Angeles, The Doors have the California sound. The electronics, the spooking organ tones, the traces of raga and sitar. Disciplined, inventive, strong in their sense of beat and form, they excel at those long, deceptively impromptu "pop songs" that last seven or more minutes. Their "Light My Fire" took off as a hit. But The Doors play at their best in "The End," a song that runs for more than eleven and a half minutes with words by Jim Morrison writing as if Edgar Allan Poe had blown back as a hippie.

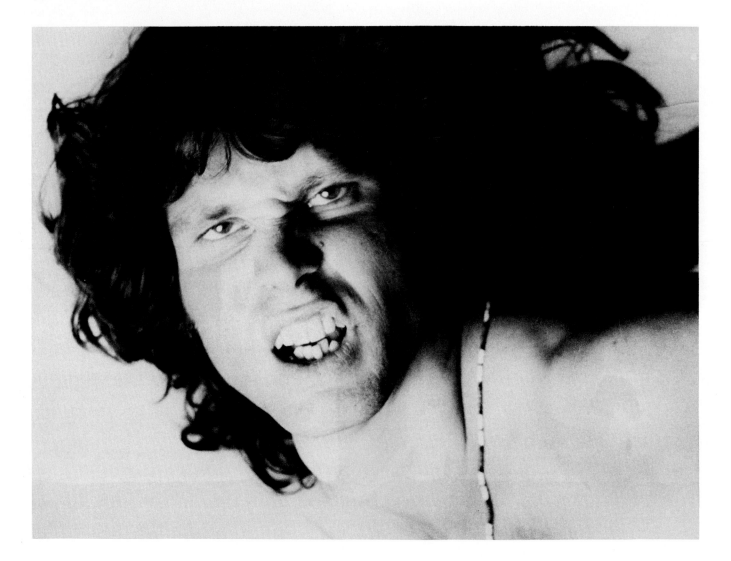

When the doors of perception are cleansed man will see things as they truly are, infinite.

        — *WILLIAM BLAKE,* as quoted in Aldous Huxley's <u>The Doors of Perception</u>

There are things known and there are things unknown and in between are the Doors.

—*JIM MORRISON*

2

STRANGE DAYS

November, 1967

THE WILLIAMS COLLEGE NEWS
FOUR DOORS TO THE FUTURE: GOTHIC ROCK IS THEIR THING · by John Stickney

"Which one is Jim Morrison?" one girl said to another. But he was not on stage, and a drummer and an organist and a guitar player looked impatiently toward a curtained door.

They sat in darkness punctuated by the steady red lights of amplifiers as tall as a man and the glow of a hundred cigarettes dancing in the evening breeze. The curtain on the door hung like velvet one inch thick.

Two hands pierced the slit of the curtain and drew it back sharply as a spotlight racked the stage and exposed a man who squinted in the brightness. There was applause that he did not care to hear, and the spotlight caught the contempt in the faces of the other musicians as Jim Morrison tentatively fingered the microphone.

He screamed and reeled, throttling the microphone and gazing at a sea of blank faces. He shouted a strung-out, distorted, and violated stream of word-images which twisted the faces into expression of shock and yet fascination.

He sang, or rather groaned, or talked to himself out loud as the group raced through "Break on Through" to lead off the set. The band and their instruments work together in complete interaction crystallizing the night air with a texture of sound which a person can run his hand over.

But Morrison gets all the attention, with black curls cascading over the upturned collar of a leather jacket worn the way all leather jackets should be: tight, tough, and somehow menacing. Some people have said that Morrison is beautiful, and others have learned the meaning of the word charisma by watching him.

And then there is "Light My Fire," and Morrison's brass and leather voice strokes the lyrics with all the subtlety in which he handles the microphone. The song deserves to be done The Doors' way, with suggestive intonation and instrumentation striving together to produce the incredible erotic pressure of the driving organ-scream climax.

After all, sex is what hard rock is all about. But there is terror in the sexuality of "The End," Morrison's black masterpiece of narrative poetry about a physical and spiritual odyssey which finishes in patricide and incest.

Morrison is at his best in this song, doing his own thing while the organist bends low and presses hard on the keys and the guitarist walks unconcernedly in and out of the spotlight. The drummer sweats.

Morrison dislodged the microphone and staggered blindly across the stage as the lyrics and screams which are "The End" poured out of his mouth, malevolent, satanic, electric, and on

fire. He stumbled and fell in front of a towering amplifier and sobbed to himself. The guitarist nudged him with the neck of his guitar, and a mouth in the audience said knowingly, "He's stoned."

But he wasn't. He sat up on his knees and stretched out his arms in an attitude of worship toward the cold amplifier, the impartial mediator between the virtues and absurdity of a music dependent upon circuits and ohms.

The audience did not know whether to applaud or not. The guitarist unplugged the electric cord which makes his instrument play, the organist stepped off left, the drummer threw his sticks to the ground in contempt and disgust, and Morrison had disappeared through the velvet curtain without a wave or a smile.

The Doors do not cater to the nameless faces

beyond the footlights. The group is not kind, and they do not entertain in any traditional sense. They allow other people to witness the manner of their existence and the pain and pleasure inherent in their imaginations.

The audience was scared, and rightly so. The Doors are not pleasant, amusing hippies proffering a grin and a flower; they wield a knife with a cold and terrifying edge. The Doors are closely akin to the national taste for violence, and the power of their music forces each listener to realize what violence is in himself.

The Doors met New York for better or for worse at a press conference in the gloomy vaulted wine cellar of the Delmonico Hotel, the perfect room to honor the Gothic rock of The Doors.

It was a good scene. Very few press people, and a lot of the city's rock hangers-on, hirsute and free, were there, all sampling a new sort of high: alcohol. Plastic chicks in mischievous miniskirts sipped daiquiris and waited for Morrison to show. No one was sure he would. But Andy Warhol walked in, and everybody breathed a sigh of relief to find that this indeed was the place to be.

There is a story of the meeting of two electric world-historical heroes; that is, Jim Morrison and Nico, underground film star and singer with Warhol's Velvet Underground. It was love at first sight, which later grew into lust, according to a friend of Morrison's. Anyway, Warhol seems to be interested in Morrison's potential as a movie star.

Suddenly all eyes turned to the door, where Morrison was making another entrance, sweeping into the room and gathering up the adulation to put in the pocket of his leather jacket.

He put his arm around a reporter, spilling

his drink, and compelled him toward the bar. A question which Morrison has been asked before came out somehow, "Jim, were you stoned up there on stage?" And the reply came back, "Man, I'm always stoned."

But apparently Morrison is not into drugs but has stuck with the old American standby, alcohol. He got his drink, spoke to the reporter in words which sailed over his head and bounced off the walls of the wine cellar like dead tennis balls. Morrison caromed off and hugged a chick. He was in his element. All eyes were his.

Morrison writes nearly all of The Doors' lyrics, and his work does have meaning. There are rock critics in our time, and when they speak of Morrison's lyrics, visions of Baudelaire, Rimbaud, Joyce, and Artaud pop out of their critiques.

But hard rock was never meant for academicism. There is truth in The Doors' beat which drives home the meaning of their fascination with symbolism, streams of consciousness, cruelty, and the bizarre in whatever form. That's where The Doors are.

The themes, symbols, and imagery of The Doors are stronger in their second album, which manages to transcend the fever-pitch intensity and macabre beauty of their first. The Doors have grown, a good sign.

Significantly titled *Strange Days*, the new album's music is just as erotic, just as hard-driving, just as compelling but twice as terrifying as their first effort.

The album contains neither the sophistication and cautious optimism of the Beatles, nor the self-conscious hedonism of the Rolling Stones. The Doors are doing their own thing, and innovation is better than stasis as far as rock is concerned. With The Doors, it's getting better all the time.

From **THE WAY OF THE SHAMAN**
by Michael Harner

Through his heroic efforts, the shaman helps his patients transcend their normal ordinary definition of reality, including their definition of themselves. The shaman shows those in his audience they are not emotionally and spiritually alone in their struggle against illness and death. The shaman shares his special powers and convinces these people, on a deep level of his consciousness, that another human is willing to offer up his own self to help them. Students in the West particularly have demonstrated again and again they can easily become initiated into the fundamentals of this ritual. This ancient way is so powerful and taps so deeply into the human mind that one's usual cultural belief and systems and assumptions about reality are essentially irrelevant.

CRAWDADDY!
THE DOORS · *by Sandy Pearlman*

Somewhere out on Long Island there is a guy who is keeping himself busy by fashioning a Jim Morrison doll. Some think he is a sick boy, a very sick boy. But maybe there was nothing better to do? Why not? So for lack of anything better to do, he did this: he took a Marine G.I. Joe model, he threw away the camouflage clothing, which left exposed a groovy pink plastic body with an unprecedentedly large number of unmutated limbs and organs, and then he got himself some soft black leather, sewed it up (learning how as he went or maybe some random girl did it) on a machine, and planned, I think, to top it off with a brownish Barbie doll wig brushed back.

R. Meltzer, too, has spoken of Morrison and leather: with Morrison, "Leather must be treated as functional—not the Warhol-Reed bit—held up in its black splendor by *metal*, or supporting a frail yet happy chuck-wagon bell." Clearly Morrison is the hero. As Gloria Stavers of *Sixteen* magazine has said: "Morrison is magic." Obviously. Morrison can inspire faith. He puts life into the scene. Ed Sullivan thinks, "Isn't he handsome." And to quote the mystic and voodoo adept L. Silvestri, "I believe him to be a being not of this earth." But, we shouldn't be entirely misled. The Doors, *as a group*, have a lot to do with faith. Morrison is merely the prettiest one dressed in leather. But, for example, who knows what evil lurks in the heart of Manzarek?

"Back Door Man" seen live many times, and then heard—at last—dead on the grooves, is a very neat thing. With all those grunts and stuff, it's where the inordinacy really starts. (As well as the leather.) "I am," Morrison says, "the back door man. The men don't know but the little girls understand." This is the spot for categorical statement. After too many years of bluesy overuse, this song can't even prove disconcerting through embarrassment. "I am." And we are in the presence of definitive charisma. Mere categorical assertion slipping up and off into arrogance. "I am." Absolutely categorical assertion has here become systematically assertive. (If you say something strangely enough it assumes an inexplicable aura of strength.) The strength of this categorical assertion is so enormous that not only does it encompass the whole world (i.e., as a systematic construc-

tion), but it becomes unnatural. That's when it surpasses all reason and arrives at Meltzer's categorical magical. Starting with household fornication we've gotten to a magical collapse of the world. This is no sly boy. This Back Door Man has absolute faith ("I am") and is also inspiring.

The Doors are spectral. Maybe more than anybody. What counts is the impression for which no significant referent detail can or should be found. The music ends and there is no detail which you can refer to to actually justify your impression. But you have that impression.

Movie music could have been a big influence. Check the surrealist organ on "Strange Days" and "Unhappy Girls," or that bass entrance on "You're Lost Little Girl" which smacks of the pulp mystery (crime-detective) movie music of the era 1940–1960. I can see The Doors scoring the "Invasion of the Body Snatchers" or even the fabulous "Mysterians." But it is your Krieger who really outdoes himself. This nice boy, often looking perplexed on stage, who may be the first with the Jimi Hendrix hair, who plays slowly with not as many notes as some, is revealed as a master of the left hand. A guitar scientist like the above Hendrix, he uses the instrument to produce explicitly technological-sounding sounds. Radically distending all sorts of notes on "Moonlight Drive." An inordinate number some might think, without realizing that with The Doors (especially on *Strange Days*) inordinacy (as with Hendrix) has become stylistic.

Disorder has been rationalized by The Doors into something both comprehensive and modular. The spirit is comprehensive so as to taint anything they turn to. And modular so as to be applicable anywhere. That's how The Doors taint the world. But understand there are kinds of purity. And the world can be purified by tainting it. Morrison has said: "It is a search, an opening of doors. We're trying to break through to a clearer, purer realm." (And along these lines don't you forget that the melody for "My Eyes Have Seen You" starts off like the Ajax ad, "Stronger Than Dirt.") Now if things have been absolutely tainted, they have also attained a certain absolute purity. An arrangement according to a perfect order.

EYE
LOVE AND THE DEMONIC PSYCHE · *by Digby Diehl*

Like some demonic vision out of a medieval hell-mouth, he hovers over the tightly packed, squirming crowd of girls at stage front. He peers into the darkness with sweat-blurred eyes. Swaying and staggering, the sonic waves exploding behind him, his distorted face registers a melting look of terror and despair.

"Faaaaaarrrruuuuugh. . . ." The screaming obscenity, massively amplified, forces the fans to recoil, while he reels and pitches even more wildly, almost falling off the stage. His mind is gone; he is a screaming, jellied blur of terror, and the excruciating vista reflected in his face is no longer the Fillmore, but an abyss of chaos, violence, and pain, like some nightmare landscape by Hieronymus Bosch. A vision of the ultimate; a vision of love and death seen once by a frozen leopard.

The insistent opening phrases of "Light My Fire" swell from the organ as he stands there with head in hands. Lost, blinded, he gropes for the microphone, at first completely incoherent, then catching the phrase "Got to love you, baby, one more time" from his mental swirl, repeating it over and over . . . gently, pleadingly, passionately, then cruelly. The "Light My Fire" background rises to a crescendo and collapses in a roar around him. The spotlight goes dark, the shell-shocked hippies disperse, and Jim Morrison and The Doors have forced the American Dream to the edge of reality once again.

This flagitious assault on the libido has proven to be the key to The Doors' confrontation with American life. *Mirabile dictu*, the public has responded to this onslaught by making their first album, *The Doors*, a million-seller, pushing *Strange Days* rapidly in the

same direction, and generally acclaiming the group as black priests of the Great Society. Drawing capacity crowds to almost all of their appearances, the newly arrived group already receives $10,000 to $12,000 for concerts.

Their music is an eerie amalgamation of primitive pulsations and beautiful lyricism that has all the hypnotic decadence of Edgar Allan Poe. Sounding more like Rimbaud than Poe, Morrison announces the philosophy of The Doors in personal terms: "I'm interested in anything about revolt, disorder, chaos, especially activity that appears to have no meaning. It seems to me to be the road toward freedom." The *hows* and *whys* of the bacchic frenzy that accompanies each of the group's concerts are puzzling to Morrison, as they are to many observers, but he suspects it has to do with the Puritan Ethic, repression, and

Vietnam. "I think there's a whole region of images and feelings inside us that rarely are given outlet in daily life. And when they do come out, they can take perverse forms. It's the dark side. Everyone, when he sees it, recognizes the same thing in himself. It's a recognition of forces that rarely see the light of day."

The shock of recognition can return people to their elemental senses, says Morrison, likening a Doors performance to a séance. "The more civilized we get on the surface, the more the other forces make their plea. We appeal to the same human needs as classical tragedy and early southern blues. Think of it as a séance in an environment which has become hostile to life; cold, restrictive. People feel they're dying in a bad landscape. People gather together in a séance in order to invoke, palliate, and drive away the dead.

Through chanting, singing, dancing, and music, they try to cure an illness, to bring harmony back into the world."

James Douglas Morrison has a soft and gentle beauty in the features of his face, very much like an angel in a Renaissance painting. This look of original innocence, joined with a genuinely shy manner and soft, youthful voice, contrasted with the black satyr on stage, is part of the Morrison enigma. He likes extremes; he lives extremes. "I think the highest and the lowest points are the important ones; all the points in between are, well, in between. I want freedom to try everything—I guess I want to experience everything at least once." He can be extremely civil, polite, even erudite; yet on other occasions, he can be gross,

There are no experts so, theoretically, any student knows almost as much as any professor."

During this period at UCLA, the noted director Josef Von Sternberg was teaching film direction in the department, and Morrison was quite influenced by the man and a retrospective of his works. In fact, he still claims that his favorite film is *Anatahan*, Von Sternberg's last film, shot in 1954 in Japan. It is a semidocumentary story of Japanese soldiers trapped on an atoll in South Pacific with one woman, and a chronicle of their psychological changes during ten years of isolation. "I like that film because it is very real. For me, films have to be either very artificial and surreal or very real and documentary. The more extreme in either tendency, the better."

or as he says, "primitive." But above all, he is electric. Dramatic. Charismatic. A figure whose very name is a study in contemporary mythology.

"The good thing about film is that there aren't any experts. There's no authority on film. Any one person can assimilate and contain the whole history of film in himself, which you can't do in other arts.

"Film is a hard medium to break into," says Morrison. "It's so much more complex than music; you need so many people and so much equipment. I like the rock medium because of its directness. The direct contact with an audience.

"Until recently, I've always had this underlying sense that something's not quite right. I felt blinders were being put on me as I grew older. I and all my friends were being funneled down a long narrowing tunnel. When you're in school, you're taking a risk. You can get a lot out of it, but you can get a lot of harm, too."

Pecos Bill, Mighty Joe Young, and John Henry would be proud to share the volume of outrageous and semiheroic acts attributed to Morrison. In addition to prodigious feats of sexuality, he is credited with some bizarre episodes of exhibitionism. At an Ivy League university, Morrison reportedly climbed the sixteen-story belltower with a willing lass; and in a moment of exuberance, swung out on the belltower shutter, two hundred feet above the heads of terrified onlookers—all this stark naked.

tainly sensuously exciting. Most viewers describe it as evil, but Morrison prefers the term *primeval*. "I was less theatrical, less artificial, when I began," he admits. "But now, the audiences we play for are much larger and the rooms are wider. It's necessary to project more, to exaggerate—almost to the point of grotesqueness. I think when you're a small dot at the end of a large arena, you have to make up for that lack of intimacy with expanded movements."

To a surprisingly literal degree, Morrison envisions a mythic role for himself as a rock singer: "Sometimes I like to look at the history of rock 'n' roll like the origin of Greek drama, which started out on a threshing floor at the crucial seasons and was originally a band of worshipers, dancing and singing.

Like his singing idol, Elvis Presley, Morrison radiates sexuality; but something is involved beyond the usual girlish fascination with a walking phallic symbol—an element of the perverse. The tortured display of staggering horror he presents is certainly a specter of masochism, but his sometimes brutal manner with the groupies or stageside sycophants is the reverse. At a California State College concert, he battered and taunted a front row of girls mercilessly with screams and gestures. The real show begins backstage, after a concert, where he often flicks live cigarette ashes at groupies.

Ignoring the ludicrous legal definitions of morality, the Morrison stage performance is most cer-

Then, one day, a possessed person jumped out of the crowd and started imitating a god. At first it was pure song and movement. As cities developed, more people became dedicated to making money, but they had to keep contact with nature somehow, so they had actors do it for them. I think rock serves the same function and may become a kind of theater."

"We are primarily a rock 'n' roll band, a blues band, just a band, but that's not all. A Doors concert is a public meeting called by us for a special kind of dramatic discussion and entertainment. When we perform, we're participating in the creation of a world, and we celebrate that creation with the audience. It becomes the sculpture of bodies in action. That's politics, but our power is sexual. We make concerts sexual politics. The sex starts with me, then moves out to include the charmed circle of musicians on stage. The music we make goes out to the audience and interacts with them; they go home and interact with the rest of reality, then I get it all back by interacting with that reality, so the whole sex thing works out to be one fine big ball of fire."

— JIM MORRISON

NEWSWEEK
THIS WAY TO THE EGRESS

Until recently, the thunderous San Francisco sound, with its electronic overdrive, had California's sonic highway all to itself. But lately, above the roar of the feedback, has been heard the sound of Los Angeles, a challenge spearheaded by the music of The Doors—vocalist Jim Morrison, pianist-organist Ray Manzarek, guitarist Robbie Krieger, and drummer John Densmore.

The impact of The Doors has been forceful enough to drive their first album (called simply *The Doors*) to the top of the charts, to make one song, "Light My Fire," one of the best-selling singles of the year, and to win sales of nearly half a million copies

for their just-released new album, *Strange Days*. The special appeal of their poetic, theatrical songs in unholy praise of forbidden joys is to college audiences like the students at the University of California at Santa Barbara, whom The Doors were haranguing with their message last week.

They come out on stage not to entertain but to preach, with all the disdain and cold fury of a revivalist preacher confronting an audience wallowing in sin. Once singer Jim Morrison gets going, it's hard to say whose soul he's trying to save, his listeners' or his own. Tall, ascetic-eyed, angelic-faced, he grinds out his songs with gyrating hips and a flat, full-bodied anguished voice that substitutes orgasmic cries for hallelujahs. "The only time I really open up is on stage," the shy, twenty-three-year-old Morrison told NEWSWEEK's John Riley. "I feel spiritual up there."

In contrast to the raucous San Francisco groups, the blues-oriented Doors are softer and smoother, blend in and out in a complex variety of melodic, rhythmic, and instrumental changes, punctuated by odd abrupt silences. They can sound as plaintive as Hawaiian strings, as decadent as Kurt Weill or as vigorous as Chuck Berry. But for the most part, they use their electrified instruments to invoke, with the chill of cold steel, weird, eerie twangs and rumblings that echo the doomsday lyrics of their sensual, primordial songs.

In such songs as "Strange Days," "People Are Strange," and their remarkable eleven-and-a-half-minute nightmare, "The End," The Doors describe and subscribe to chaos, to a world of alienation where night is preferred to day, to a Halloween world where darkest human impulses are welcomed into consciousness. What they deplore in such existentialist songs as "The Crystal Ship" and "Unhappy Girl" is anything that interferes with absolute personal freedom. And what they advise, in such exhortative songs as "Break on Through," the orgiastic "Light My Fire," and "Moonlight Drive," is to break the rules, taste the forbidden fruit, usually in a frankly sexual encounter.

The perverse and rather fuzzy salvation of which they sing, and the obtuse language with which they communicate, reflect The Doors' own spiritual search and youthful confusion. Krieger and Densmore eat macrobiotic foods and study meditation with the Beatles' mentor, Maharishi Mahesh Yogi. Morrison lives in a shack in Laurel Canyon. They no longer use drugs. "That was a transitory stage," says Manzarek. And Morrison, who writes most of the lyrics, adds: "It's a search, an opening of doors. We're trying to break through to a cleaner, purer realm." While they all wear their hair long, they choke on the label "hippie." "Think of us as erotic politicians," says Morrison. After that there seems to be nothing left to say.

TIME
POP MUSIC: SWIMMING TO THE MOON

"I'm interested in anything about revolt, disorder, chaos, especially activity that appears to have no meaning. It seems to me to be the road toward freedom." Thus twenty-three-year-old Jim Morrison states the philosophy behind The Doors, the rock group for which he is the chief songwriter and singer. Not surprisingly, The Doors are based in Los Angeles, where they find their peculiar mysticism perversely congenial. "This city is looking for a ritual to join its fragments," says Morrison. The Doors are looking for such a ritual, too—in Morrison's words, "a sort of electric wedding."

The search takes them not only past such familiar landmarks of the youthful odyssey as alienation and sex, but into symbolic realms of the unconscious—eerie night worlds filled with throbbing rhythms, shivery metallic tones, unsettling images. Swim to the moon, they sing, and "penetrate the evening that the city sleeps to hide."

Preaching passion of both the metaphysical and physical order, The Doors have a style at once more plaintive and dramatic than the droning, hypnotic waves of sound poured out by other West Coast groups such as the Jefferson Airplane and Grateful Dead. They startle and bemuse with a uniquely mournful and moody tone that shades Morrison's dusky voice seamlessly into a dark-textured background; the haunting organ, piano, and bass of Ray Manzarek, twenty-four; the sinuous guitar of Robbie Krieger, twenty-one; the nimble drums of John Densmore, twenty-two.

When The Doors finally bring off their electric wedding, it may well take the form of a small-scale musical play. The prototype is "The End," their enigmatic, eleven-and-a-half-minute string of visions apparently revolving around an Oedipus situation, in which Morrison portrays several roles—some behind a red mask. Last week, opening an engagement at San Francisco's Fillmore Auditorium, they introduced "The Unknown Soldier," an anti-war philippic with martial music, shouted commands, the loading click of a rifle, and shots mixed in with instrumental passages.

The Doors ultimately envision music with "the structure of poetic drama." Such a forbidding structure could cramp their financial fortunes, which at the moment are wide open: Both of their albums, *The Doors* and *Strange Days,* are among the top five on the sales charts; "Light My Fire" has been one of the smash singles of the year. But they don't seem worried, since the more complex forms come closer to fulfilling their apocalyptic imagination. Says Morrison: "We hide ourselves in the music to reveal ourselves."

HAPPENING
THE DOORS AT THE HULLABALOO · *by Hank Zevallos*

At the Hullabaloo, an excited, superpacked crowd waited restlessly for The Doors. This show, their last before going east, had been put together at the last minute and had hardly been advertised. Manzarek himself hadn't known about it, and that's why there was the tensed delay as people tried to locate him.

Outside, however, enough people to fill the house another two times waited in a long, thick, impatient line.

Morrison, however, appeared little concerned. He had gotten together with a freaky girl in dark, bizarre clothing, and was now lurking about with her backstage.

Finally, the revolving stage turned toward the screaming audience with The Doors on it, already beginning to play their music. Morrison slouched at the microphone. Instamatic flashcubes strobing and silhouetting him. And when the stage stopped moving, and The Doors faced the audience full on, and

Morrison began singing, girls began screaming louder and rushed, pushing and pressing toward the stage. Guys whistled. Flashcubes strobing from all over. Morrison singing and screaming with the music, soon raping the microphone stand between his legs.

Then, by honest accident, Morrison tripped because of the mike and fell hard on the stage. But it happened with a musical climax, and it looked like this was how it was supposed to have happened. Girls screamed. Rushed, pressing harder against the stage. Camera flashlights continued to strobe the intense scene wildly. Morrison got up, angry, picked up the mike stand, and began wildly swinging and throwing it about hard. Destroying it. The girls right up front were in very real danger of being accidentally but seriously hurt. And their faces showed the terror. But something else also showed. It looked as if they were having a frenzied orgasm. Going insane with unbelievably wicked delight.

TEENSET
WHO'S AFRAID OF JIM MORRISON? · by Judith Sims

In an effort to learn more about Jim Morrison, TEEN-SET spoke with anyone we could find who knew him and read everything we could find that had been written about him (a surprising amount for such a relatively new group). Our efforts culminated in the frustrating realization that we may never "get to know" Jim Morrison by talking to him or those who know him, nor by reading what other similarly frustrated people have written about him. Jim Morrison's lyrics tell more about him than any conversation or article ever could, but his songs are often uncomfortable for us to hear and difficult to absorb and understand. His lyrics go far beyond the acceptable psychological limits of pop music; we must reframe our references when we listen to him. He isn't afraid to expose his fears and hangups—the same fears and hangups which most of us share in varying degrees and spend most of our lives trying to suppress, overcome or "cope with."

LIFE

WICKED GO THE DOORS An Adult's Education
by the Kings of Acid Rock · by Fred Powledge

I suppose it was a combination of White Power, being thirty-three years old, *Sergeant Pepper,* and my nine-year-old daughter, Polly, that made me want so urgently to understand rock music.

We bought *Sergeant Pepper's Lonely Hearts Club Band* and considered it good entertainment, suitable for the whole family. We realized as we played *Sergeant Pepper* more and more that the album was not just a collection of thirteen songs, but a successful attempt at presenting a *whole* of something, the way a symphony is a totality made up of several movements. But we didn't exactly know what the totality of *Sergeant Pepper was.*

Gradually my wife and I found that we were no longer moved by what had been our regular music. We were spending more and more time humming "Lucy in the Sky With Diamonds" to ourselves.

The new music I most wanted to understand was that of a group called The Doors, who took their name from a line by poet William Blake about "the doors of perception." My wife and I heard the first Doors album at a party a year ago, bought it for ourselves, and played it a few times.

The sound of the album slowly got inside my head. There was something about The Doors' music—most of it electronic but never superficial—and their lyrics—very obscure to me at first, then less obscure but never completely understandable—that convinced me their work was significant. This was at a time when hardly anybody else knew about The Doors. I called Elektra Records and asked if there was a second Doors album on the way. Elektra wasn't sure.

The Doors' music, unlike the Beatles', is satanic,

sensual, demented, and full of acid when you first hear it, and it becomes even more so when you play it over and over again.

The most satanic thing about The Doors is Jim Morrison, the lead vocalist and author of most of the group's songs. Morrison is twenty-four years old, out of UCLA, and he appears—in public and on his records—to be moody, temperamental, enchanted in the mind, and extremely stoned on something. Once you see him perform, you realize that he also seems dangerous, which, for a poet, may be a contradiction in terms.

He wears skintight black leather pants, on stage and away from it; and when he sings, he writhes and grinds and is sort of the male equivalent of the late Miss Lilly Christine, the Cat Girl. But with Lilly Christine you had a good idea that the performance was going to stop short of its promised ending-point. You don't know that with Morrison.

Morrison is a very good actor and a very good poet—one who speaks in short, beautiful bursts like the Roman Catullus. His lyrics often seem obscure, but their obscurity, instead of making you hurry off to play a Pete Seeger record that you can *understand*, challenges you to try to interpret. You sense that Morrison is writing about weird scenes he's been privy to, about which he would rather not be too explicit.

The words are not what you'd call simple and straightforward. You can't listen to the record once

or twice and then put it away in the rack. And this is one of the exciting characteristics of the new music in general: you really have to *listen* to it, repeatedly, preferably at a high volume in a room that is otherwise quiet and perhaps darkened. You must throw away all those old music-listening habits that you learned courtesy of the Lucky Strike Hit Parade and Mantovani.

You are reminded that the music is a plastic reflection of our plastic world. The sounds are transistorized, sharper than sharp, just as the plastic lettering over a hot dog stand is redder than red. Out of this context the music—even the conventional sounds of the church organ or the street noises—is unreal; in it, it is marvelously effective in reflecting what's going on in our society. It dances close to disharmony, to insanity; sometimes it does sound insane and disharmonious, but then you listen closer and find a harmony hidden deep within it.

Everyone with whom I talked about The Doors had made the point that concerts were a lot like Living Theater, a lot like the theater of Kurt Weill and Bertolt Brecht—artistic comments on a society that was rushing, pell-mell, toward something it did not understand. I decided to catch The Doors' next performance.

I had promised my wife and Polly a trip to New Haven and a preconcert visit backstage with John Densmore, Polly's favorite Door. We got to the New Haven Arena early, but getting to the dressing room proved to be a difficult matter. Policemen stood in the corridors, making sure that nobody got backstage.

The only man who apparently had the authority to conduct us to the dressing room was a Lieutenant James P. Kelly, head of the New Haven Police Department's Youth Division, and he was busy unblocking a fire exit. We talked to a patrolman while we waited for Lieutenant Kelly. Polly and I were interested in a black aerosol can the policeman wore on his belt. "Mace," he said, giving the name of the chemical spray now in use by many police departments; it renders a suspect harmless when it is ejected in his face. I shuddered, looked at my wife, and changed the subject.

"Do you like this kind of music?"

"Yeah," said the patrolman, who was chubby and young and pleasant enough. "My brother's in a local rock band."

Lieutenant Kelly arrived. At first he didn't want to take us to the dressing room, but he relented when I asked him how to spell his name, K-e-l-l-y or K-e-l-l-e-y?

On the way to the dressing room, we joked about the natural antipathy between cops and reporters, and how each had to give the other a hard time in order to get his job done. Polly saw The Doors, collected their autographs, and as we went for our seats for the concert she started calculating her relative stature in the fourth grade in Brooklyn on the following Monday.

The New Haven audience was much sharper than the college students at Troy had been the previous evening, and Morrison felt the difference. He stood before the six powerful amplifiers in his black leather pants and gyrated, sang, undulated, jumped, crouched, fondled, jerked, twisted, and projected poetry, at more than 1,300 watts, into the old sports arena. The crowd applauded at the right times.

There were maybe 2,000 people there, and most of them were getting bammed on the music and the words. Morrison bummed a cigarette from someone in the audience, and a little later he threw a microphone stand off the stage. A few policemen moved around in front of the audience, clearing away the little girls who had come down close to the stage with their Instamatics to take Morrison's picture. On another occasion Morrison spat toward the first row, but it fell short and nobody seemed to care. It was like *Marat/Sade*. I was in the second row, and I didn't care.

He *was* dangerous, but danger was part of the show. I understood now what Paul Rothchild was talking about when he spoke of the rock musicians' *theater*, and all the references to Living Theater and Kurt

Weill and Bertolt Brecht, and I understood what John Densmore meant when he said you had to see The Doors in concert to really appreciate them.

Manzarek continued on the electronic organ, Krieger on the guitar, Densmore on the drums; and Morrison started talking:

"I want to tell you about something that happened just two minutes ago right here in New Haven . . . this is New Haven, isn't it, New Haven, Connecticut, United States of America?"

The crowd grew quieter. Morrison started talking about having eaten dinner, and about having had a few drinks, and about somebody's having asked for his autograph at the restaurant, and about having talked with a waitress about religion, and about coming over to the New Haven Arena for the concert, and going into the dressing room, and about meeting a girl there, and talking with her.

"We started talking," he said, still writhing, still keeping the rhythm that Densmore was beating behind him, twisting at the microphone, making you understand that he was on the black, evil side.

> And we wanted some privacy
> And so we went into this shower-room
> We weren't doing anything, you know,
> Just standing there and talking.
> And then this little man came in there,
> This little man, in a little blue suit
> And a little blue cap,
> And he said,
> "Whatcha doin' there?"
> "Nothin'."
> But he didn't go 'way,
> He stood there
> And then he reached 'round behind him
> And he brought out this little black can
>   of somethin'
> Looked like shaving cream,
> And then he
> Sprayed it in my eyes.
> I was blinded for about thirty minutes . . .

The lights came on. Morrison blinked out into the audience. He asked why they were on. There was no reply. Ray Manzarek walked over and whispered something into his ear. Morrison asked if the crowd wanted more music. The audience screamed, "Yes!"

"Well, then turn off the lights. TURN OFF THE LIGHTS!"

A policeman walked onto the stage, Lieutenant Kelly was suddenly there, arresting the singer. Morrison was nonchalant at first; he even pointed the mike at Kelly and said, "Say your thing, man." But then a policeman snatched the microphone from Morrison's hand. People scrambled off the stage. Bill

Siddons, The Doors' road manager, a handsome, clean-cut young man who wears a peace button, tried to protect Morrison's body from the cops with his own. Then they took Morrison away, and Siddons tried to protect the equipment—the six amplifiers and the electronic organ and drums and guitar, and he thrashed around on the stage as more policemen ran in.

Some of the crowd started to leave; some stayed around and in protest pushed over the folding wooden chairs. Outside, Tim Page, a photographer just back from Vietnam, was taking pictures of several cops arresting a young man. One of the policemen saw him and pushed him out into the street. Tim protested to Lieutenant Kelly; the lieutenant said he was sorry and that he would speak to the patrolman as soon as things calmed down.

Then, as Kelly hurried along, the patrolman came back and arrested Tim, then arrested Yvonne Chabrier, a LIFE reporter, then arrested Michael Zwerin, the jazz critic for *The Village Voice*, all for no apparent reason. They had breached the peace, said the police later. An unknown number of teen-agers were hauled off. The charge against Jim

Morrison was that he had breached the peace, given an indecent and immoral exhibition, and resisted arrest. He was placed under $1,500 bond. His road manager posted the money from concert receipts.

I sought out Lieutenant Kelly and told him about the arrests. I thought he could undo what was being done. He seemed surprised. "It's sickening," he said. "It's terrible what went on here."

I saw the chubby policeman who had showed Polly the can of Mace earlier—the cop who had a brother in a local rock band. Did he still like the music? He said, "Sure," as he pushed teenaged girls

and boys toward the exits. His face was hard and strained.

I looked down at Polly. "Why can't Lieutenant Kelly stop this?" she asked.

She stood there, in the midst of it all, the cops and teenagers swirling around her, Tim and Yvonne and Michael being led toward a paddy wagon; she was not afraid, as I was. Her little-girl face was angry, her fists were clenched, her eyes pinched but still seeing everything that was happening. And understanding it. She was seeing it live this time.

Not on tape. Not on film. No lip-synch.

THE NEW YORK TIMES
NEW HAVEN POLICE CLOSE "THE DOORS"

NEW HAVEN—The police stopped a rock 'n' roll concert at the New Haven Arena, forcibly removed the lead singer of "The Doors" group and arrested three journalists late last night.

Those arrested were Jim Morrison, twenty-four years old, of Los Angeles, leader of "The Doors," one of the nation's leading rock groups; Michael Zwerin, music critic for *The Village Voice*; Tim Page, a freelance photographer on assignment for LIFE magazine, and Miss Yvonne V. Chabrier, researcher for LIFE.

According to the police, Mr. Morrison was giving an "indecent and immoral exhibition" when he was off the stage.

One witness, Fred Powledge, a writer working on a rock 'n' roll story, said Mr. Morrison started singing a song and then began a monologue concerning an earlier confrontation with a policeman in a dressing room.

"Morrison," Mr. Powledge said, "told the audience of about two thousand persons that he was talking to a girl in the dressing room when a policeman came and told the couple to move. Morrison said he hesitated, and the officer sprayed Mace in his eyes."

Mace is a form of tear gas that police use in attempting to quell persons who become violent.

The police gave a different version of what had happened in the dressing room.

Lieutenant James P. Kelly wrote in his arrest report that Mr. Morrison and an eighteen-year-old coed from nearby Southern Connecticut State College were "standing and kissing" in the dressing room.

The patrolman said he asked the performer to leave and a scuffle broke out. The officer said he used Mace on Mr. Morrison to subdue him.

At this point, Mr. Morrison's agent pleaded with the police not to arrest the singer so he could appear with his act. The police agreed, and Mr. Morrison was allowed on stage with "The Doors"—the last act in the show being staged for a New Haven college scholarship fund.

Mr. Powledge said that when Mr. Morrison began his narrative of the dressing-room incident, "the lights came on and six officers dragged Morrison off the stage."

Lieutenant Kelly told the audience the show was over.

The police contended they had received complaints from audience members who did not like foul language that the performer allegedly used.

The audience left the arena, and several scuffles broke out between the police and the crowd.

Mr. Page, the photographer, said he was arrested while taking a picture of a policeman "roughing up a kid."

The police said Mr. Page, Mr. Zwerin, and Miss Chabrier were arrested for "breach of the peace, interfering with an officer, and resisting arrest." They were released on $300 bond each.

Mr. Morrison, in addition to the indecent exhibition charge, was cited with breach of the peace and resisting a policeman. He was released on $1,500 bond.

MORRISON/SUGERMAN INTERVIEW

Danny Sugerman: What's it like to be a sex symbol?

Jim Morrison: For some reason I'm not fully sure of, certain archetypal roles exist in human society, which society demands be filled, and I think it's just a matter of chance who comes along to fill them. Anyway, the only place where that kind of thing has any reality at all is in a few magazines and newspapers.

Danny: What about being hailed as the "King of Orgasmic Rock"?

Jim: I consider it a high compliment. Music is very erotic. One of the functions is a purgation of emotion. To call our music orgasmic means that we are able to move people to a kind of emotional orgasm through the medium of words and music.

A concert clicks when the musicians and the audience reach a kind of united experience. It is stirring and satisfying to know that the various boundaries which separate people from other people are lowered for the space of one hour.

LOS ANGELES FREE PRESS • *Strange Days*
by Gene Youngblood

The Doors' new album, *Strange Days*, is a landmark in rock music. It ventures beyond the conventional realm of musical expression: It has become the theater. The cruel theater of Artaud, and of *Marat/Sade*. The theater of shock, and of McClure's *The Beard*. The theater of the absurd, Grand Guignol in electronic shrieks. The erotic demons of Bosch wiggling across the musical stage.

Even the record label—Elektra—is apropos, for the music of The Doors is electric both in fact and fantasy: it doesn't soothe, it assaults; it doesn't encourage, it intimidates; it doesn't touch the heart, it tickles the prostate. The Beatles and the Stones are for blowing your mind; The Doors are for afterward, when your mind is already gone. It's like screeching your fingernails on glass.

The music of The Doors is the music of total abandon. If the Beatles find their cinematic equivalent in Fellini ("For the Benefit of Mr. Kite") or Antonioni ("A Day in the Life"), The Doors conjure up the eyeball-slashing of Luis Buñuel (*Un Chien Andalou*) and the baroque orgies of Anger's *Inauguration of the Pleasure Dome*. Indeed, the wickedness of the Doors' psycho-sexual musico-literary tapestries can be found in the UCLA student films of Ray Manzarek, *Evergreen* and *Induction*. Though not yet fully realized, they embodied the same black humor and ominous moods which now inform The Doors' lyrics:

> Strange eyes fill strange rooms
> Voices will signal their tired end
> The hostess is grinning
> Her guests sleep from sinning
>
> Hear me talk of sin
> And you know this is it.

The Doors' music is the music of outrage. It is not sham. It probes the secrets of truth. It is avant-garde in content if not technique: it speaks of madness that dwells within us all, of the Velvet Underground, of depravity and dreams, but it speaks of them in relatively conventional musical terms. That is its strength and its beauty—a beauty that terrifies.

The music of The Doors is more surreal than psychedelic, it is more anguish than acid. More than rock, it is ritual—the ritual of psycho-sexual exorcism. The Doors are the warlocks of pop culture. The agonized grunts and screams that fly from Jim Morrison's angelic mouth are indeed as enigmatic as the idea of a butterfly screaming. The Doors are saying there are screams we don't hear, and they're trying to give them shape. Morrison IS an angel; an exterminating angel. He and The Doors are a demonic and beautiful miracle that has risen like a shrieking Phoenix from the burning bush of the new music.

CIRCUS • *Strange Days*
by Eric Van Lustbader

All things considered, *Strange Days* is The Doors' best album, despite the fact that it never sold as well as their first. And maybe, here at last, we have a clue to Morrison. Certainly this LP, revolving around one concept, from brilliant music to brilliant cover, is The Doors' most cohesive effort (*Waiting for the Sun*, for instance, their third LP, contains excellent songs, but they don't fit together; there's no motion from one to another, no continuity, as if tracks that had to be left off other albums for one reason or another, had accumulated here), and certainly at least two years ahead of its time. If it were to be released now, it would be hailed as a masterpiece.

Listening to *Strange Days* is like watching Fellini's *Satyricon*. Morrison's words are so cinematic that each song begins to form pictures in the mind. More than any other American songwriter—lyricist, if you will—he has this quality. Like the film, *Strange Days* builds its storyline (of people trying desperately to reach each other through the choking haze of drugs and artificial masks) through the images and characters in a series of vignettes. And the whole becomes more and more visible the deeper one gets into the film and/or the album. Because *Strange Days* has been set up that way.

THE VILLAGE VOICE • *Strange Days*
by Richard Goldstein

The Doors have had ample practice being themselves. They are one of the most oft-appearing groups in pop music and this constant attention to live effect has produced a crackling confidence in each other's style which shows on their new album, *Strange Days* (Elektra). The music is as tight, as controlled, as satisfying of its own aims as any I have heard in hard rock. Robbie Krieger's guitar slides and slithers around Jim Morrison's voice like a belly dancer. Ray Manzarek's rock organ continues to speak in an impressive array of languages (this album should enlarge the coterie of young musicians now applying a driving-yet-cool approach). Paul Rothchild's production is tastefully cut and tapered, and the album's jacket (let us offer thanks) is not in art nouveau.

Lizze James: *I think fans of The Doors see you as a savior, the leader who'll set them all free. How do you feel about that? It's kind of a heavy burden, isn't it?*

Jim Morrison: It's absurd. How can I set free anyone who doesn't have the guts to stand up alone and declare his own freedom? I think it's a lie—people claim they want to be free—everybody insists that freedom is what they want the most, the most sacred and precious thing a man can possess. But that's bullshit! People are terrified to be set free—they hold on to their chains. They fight anyone who tries to break those chains. It's their security. . . . How can they expect me or anyone to set them free if they don't really want to be free?

Lizze: *Why do you think people fear freedom?*

Jim: I think people resist freedom because they're afraid of the unknown. But it's ironic. . . . That unknown was once very well known. It's where our souls belong. . . . The only solution is to confront them—confront yourself—with the greatest fear imaginable. Expose yourself to your deepest fear. After that, fear has no power, and fear of freedom shrinks and vanishes. You are free.

Lizze: *What do you mean when you say "freedom"?*

Jim: There are different kinds of freedom—there's a lot of misunderstanding. . . . The most important kind of freedom is to be what you really are. You trade in your reality for a role. You trade in your senses for an act. You give up your ability to feel, and in exchange, put on a mask. There can't be any large-scale revolution until there's a personal revolution, on an individual level. It's got to happen inside first. . . . You can take away a man's political freedom and you won't hurt him—unless you take away his freedom to feel. That can destroy him.

Lizze: *But how can anyone else have the power to take away from your freedom to feel?*

Jim: Some people surrender their freedom willingly—but others are forced to surrender it. Imprisonment begins with birth. Society, parents—they refuse to allow you to keep the freedom you are born with. There are subtle ways to punish a person for daring to feel. You see that everyone around you has destroyed his true feeling nature. You imitate what you see.

Lizze: *Are you saying that we are, in effect, brought up to defend and perpetuate a society that deprives people of the freedom to feel?*

Jim: Sure . . . teachers, religious leaders—even friends, or so-called friends—take over where parents leave off. They demand that we feel only the feelings they want and expect from us. They demand all the time that we perform feelings for them. We're like actors—turned loose in this world to wander in search of a phantom . . . endlessly searching for a half-forgotten shadow of our lost reality. When others demand that we become the people they want us to be, they force us to destroy the person we really are. It's a subtle kind of murder . . . the most loving parents and relatives commit this murder with smiles on their faces.

Lizze: *Do you think it's possible for an individual to free himself from these repressive forces on his own—all alone?*

Jim: That kind of freedom can't be granted. Nobody can win it for you. You *have* to do it on your own. If you look to somebody else to do it for you—somebody outside yourself—you're still depending on others. You're still vulnerable to those repressive, evil outside forces, too.

Lizze: But isn't it possible for people who want that freedom to unite—to combine their strength, maybe just to strengthen each other? It must be possible.

Jim: Friends can help each other. A true friend is someone who lets you have total freedom to be yourself—and especially to feel. Or not feel. Whatever you happen to be feeling at the moment is fine with them. That's what real love amounts to—letting a person be what he really is. . . . Most people love you for who you pretend to be. . . . To keep their love, you keep pretending—performing. You get to love your pretense. . . . It's true, we're locked in an image, an act—and the sad thing is, people get so used to their image—they grow attached to their masks. They love their chains. They forget all about who they really are. And if you try to remind them, they hate you for it—they feel like you're trying to steal their most precious possession.

Lizze: It's ironic—it's sad. Can't they see that what you're trying to show them is the way to freedom?

Jim: Most people have no idea what they're missing. Our society places a supreme value on control—hiding what you feel. Our culture mocks "primitive cultures" and prides itself on suppression of natural instincts and impulses.

*Lizze: In some of your poetry, you openly admire and praise
primitive people—Indians, for instance. Do you mean that
it's not human beings in general but our particular society
that's flawed and destructive?*

Jim: Look at how other cultures live—peacefully, in harmony with
the earth, the forest—animals. They don't build war machines and invest millions of dollars in attacking other coun-
tries whose political ideals don't happen to agree with their
own.

Lizze: We live in a sick society.

Jim: It's true . . . and part of the disease is not being aware that
we're diseased. . . . Our society has too much—too much
to hold on to, and value—freedom ends up at the bottom
of the list.

*Lizze: But isn't there something an artist can do? If you didn't
feel you, as an artist, could accomplish something, how
could you go on?*

Jim: I offer images—I conjure memories of freedom that can still
be reached—like The Doors, right? But we can only open
the doors—we can't drag people through. I can't free them
unless they want to be free—more than anything else. . . .
Maybe primitive people have less bullshit to let go of, to give
up. A person has to be willing to give up everything—not
just wealth. All the bullshit he's been taught—all society's
brainwashing. You have to let go of all that to get to the
other side. Most people aren't willing to do that.

"I think there's a whole region of images and feelings inside us that rarely are given outlet in daily life. And when they do come out, they can take perverse forms. It's the dark side. Everyone, when he sees it, recognizes the same thing in himself. It's a recognition of forces that rarely see the light of day."

— JIM MORRISON

3

WAITING FOR THE SUN

July, 1968

From THE WHITE ALBUM
WAITING FOR MORRISON · *by Joan Didion*

It is six, seven o'clock of an early spring evening, and I am sitting on the cold vinyl-tile floor of a sound studio on Sunset Boulevard, watching a rock group called The Doors record a rhythm track. On the whole my attention is less than entirely engaged by the preoccupations of rock groups (I have already heard about acid as a transitional stage and also about the Maharishi and even about universal love, and after a while it all sounds like marmalade skies to me), but The Doors are different. The Doors interest me. They have nothing in common with the gentle Beatles. They lack the contemporary conviction that love is brotherhood and the *Kama Sutra*. Their music insists that love is sex and sex is death and therein lies salvation. The Doors are the Norman Mailers of the Top 40, missionaries of apocalyptic sex.

Right now they are gathered together in uneasy symbiosis to make their album, and the studio is cold and the lights are too bright and there are masses of wires and banks of the ominous blinking electronic circuitry with which the new musicians live so casually. There are three of the four Doors. There is a bass player borrowed from a group called Clear Light. There are the producer and the engineer and the road manager and a couple of girls and a Siberian Husky named Nikki with one gray eye and one gold. There are paper bags half-filled with hard-boiled eggs and chicken livers and cheeseburgers and empty bottles of apple juice and California *rosé*. There is everything and everybody The Doors need to cut the rest of this third album except one thing, the fourth Door, the lead singer, Jim Morrison, a twenty-four-year-old graduate of UCLA who wears black vinyl pants and no underwear and tends to suggest some range of the possible just beyond a suicide pact. It is Morrison who describes The Doors as "erotic politicians." It is Morrison who defines the group's interests as "anything about revolt, disorder, chaos about activity that appears to have no meaning." It is Morrison who got arrested in New Haven in December for giving an "indecent" performance. It is Morrison who writes most of The Doors' lyrics, the peculiar character of which is to reflect either an ambiguous paranoia or a quite unambiguous insistence upon love-death as the ultimate high. And it

is Morrison who is missing. It is Ray Manzarek and Robbie Krieger and John Densmore who make The Doors sound the way they do, and maybe it is Manzarek and Krieger and Densmore who make seventeen out of twenty interviewees on *American Bandstand* prefer The Doors over all other groups, but it is Morrison who gets up there in his black vinyl pants with no underwear and projects the idea, and it is Morrison they are waiting for now.

Ray Manzarek is hunched over a Gibson keyboard. "You think *Morrison's* gonna come back?" he says to no one in particular.

No one answers.

"So we can do some vocals?" Manzarek says.

The producer is working with the tape of the rhythm track they just recorded. "I hope so," he says without looking up.

"Yeh," Manzarek says. "So do I."

It is a long while later. Morrison arrives. He has on his black vinyl pants, and he sits down on a leather couch in front of the four big blank speakers, and he closes his eyes. The curious aspect of Morrison's arrival is this: No one acknowledges it by so much as a flicker of an eye. Robbie Krieger continues working out a guitar passage. John Densmore tunes his drums. Manzarek sits at the control console and twirls a corkscrew and lets a girl rub his shoulders. The girl does not look at Morrison, although he is in her direct line of sight. An hour or so passes, and still no one has spoken to Morrison. Then Morrison speaks to Manzarek. He speaks almost in a whisper, as if he were wresting the words from behind some disabling aphasia.

"It's an hour to West Covina," he says. "I was thinking, maybe we should spend the night out there after we play."

Manzarek puts down the corkscrew. "Why," he says.

"Instead of coming back."

Manzarek shrugs. "We were planning to come back."

"Well, I was thinking, we could rehearse out there."

Manzarek says nothing.

"We could get in a rehearsal, there's a Holiday Inn next door."

"We could do that," Manzarek says. "Or we could rehearse Sunday, in town."

"I guess so." Morrison pauses. "Will the place be ready to rehearse Sunday?"

Manzarek looks at him for a while. "No," he says then.

I count the control knobs on the electronic console. There are seventy-six. I am unsure in whose favor the dialogue was resolved or if it was resolved at all. Robbie Krieger picks at his guitar, and says that he needs a fuzz box. The producer suggests that he borrow one from the Buffalo Springfield in the next studio. Krieger shrugs. Morrison sits down on the leather couch again and leans back. He lights a match. He studies the flame awhile and then very slowly, very deliberately, lowers it to the fly of his black vinyl pants. Manzarek watches him. The girl who is rubbing Manzarek's shoulders does not look at anyone. There is a sense that no one is going to leave the room, ever. It will be some weeks before The Doors finish recording this album. I do not see it through.

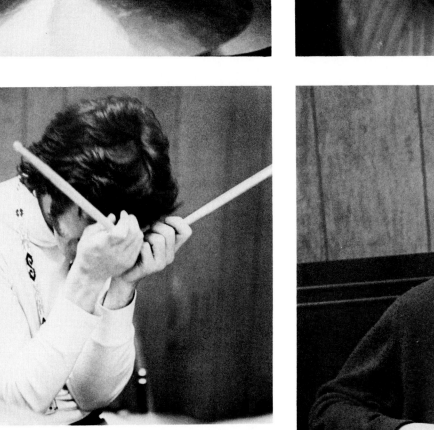

"The shaman . . . he was a man who would intoxicate himself. See, he was probably already an . . . uh . . . unusual individual. And, he would put himself into a trance by dancing, whirling around, drinking, taking drugs—however. Then, he would go on a mental travel and . . . uh . . . describe his journey to the rest of the tribe."

—*JIM MORRISON*

He comes to meet you in superstar fatigues: a slept-in pullover, and the inevitable leather pants. A lumpy hat covers most of his mane. You mutter "groovy" at each other in greeting, and split for the beach. His most recent song comes on the radio. You both laugh as he turns up the volume, and fiddles with the bass controls. It's a perfect afternoon, so he picks up his girl. She says, "Your hat makes you look like a Rembrandt, Jim," and he whispers, "Oh, wow," riding the image as though it were a breaking wave.

The official interview takes place in a sequestered inlet at the Garden of Self-Realization, an ashram Hollywood style. You sit not far from an urn certified to contain Mahatma Gandhi's ashes. Music is piped in from speakers at the top of a stucco arch with cupolas sprayed gold.

Amid a burst of strings from the hidden speakers, you ask the trial question. Jim answers in a slithering baritone. "I dunno . . . I haven't thought about it." The garden supplies Muzak hosannas.

"When you started, did you anticipate your image?"

"Nahhh. It just sort of happened . . . unconsciously."

"How did you prepare yourself for stardom?"

"Uh . . . about the only thing I did was . . . I stopped getting haircuts."

"How has your behavior on stage changed?"

"See, it used to be . . . I'd just stand still and sing. Now, I . . . uh . . . exaggerate a little bit."

His voice drops an octave at the sight of a tape recorder, and the surrogate audience it represents. He gives a cautious mischievous interview, contemplating each question as though it were a hangnail, and answering with just a trace of smile in the corners of his quotation marks. But he gets his scene across.

"I'm beginning to think it's easier to scare people than to make them laugh.

"I wonder why people like to believe I'm high all the time. I guess . . . maybe they think someone else can take their trip for them.

"A game is a closed field . . . a ring of death with . . . uh . . . sex at the center. Performing is the only game I've got, so . . . I guess it's my life."

His statement, like his songs, is an unpunctuated puzzle. You connect the dots between images, and

become involved. "I'm a word man," he exults. In discussing his craft, he sputters with esthetic energy. "See, there's this theory about the nature of tragedy, that Aristotle didn't mean catharsis for the audience, but a purgation of emotions for the actors themselves. The audience is just a witness to the event taking place on stage."

He suggests you read Nietzsche on the nature of tragedy to understand where he is really at. His eyes glow as he launches into a discussion of the Apollonian-Dionysian struggle for control of the life force. No need to guess which side he's on.

"See, singing has all the things I like," he explains. "It's involved with writing and with music. There's a lot of acting. And it has this one other thing . . . a physical element . . . a sense of the immediate. When I sing, I create characters."

"What kinds of characters?"

"Oh . . . hundreds. Hundreds of 'em."

"I like to think he just arrived—you know, came out of nowhere"

A FAN

The Doors, however, are an inner theater of cruelty. Their musical dramas have made fear and trembling part of the rock lexicon. These days every band worth its psychedelic salt has a local lunatic singing lead. But The Doors have already transcended their own image. Now, they are in search of total sensual contact with an audience. They may yet appear at a future concert in masks. As Ray Manzarek explains: "We want our music to short-circuit the conscious mind and allow the subconscious to flow free."

That goal is a realization of all that was implicit in Elvis Presley's sacred wiggle. But if Elvis was an unquestioning participant in his own hysteria, The Doors celebrate their myth as a creative accomplishment. Playing sorcerer is Jim's thing—not a job, or a hobby, or even one of those terribly necessary rituals we sanctify with the name Role. Jim calls it "play":

The Lizard King slithers down Sunset Strip in a genuine snakeskin jacket and leather tights. Bands of teenyboppers flutter about like neon butterflies, but he is oblivious to their scene. He moves past ticky-tacoramas and used-head shops, into the open arms of recording studio B, where his true subjects wait.

He greets us with a grin out of *Thus Spake Zarathustra,* and we realize instantly that Jim is loaded. Juiced. Stoned—the old way. Booze. No one is surprised; Jim is black Irish to the breath. He deposits a half-empty quart bottle of wine on top of the control panel and downs the remnants of somebody's beer.

"Hafta' break it in," he mutters, caressing the sleeves of his jacket. It sits green and scaly on his shoulders, and crinkles like tinfoil whenever he moves.

"It's—very Tennessee Williams, Jim."

Grunt. He turns to producer Paul Rothchild with a spacious grin that says, "I'm here, so you can start." But Rothchild makes little clicking noises with his tongue. He is absorbed in a musical problem, and he offers only a perfunctory nod to the tipsy titan at his side.

Behind a glass partition three musical Doors hunch over their instruments, intent on a rhythm line that refuses to render itself whole. The gap between Morrison and the other Doors is vast in the studio, where the enforced cohesion of live performance is missing. On their own, they are methodic musicians.

Densmore drums in sharp, precise strokes. Krieger's guitar undulates like a belly dancer—sinuous but sober. And at the organ, Manzarek is cultivated and crisp. With his shaggy head atop a pair of plywood shoulders, he looks like a hip undertaker.

Jim walks into the studio and accosts a vacant mike. He writhes in languid agony, jubilant at the excuse to move. But Rothchild keeps the vocal-mike dead, to assure maximum concentration on the problem at hand. From behind the glass partition, Jim

looks like a silent movie of himself, speeded up for laughs. The musicians barely bother to notice. When he is drinking, they work around him. Only Ray is solicitous enough to smile. The others tolerate him, as a pungent but necessary prop.

He teeters about the tiny room, digging his boots into the carpeting. Between belches, he gazes at each of us, smirking as though he has found something vaguely amusing behind our eyes. But the séance is interrupted when Rothchild summons him. While Jim squats behind the control panel, a roughly recorded dub of his "Celebration of the Lizard" comes over the loudspeakers.

Gently, almost apologetically, Ray tells him the thing doesn't work. Too diffuse, too mangy. Jim's face sinks beneath his scaly collar. Right then, you can sense that "The Celebration of the Lizard" will never appear on record—certainly not on the new Doors album. There will be eleven driving songs, and snatches of poetry, read aloud the way they do it at the Ninety-second Street Y. But no Lizard King. No monarch, crowned with lovebeads, and holding the phallic scepter in his hand.

"Hey, bring your notebook to my house tomorrow morning, okay?" Rothchild offers.

"Yeah," Jim answers with the look of a dog who's just been told he's missed his walk. "Sure."

Defeated, the Lizard King seeks refuge within his scales. He disappears for ten minutes and returns with a bottle of brandy. Thus fortified, he closets himself inside an anteroom used to record isolated vocals. He turns the lights out, fits himself with earphones, and begins his game.

Crescendos of breath between the syllables. His song is half threat, and half plea:

> Five to one
> One in five
> No one here
> Gets out alive

Everyone in the room tries to bury Jim's presence in conversation. But his voice intrudes, bigger and blacker than life, over the loudspeakers. Each trace of sound is magnified, so we can hear him guzzling and belching away. Suddenly, he emerges from his Formica cell, inflicting his back upon a wall, as though he were being impaled. He is sweat-drunk, but still coherent, and he mutters so everyone can hear: "If I had an axe . . . man, I'd kill everybody . . . 'cept . . . uh . . . my friends."

Sagittarius the hunter stalks us with his glance. We sit frozen, waiting for him to spring.

"Ah—I hafta get one o' them Mexican wedding shirts," he sighs with brandied breathiness.

Robbie's girl, Donna, takes him on: "I don't know if they come in your size."

"I'm a medium . . . with a large neck."

"We'll have to get you measured, then."

"Uh-uh . . . I don't like to be measured." His eyes glow with sleep and swagger.

"Oh Jim, we're not gonna measure all of you. Just your shoulders."

MINNEAPOLIS DAILY
DOORS HAMM IT UP IN CONCERT · *by Tim Boxell*

The Doors' latest album, *Waiting for the Sun*, wasn't half what it would have been if the original plan to include Jim Morrison's "Celebration of the Lizard" had succeeded.

With this in mind, I looked forward eagerly to The Doors' concert. Even as influenced as it was by too much Hamm's beer (throughout the concert, The Doors, particularly lead singer Morrison, kept swigging from sixteen-ounce cans), it was something else.

People who came to hear cuts from their albums flawlessly duplicated must have been disappointed, for Morrison seemed quite bored by all the old Doors' material, which with the beer and the standard performers' response to playing sleepy old Minneapolis added up to ineffectively delivered numbers laden with ad libs and vulgarities.

The appearance of local blues harpist Tony Glover and a change to blues material brought Morrison around. Ray Manzarek, organist for The Doors, seemed to respond as well.

Backed by Densmore's beat, Morrison managed to do some of the singing that he has become known for. The standard closing "Light My Fire" was a return to Morrison's lethargy in spite of a dynamic effort by the rest of the group.

The concert was a success only by grace of Morrison's initial effect as a superstar and a very good poet and by the hard work of the rest of the band. Morrison broke off in nearly every song after the first couple of stanzas, leaving it up to the others to improvise until he was ready to sing again. This may be one reason why the rest of the group is so good.

Watching Morrison himself was a great part of the show, and he could hold your attention sitting down, but in the rows farther back people were more dependent on their ears than their eyes and it must have really dragged at times.

Yet a concert by The Doors is supposed to be something out of the ordinary. People come to see The Doors as much for their unpredictability as for their music. The Doors come to affect you and create a response, and the one they created depends on you and on what they want to do.

Morrison instrumented the effect this time. He didn't give the audience what they expected. He gave them what they wanted. He gave them The Doors.

PHOENIX GAZETTE
7 DETAINED AT COLISEUM AFTER ROCK-GROUP RUCKUS

One member of a "rock" singing group made obscene gestures, used obscene language, and almost created a full-scale riot among 10,000 teenagers and young adults at Veterans Memorial Coliseum, officials said today.

At least seven persons were detained after last night's appearance at the Coliseum by The Doors, and Arizona Highway Patrol Captain Bill Foster said he feared the incident was going to develop into a full-scale riot.

"For a little while there, I didn't know which way it was going to go," Foster said.

There were fifty-five security men on duty in the Coliseum, including highway patrolmen, Phoenix police, and private security forces. They had to shove and push many of the youngsters from the building and then disperse a crowd gathering outside.

Phoenix Gazette photographer Brian Lanker said the singer, identified as Jim Morrison, invited the youngsters to leave their seats and approach the stage. The youngsters milled in the aisles, threw things on stage, and pushed against a line of security police ringing the stage.

Witnesses said Morrison made obscene gestures with a scarf and then threw it into the crowd of screaming youngsters.

Foster said the singer "made many raw statements," including four-letter words not usually heard in public.

The singer reportedly commented on the presidential race by saying:

"Four more years of mediocrity and h——s——. If he (President-elect Richard Nixon) does wrong, we will get him."

Dick Smith, vice-chairman of the State Fair Board, said the group "won't be back here. They certainly shouldn't be in our building."

Smith said there had been no trouble or reports of trouble from the group, and he repeated: "They shouldn't be allowed there (Veterans Memorial Coliseum)."

Captain Foster said the singer, Morrison, "certainly encouraged and invited the problem." Foster said if the singer had not called for the youngsters to leave their seats, "there would have been no problem like this."

Asked why Morrison was not arrested for using vulgar and obscene language, Foster admitted that he (Foster) "was right on the brink" several times.

Phoenix police said today they were holding four persons, including one girl, in connection with use of vulgar language, one person accused of assault, and also had detained two juveniles accused of disturbing the peace.

THE MILWAUKEE JOURNAL
"ACID" ROCK SINGERS ETCH THEIR MESSAGE

The Doors to acid rock opened at the Arena Friday night to a large crowd that held the proper key: Youth.

The Doors, to the uninitiated, are no wooden set of guitar pickers and brassy vocalists. They are perhaps the leading popular exponents of acid rock—acid in terms of drug-oriented, perhaps; acid in terms of social commentary, certainly.

Jim Morrison, the white James Brown who leaps and sprawls across the stage, slink bops back and forth, and makes love to microphone stands, is the leader.

In a society that does not pay poets well, he is a poet. He sings for a living. Not well, but that isn't the idea. He writes his own lyrics and has a lot to say. Poetry these days comes with guitar, organ, and drum accompaniment.

"We want the world and we want it NOW!" he tells his audience of stylishly hippie-clad teens, all of whom are trying to grow up fast and want that world.

They plug into Morrison and 1,300 watts of amplified sound blast into their minds, a sound so loud it drives thought out, a sound so loud it pins the value judgments of the adult world to the far wall of the Arena and leaves them squirming helplessly.

BRIDGEPORT (CONNECTICUT) TELEGRAM
DOORS SHOUT AND SHRIEK TO 5,000 IN JFK STADIUM · *by Charles S. Gardner*

The four-man rock group, The Doors, authors of today's number one tune "Hello I Love You," performed before 5,000 in Kennedy Stadium last night, singing, among others, the song that earned them their initial popularity, "Light My Fire."

The audience was young, with a predominance of the long-haired, scruffy variety, which made a colorful show for a summer's evening.

Jim Morrison, spiritual leader of the group, attired from head to toe in leather, caresses the mike, and sings his poetry, much of which is vaguely mystical, some of which is love song, and more of which is his special brand of revolutionary, anti-police, anti-older generation rock, invariably couched in the sensuality Morrison seems to exude.

In his role as poet, Morrison chants, sometimes metaphorically, often directly, of man's misadventures.

The Doors clearly are speaking to their peers, and their language is not communicable to any others. Their music is harsh, and, with the exception of the almost rollicking organ, too aggressive. But then Morrison slinks across the stage, eyes shut, dazed, and croons huskily, off-key into the mike. The effect is startling. The audience, instead of screaming as in the early Beatle days is silent, focuses on Morrison, and listens to what he says.

Morrison performs with an economy of motion which lends his every act a strange significance. The effect is eerie; he, Morrison, is evil, and the world behind his closed eyelids is enticing, yet forbidding. The Morrison mystique speaks as eloquently to his audience as he seems to threaten the police lining the stadium.

Morrison, the police, the green playing-field, and the huge enthusiastic audience under the thunderstorm which did appear, gave the entire performance a surrealistic touch which might not have been merited in daylight. Yet the sort of energy The Doors seem to command from their audiences cannot be excused with the usual platitudes. The 5,000 youths packed in the Kennedy Stadium responded, almost too readily, to the image The Doors seem to portray to them. Rather than be accused of stirring their audience, The Doors can only be applauded for touching something in them not available through more conventional means.

The Doors concluded their show with "Little Red Rooster" and "Unknown Soldier," a desperately anti-war ballad climaxing with Morrison's being thrown to the floor in a burst of exploding electronic feedback. The whining rises, the audience rises to their feet, The Doors retreat out the back.

MADISON (WISCONSIN) JOURNAL
THE DOORS PROVE A SLAM HERE · *by John W. English*

Jim Morrison, lead vocalist of The Doors, demonstrated his explosive style Friday before a half-filled Dane County Memorial Coliseum crowd of hard-rock devotees.

The effect was both chilling and numbing. The Doors' music, while emphasizing mood rather than meaning, switched from gentleness and love to death, pain, and even violence.

At one point during "Light My Fire," Morrison even destroyed his microphone but continued his intense performance in his uninhibited style.

When Morrison took over, the show turned into a musical séance. His abandon and sexuality stirred the audience's emotion. Many fans who were sitting far away from the stage poured down onto the floor, but were chased out of the aisles by police and ushers.

Morrison began with "Back Door Man," and mixed poetry and wails along with his screaming singing. During "The End," he reached his fans with his screech, "We want the world and we want it now."

After a cigarette break (the Coliseum forbids smoking), The Doors concluded their concert with a theater event, a relatively new happening in music called "Celebration of the Lizard."

A stream of poetry containing numerous images and a theater-like enactment, along with musical accompaniment, kept the audience involved and left them unable to muster an applause for the finale.

It was clear that The Doors' fans were impatient to hear the Elektra recording stars. Morrison and company, who command five-figure dollars for their show, finally put on the spellbinding musical entertainment the crowd had come to see.

VARIETY
DOORS PULL NEAR—SRO 75G IN SINGER BOWL GIG MARKED BY MELEE

City streets are not the only place where there is unrest and mobs get out of hand. On Friday night at the Singer Bowl, which is located on the grounds of the old New York World's Fair, a melee broke out involving several young patrons of a concert headlining The Doors, and The Who, both top rock combos.

The youngsters charged the stage area and threw chairs on stage, damaging some of The Doors' equipment. The Doors were just wrapping up their slot shortly past midnight. Three persons were hurt; one of them was arrested.

The kids were restless due to the concert's late start, a long intermission, and the addition of a third act, The Kangaroo. Perhaps topping off these events were The Doors' lyrics, many of which refer to death, power, violence, and comment on society's bizarre aspects, and the wild theatrics of the group's lead singer and new contemporaneous sex symbol, Jim Morrison.

Adding to the climactic moment, was that, per plan, The Who had performed with the house lights on, but these were turned off for The Doors. And the tension was further spurred by breakdown of the revolving stage which, when operative, made it possible for the act to be seen from all angles.

The Doors have been gaining a reputation for exciting audiences beyond the norm. They have had several such incidents, the most recent of which was a larger-scaled riot the previous weekend in Cleveland. Rushing the performers is, of course, not new to pop music in general, let alone r & r specifically. But it seems to be only of late that destructiveness has become a key threat.

NEW YORK POST
END OF POP CONCERT STARTS QUEENS MELEE

Two persons were arrested and three others slightly injured early today during a chair-throwing melee at the close of a pop music concert in the Singer Bowl in Queens, attended by 8,000 persons, mostly teenagers.

The violence began when Jim Morrison, lead singer of The Doors, ended his last song, called "The End," by falling back on the stage and screaming.

Some of the audience began throwing paper cups, others broke chairs and threw the legs at the stage, and still more threw whole chairs. None of the performers were injured.

Fifteen private policemen held back part of the audience from the stage, but others outflanked them and stormed the stage. The entertainers fled.

One youth was arrested for disorderly conduct and another for harassing a policeman. The injured did not require hospitalization.

NEWARK (NEW JERSEY) EVENING NEWS
IRATE TEENS BREAK UP N.Y. CONCERT

Three persons were injured and two were arrested early today when a teenage audience at a folk-rock concert suddenly charged the stage.

Police said about 200 teenagers in a capacity audience of 10,000 listening to a group called "The Doors" began breaking up the wooden chairs at the Singer Bowl in Flushing Meadows Park, Queens.

As the group was completing its last two numbers, the teenagers ran for the stage, forcing the musicians to retreat, leaving their equipment behind. A witness said students armed with pieces of chairs began smashing the equipment on stage before guards could stop them.

One teenager was arrested when he punched and kicked a patrolman, police said. The youth was treated at a hospital for a cut on his head.

Two girls were treated at the hospital for minor injuries and another person was arrested.

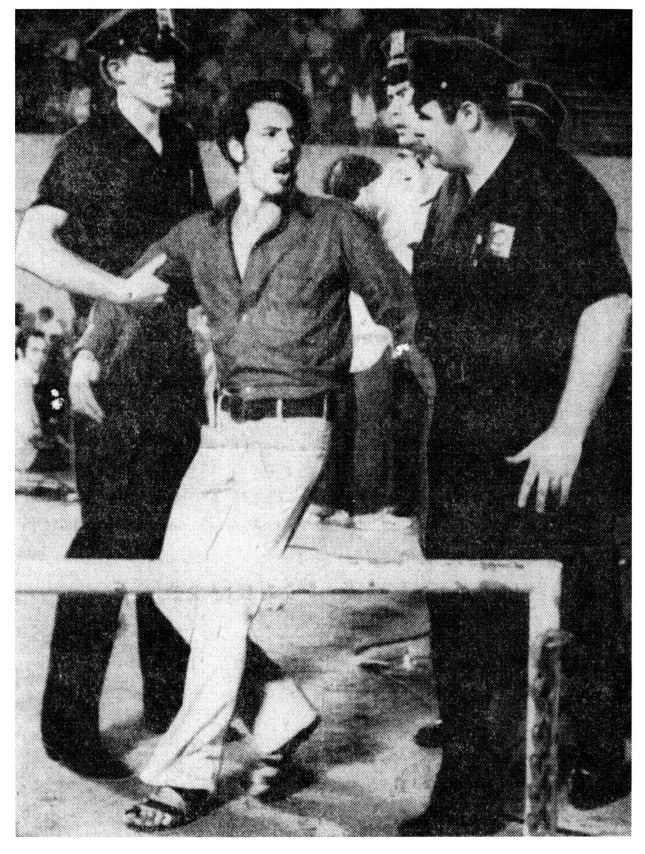

CONCERT AUDIENCE STAGES CLIMAX

Police arrest young man at New York's Singer Bowl after disturbance erupted Friday night at performance by "The Doors," a folk-rock group. Police said about 200 youths in the crowd of 10,000 suddenly rushed the stage, forcing the musicians to flee, and began smashing their equipment on stage before police intervened.

VARIETY
DOORS LATCH SRO BIZ AT FILLMORE EAST, N.Y.

Apparently death is a popular topic among hippies, yippies, or whatever disenchanted youths call themselves this year. This is a conclusion that can be reached from the sellout performances of The Doors last weekend at Fillmore East, Bill Graham's new rock 'n' roll hq in New York. A total of 10,000 buffs showed up for four performances spread over Friday and Saturday nights at the 2,500-seat site, which was scaled to a $5 top.

The Doors, Elektra Records' hot quartet from Los Angeles, imply that the death of the world is imminent, and they want to record a lot in the annals of history before they go. They essay some highly inventive musical and ideological concepts with a bizarre treatment that seems somehow permanent and constructively artful in its pessimism.

Led by a wayout vocalist, Jim Morrison, whose animalism has prompted some observers to dub him some sort of sex symbol, they wrap up one of the philosophies of their generation in an opus entitled "When the Music's Over," which says that music is the vibrant force of communication and fraternity.

CRAWDADDY!
OH CAROLINE: THE DOORS AT THE FILLMORE EAST · by Kris Weintraub

Oh Caroline, I want to go back.

He's beautiful!

Debbie, Robin, and I were close enough to see faces. Beautiful faces.

Finally Ray came wandering across the purple-lit stage. He must be over six feet tall, very blond, and very thin. He was wearing a beautiful cream-colored suit with a long jacket (double vents to the waist in back). It was perfect for him. He sat at his organ on the left facing center.

John came out—loped out—he's very long-legged—and sat at his drums. He has this really great face. It's very intense but you know all the time that he's smiling inside. He was dressed in red velvet and the front of the pullover top was like a striped woven bib with tassels on the bottom. Very interesting. He looked comfortable.

Robbie materialized out of nowhere. I looked and there he was, standing there in a black denim street cowboy suit. You know the kind. It looked like

he's been wearing it for seven or eight years and it's all stretched out to fit his bumps. His hair is incredible. It has no arrangement. How do you describe it? Avant-garde Garfunkel? A haystack in a high wind? So what.

Robbie and Ray threw notes back and forth across the stage tuning up and John bashed around

a little so we wouldn't forget he was there. This went on until everyone was crazy from excitement—then they started the introduction to "When the Music's Over."

I couldn't believe they'd start with that. How do you follow it?

But they did.

They went on playing this endless introduction until everyone was leaning out of their seats in anticipation. . . .

Debbie kept saying, "I bet he isn't here" until I was ready to hit her. . . .

Then a shadow came out of the wings.

A beautiful phantom in a sloppy pea jacket, floppy light brown leather cowboy hat, hair down to here, and these impossible tight leather pants. . . .

There was instant applause and cheering.

He stepped to the microphone, grabbed the top with his right hand and the stand with his left fingertips, and looked up so the light hit his face.

The world began at that moment.

I felt like it was all a dream before that. Nothing was real except his incredible presence. Jim Morrison was there in that room and, baby, you better believe it.

There isn't another face like that in the world. It's so beautiful and not even handsome in the ordinary way. I think it's because you can tell by looking at him that he IS God. When he offers to die on the cross for us it's OK because he IS Christ. He's everything that ever was and all that ever can be and he KNOWS it. He just wants to let us know that so are we.

That's why we love him. (His soul has been around for a long time. It's seen things he only hints

at but I remember things from a million years ago when he sings. He has one of the really old souls.)

He starts out shrieking, eating the microphone, pressing his thin leather leg against the stand. (The teenyboppers are coming all over the place. There are incredible sexual groans from the girls down the aisle at his every whisper.)

There were a few times when he scared me to death. He grabbed the mike in both hands and screamed and shook until everyone was sure he was being electrocuted. Purely for effect.

And even though he tries to hold it back—once in a while he breaks into a smile that is so beautiful you want to hug him.

He loves us and wants to show us that all we have to do is open up to ourselves and be honest with what is inherently US. That by putting him on a pedestal we can only elevate ourselves because he is determined to pull us up with him. He wants us to KNOW that and we sense it—at least subconsciously.

He's really an artist. I kept feeling that he was creating right in front of me. The sound waves are his canvas, the group is his brush, and their talents are his colors. Right there he has more than enough to create a masterpiece. Then he puts himself into the center of it and becomes part of his art. It frames him and he IS and CREATES at the same time.

But there's more.

Ever since I got so deeply involved with their albums I've realized that Jim has or will say everything that needs to be said. Everything that *can* be said.

His poetry isn't personal like Dylan's. Anyone can understand it and realize that it's there to make it a better world. To make us better people.

Jim and his old soul are deeply tied in with the collective unconscious and he is great because he makes us remember ourselves or whoever we were in the past.

He unlocks something in the cells. That's very important.

Go see them if you ever have the chance.

Los Angeles Free Press
JOHN CARPENTER INTERVIEW WITH JIM MORRISON

John Carpenter: How did the cover on Strange Days *come about?*

Jim Morrison: I hated that cover on the first album. So I said, "I don't want to be on this cover. Where is that? Put a chick on it or something. Let's have a dandelion or a design." The title, *Strange Days*, came and everybody said, yeah, 'cause that was where we were, what was happening. It was right.

Originally I wanted us in a room surrounded by about thirty dogs, but that was impossible 'cause we couldn't get the dogs and everybody was saying, "What do you want dogs for?" And I said that it was symbolic that it spelled God backwards. (Laughs) Finally we ended up leaving it up to the art director and the photographer. We wanted some real freaks though, and he came out with a typical sideshow thing. It looked European. It was better than having our fucking faces on it though.

Carpenter: What place do albums have as art forms to you?

Morrison: I believe they've replaced books. Really. Books and movies. They're better than movies 'cause a movie you may see once or twice, then later on television maybe. But a fucking album, man, it's more influential than any art form going. Everybody digs them. They've got about forty of them in their houses and some of them you listen to fifty times, like the Stones' albums or Dylan's.

You don't listen to the Beatles much anymore, but there are certain albums that just go on and on. You measure your progress mentally by your records, like when you were really young, what you had then, Harry Belafonte, you know, Calypso, Fats Domino. Elvis Presley.

Carpenter: You guys are only working weekends now, aren't you?

Morrison: Not really. I think we work a lot. More than most people think. Like after the Bowl we go to Texas, then to Vancouver, Seattle, then jump to the East Coast, Montreal and blah, blah, blah. Take three weeks off in August for the film, then we go to Europe. Man, we work an awful lot!

Carpenter: Do you still read a lot?

Morrison: No, not as much as I used to. I'm not as prolific a writer either. Like when, a while ago, I was living in this abandoned office building, sleeping on the roof, you know the tale. (Laughs) And all of a sudden, I threw away all my notebooks that I'd been keeping since high school and these songs just kept coming to me. Something about the moon, I don't remember.

Well, I'd have to make up words as fast as I could in order to hold on to the melody—you know a lot of people don't know it, but I write a lot of the melodies, too—later, all that would be left would be the words 'cause I couldn't hold on to them. The words were left in a sort of vague idea. In those days when I heard a song, I heard it as an entire performance. Taking place, you know, with the audience, the band and singer. Everything. It was kind of like a prediction of the future. It was all there.

LOS ANGELES FREE PRESS
AT THE HOLLYWOOD BOWL · by Harvey Perr

The Doors' concert at the Hollywood Bowl could have (and should have) been great theater. There was Jim Morrison, moving with animal grace, exuding his own peculiar sexuality, obviously in a good mood and ready to give his audience everything they wanted and possibly more.

Morrison represents a specific kind of dramatic experience: one in which a shrewd and skillful performer, fully aware of his electrically charged relationship to his admirers, chooses to complement the natural sensuality inherent in his act with what is essentially a cerebral tragi-comedy (evidenced by the hard common sense of his poetry); it is a performance that both involves and alienates, a Brechtian epic reality.

And then the sense of unpredictability and spontaneity, so important to the success of such an evening, was missing (except for one movement when a kid climbed over the wall and managed a little game of cat and mouse with the cops right on stage while Morrison kept singing). What The Doors apparently felt their audience wanted was exactly what they didn't want.

I think they wanted temperament, the tension that snaps when an artist has a healthy antagonism toward the natural elements in the atmosphere. When the lights didn't go down at one moment, they didn't want Morrison to stay cool and go on singing. At the core, they wanted him to walk off the stage. And if he didn't come back, they might have screamed for refunds but they would have understood and they would have been satisfied.

But everything went smoothly, too smoothly. And restlessness set in. And the impact of "Light My Fire" (despite the random sparklers that were lit and thrown) or "The Unknown Soldier" or "When the Music's Over" was dissipated, because we weren't listening to words of death and passion and love and violence; we were spectators at a sport in which nothing of crucial significance was affecting our existence. It was a good show and nothing more. The mystique had turned mundane.

Perhaps the Bowl itself is to blame. It's a forbidding place, forcing us to keep our distance from whatever is happening on the stage. Even The Orchestra could get lost up there. But at the heart of the matter, the evening failed not only as Theater but it failed, as well, as a rock concert.

I AM NOT AN ADVOCATE FOR FREQUENT
CHANGES IN LAWS AND CONSTITUTIONS.
BUT LAWS AND INSTITUTIONS MUST GO
HAND IN HAND WITH THE PROGRESS
OF THE HUMAN MIND. AS THAT BECOMES
MORE DEVELOPED, MORE ENLIGHTENED,
AS NEW DISCOVERIES ARE MADE, NEW
TRUTHS DISCOVERED AND MANNERS AND
OPINIONS CHANGE, WITH THE CHANGE
OF CIRCUMSTANCES, INSTITUTIONS
MUST ADVANCE ALSO TO KEEP PACE
WITH THE TIMES. WE MIGHT AS WELL
REQUIRE A MAN TO WEAR STILL THE
COAT WHICH FITTED HIM WHEN A BOY
AS CIVILIZED SOCIETY TO REMAIN
EVER UNDER THE REGIMEN OF THEIR
BARBAROUS ANCESTORS.

LIFE
DOORS OPEN AND CLOSE

The sound of The Doors is primitive and mystical, the erotic rushes of the organ, the pirouetting of the guitar, the compulsive hide-and-seek of the drums, the dark green lyrics. The music has no meaning, just mood. "Rather than start from the inside," says Morrison, "I start on the outside and reach the mental through the physical." He seeks an unlicensed freedom "to try everything," his mind playing host to angels and devils. He tries to share a catharsis with his audience. "Today is the age of the heroes, who live for us and through whom we experience the heights and depths of emotion. The spectator is a dying animal and the purgation of emotion is left up to the actor, not the audience." He suddenly quotes William Blake: "If the doors of perception were cleansed, man would see things as they are, infinite." Then adds, "We are The Doors, because you go into a strange town, you check into a hotel. Then after you've played your gig, you go back to your room down an endless corridor lined with doors until you get to your own. But when you open the door, you find people inside and you wonder: Am I in the wrong room? Or is this some kind of party?"

CRAWDADDY!
THE UNKNOWN SOLDIER · *by Michael Horowitz*

In the spring of 1968 the world expected The Doors' third album. They didn't get it. What they got instead was a three-minute sound-tracked film called *The Unknown Soldier*.

The work is typical later Morrison, revealing fully his current potential. The film opens at the breakfast table, an archetypical family scene. The action switches to a California beach, Morrison's favorite setting. Our Hero is tied to a tree by ropes, command orders are given, and he is shot to death. After his burial, the whole world celebrates wildly, while Morrison sings hysterically on the sound track: "It's all over, baby! The war is over!"

When the film played at the Fillmore East, a young audience brimming with anti-war frustration broke into pandemonium. "The war is over!" cried teenyboppers in the aisles. "The Doors ended the fucking war!" The Doors' little passion play had grabbed the audience. Jimmy and the boys had done it again.

But what about that dead soldier? Morrison attains a bizarre duality in *The Unknown Soldier*. He is killed on the screen but survives triumphantly in sound. He is both victim and victor, martyr and apostle.

"It's a little early to be disillusioned," suggests Dr. Albert Goldman. "But my hunch is that The Doors are stalling. And they're slipping—as you must in this business when you stall—into the teenybopper circuit. Their audiences are getting younger. They'll be getting more mechanically repetitive. And it may

THE (PHILADELPHIA) INQUIRER ·
Waiting for the Sun

by Pete Johnson

The new album from The Doors, *Waiting for the Sun*, is that difficult third LP which seems to thwart a number of contemporary pop groups.

The Doors have succeeded. Their first two LPs, *The Doors* and *Strange Days*, were quite similar both in structure and in mood. Each contained an eleven-minute fantasy number and some shorter songs whose fabric was trimmed from nightmarish visions and sexual images. Both were more grotesque than pretty. Both also were powerful enough to establish The Doors as the hottest group in the United States.

Waiting for the Sun contains the fewest snakes, the least ugliness, the lowest number of freaks and monsters, and the smallest amount of self-indulgent mysticism of the trio of Doors' LPs. They have traded terror for beauty and the success of the swap is a tribute to their talent and originality.

end up with Morrison sort of peeling off and becoming a movie star.

"I worry about the militarism in *The Unknown Soldier*," Goldman complains. "Morrison has an authoritarian personality. When The Doors sit down to dinner, he sits at the head of the table. I think he's more like his father than he realizes. In *The Unknown Soldier* there is an inversion. Instead of the officer, he's the deserter. But it's the same thing."

Not that Goldman isn't sympathetic to Morrison's current artistic problem. Having posed as the rebel, the vocalist now finds himself with a measure of victory. But it is difficult to transcend rebellion and it comes as no surprise to see Morrison rehashing the theme of authority rather than following through.

"The initial vision was essentially a vision of breakthrough," Goldman recounts. "What they offered you was a coal with blue-black embers on the outside and a ferocious center leaping through. Occasionally they gash the outside of the ember and the real frenzy in the core breaks through.

"That was the spirit of their first album. That's what got us all excited. That's what raised all the sunken continents in everybody's mind, you see.

"They evangelically converted everyone. Then came the moment of truth. You've got the world on your side. But where are *you* at, baby? What are you going to do about it? You made the girl love you. Now, do you love the girl? Do you want to marry her?

"At that moment they really began to go into their problem. The flip side of breakthrough is estrangement. Once you've broken away, it's pretty bleak out there. The rebel cuts himself off. It's Christ in the garden."

4

EUROPEAN TOUR

August, 1968

MELODY MAKER
JIM MORRISON—IS HE THE AMERICAN MICK JAGGER?

Look out, England! Jim Morrison is coming to get you!

Fresh from being busted by New Haven police for a breach of the peace, giving an indecent and immoral exhibition and resisting arrest, Doors singer Morrison will be in England this autumn for a tour. Exact details are being worked out at the moment.

Meanwhile, The Doors' new album, *Waiting for the Sun,* sold enough copies on its first day to qualify for a golden disk and a single from the album, "Hello, I Love You," is already at number one in the American chart.

Like Jagger and the Stones, much of The Doors' image is centered upon twenty-four-year-old Morrison, who comes on like a 50s-style rock idol in skin-tight leather pants, but is actually a poet of some stature.

Visually, he is sufficient to make any writer reach for his stock of adjectives—satanic, fallen angel, dangerous, with curly black hair (recently shortened, but still luxuriant by conformist American standards) falling around a panting face like a spoilt Greek statue.

His movements have something of Elvis eroticism in them with this difference: his audiences know he isn't kidding. This is no come on. When he sings, "Come on and light my fire," his audiences know exactly what he means.

Sociologists are beginning to think that the sexual revolution of recent years has a wider significance than merely who sleeps with whom. Certainly, in Morrison's completely unambiguous lyrics, it seems to be part of a wider scene where all the comfortable assumptions are challenged.

The highbrow critics like comparing a Doors show with the Marat-Sade "theatre of cruelty," which it does resemble in a way. But it wouldn't be quite so powerful if it wasn't also just very, very good pop.

RAVE
THE EXPLOSIVE JIM MORRISON · *by Mike Grant*

Jim Morrison lives in exaggerations—the dragged-out half stumble and the sloth-like stance on stage, the upturned, pouting face with eyes clenched shut, the ponderous but precise speaking voice which is out of the best Brando mould.

James Douglas Morrison, Superstar, Poet, and idol of America's rising generation, would be a perfect target for the satirist.

That apart, he is not as black as he has been painted.

Already prewarned by colleagues of Morrison's erratic behaviour toward the British press during The Doors' recent and eventful stay here, it did not cool my apprehension any to read, on my way to see Mr. Morrison, his publicist's claim that he can be civil, polite, even erudite one day; yet gross or, as Jim says, "primitive" the next. Which extreme was I about to face?

"He's been quite good today," said his British publicist at Polydor-Elektra Records, with the air of a keeper talking about London Zoo's naughtiest lion.

I was ushered into a small room containing The Doors and sundry people flitting back and forth with no apparent purpose. Most of them were hovering on the edge of Morrison's conversation and it was Jim, in open-necked shirt and tight black leather jeans, who dominated the room.

Among those present with some purpose were three gentlemen in a Granada Television team filming the whole Doors visit with a rare degree of dedication. A bored-looking Robbie Krieger, Doors' guitar man, was to tell me later that they had even followed one of them to the toilet!

Next to Robbie was drummer John Densmore, an active Maharishi student, colourfully attired, who was sitting cross-legged on his chair, saying little and watching the chaos that was supposed to be a press conference. In another corner sat organist Ray Manzarek with a polite smile on his face and a polite line in answers.

Krieger, hiding behind dark glasses and an uncontrolled growth of beard, had some interesting things to say about Morrison in the short interview which came to a sharp end at the sight of a Granada man crawling along the floor and pushing a huge mike up into our faces. A camera was meanwhile probing the recesses of my left ear.

What of Jim's reported moods? "It depends," said Robbie, "which day of the week you get him. It is just the way he is. I think I understand him as well as anybody through being with him for three years, but I still don't understand him completely."

Morrison certainly knows how to project himself and has an actor's feel for presence. Questions are met by prolonged periods of deep thought accompanied by closed eyes and an intense expression downward. He can often take so long to answer that the poor interviewer finds he's lost track of his precise inquiry. Answers themselves, delivered in a half-stumbling tone reminiscent of Jim's movements on stage, are accompanied by intense glances skyward.

He first wished to extend his praise for the behaviour of the audiences during The Doors' two London concerts at the Roundhouse. "They were one of the best audiences we've ever had. Everyone seemed to take it so easy. It was like going back to the roots again and it stimulated us to give a good performance. They were fantastic. That's all I can say. 'Cept that we enjoyed playing at the Roundhouse more than any other date for years."

While on the subject of their stage act, I asked Jim how important the sex angle was.

"Sex is just one part of my act. There are a lot of other factors. It is important I guess, but I don't think it is the main thing, although all music is a very nature-based thing. So they can't be separated.

"But the sex thing has been picked out because it sells papers."

How important then were politics in his writing?

"I don't think so far politics has been a major theme in my songs. It is there in a few songs, but it is a very minor theme. Politics is people and their interaction with other people, so you cannot really separate it from anything."

I became aware at this point that there was a hint, only a hint, about Morrison that he was reluctant to take himself seriously. The journalist faithfully transcribing Morrison's thoughts to paper would be

well advised to glance up from his work for a second—and there you may see just the trace of an inward smile on the handsome countenance.

Jim acknowledges that Elvis Presley along with the other giants of the era, Little Richard, Jerry Lee Lewis, Fats Domino, Gene Vincent, was an early and strong influence on him. He says: "Their influence was due to their music and the fact I heard them at an age when I was kinda ready for an influence."

Jim was courteous enough to me. But a glimpse of what the "primitive" Morrison could be like came out at the questioning of one persistent reporter who asked him first about the comparisons between him and Mick Jagger.

"I've always thought comparisons were useless and ugly. It is a short cut to thinking," replied Jim, in what seemed to be too glib an answer to an off-the-cuff comment. He went into deep thought, with eyes closed and down, and finally replied, "Well, how do you see yourself?"

The questioner pressed for an answer. More deep thought. "That's a rhetorical question and I have given you a rhetorical answer. You might as well ask me how do I see my left palm."

I asked him if he found the group's followers coming to him to be taught how to live. "I get incredible letters," he replied, "but they teach *me* how to live rather than me teach them. My fans are intelligent youngsters and *very* sensitive."

On a par with Morrison's writing is his stage performance—often described as evil. Jim prefers the term primeval. "I was less theatrical, less artificial when I began," he says, "but now the audiences we play for are much larger and the rooms wider. It's

necessary to project more. I think when you're a small dot at the end of a large arena, you have to make up for that lack of intimacy with expanded movements."

MELODY MAKER
DOOR JIM COLLAPSES ON STAGE
Morrison Rushed to Hospital

Doors lead singer Jim Morrison collapsed before a concert in Amsterdam on Sunday and was rushed to a hospital. He was detained but it is not known what he is suffering from.

A spokesman for the group told the MM from Amsterdam on Monday: "We don't know what is wrong with Jim but we hope he'll be discharged today or tomorrow." The spokesman said he hoped the singer would be fit for a concert in Stockholm on Wednesday.

The other three Doors went on stage on Sunday at Amsterdam's Concert Hall and played for the fans handling the vocals between them.

5

THE SOFT PARADE
MIAMI

July, 1969

DAILY NEWS
OOO, *THEY LIT THE GARDEN'S FIRE!*

A West Coast rock group called The Doors slammed into Madison Square Garden last night and 20,000 screaming teenyboppers tried to rip them off their hinges.

The Doors, for the benefit of any squares who read this, are the new Beatles led by an Elvis Presley type named Jim Morrison, who cranks up kids as effectively as a shot of LSD. The music isn't called acid rock for nothing.

They came out onto the stage at the Garden at 9:30 P.M.—Morrison, drummer John Densmore, guitarist Robbie Krieger, and organist-pianist Ray Manzarek—to a roll of thunder from the teenyboppers that sounded like the crack of doom.

The kids swarmed all over the place like lemmings, filling up every empty spot in the aisles, squirming as close as possible to adore their idols as they blasted out their biggest hit, "Light My Fire."

This song drives the kids right up the wall, and virtually blows their minds. If nothing else, it should deafen them because The Doors believe in using loudspeakers—like about one to a person.

"They got more amplification on that stage tonight than they usually have in the whole Gar-

den," an electrician sighed jealously.

The kids, dressed every which way from Brooks Brothers modern to East Village raggedy, lighted up the Garden with a steady flare of their camera flashbulbs, turning the joint into a rocking, ear-splitting psychedelic trip.

Densmore flung a series of drumsticks into the throng, sending the kids elbow over ponytail after those souvenirs from on high.

And then Morrison majestically let fly with an eloquent belch and flung his jacket into the audience. The jacket went like a cow in a river swarming with piranhas, as the kids shredded it in seconds.

"I thought his belch was very original," cooed Holly Chiger, twenty-one, a City College student.

Among the scattering of non-teenyboppers there was City Council President Francis X. Smith. Asked if he dug the sound, Smith said, "No, but my five kids do."

The affair was a sellout as of Monday, officially, but rock nuts say it was locked up a month ago.

Their agent confided that The Doors will pick up "a big percent" of the $105,000 gross.

THE VILLAGE VOICE
RIFFS: JIIIMMIEEEEE!

Jim Morrison carefully wrapped his black leather jacket into a shape suitable for air travel, then heaved it far into the $6.50 seats. It was early on in the proceedings Friday night at Madison Square Garden and, if there had been any question earlier whether The Doors concert was going to be anything but predictable, it was answered then. Morrison wasn't on his knees once, however: He doesn't need to engage in strenuous theatrics anymore to set the teenyboppers hysterical. All he has to do is strike a pose, bathed in crimson lights, and it's all over. And he knows now how to turn it off just as well as how to get it started. The instrumentalists in the group play their axes, Morrison plays the audience. The guards at the Garden were up for it, too, setting up one imaginary and one real Maginot Line for the stage-level standees, and the standees honored the charade, going back to the imaginary line when the guards insisted, rushing forward to the real one, but no farther, when the guards returned to their stations. The game worked. No trouble Friday. There is something about that hysteria that is as spurious as Morrison's performance is calculated.

Well, the teenies got their show and The Doors and the promoters got lots of money, and money is really all that these monster events, indoors and out, are all about. The music? Who knows? The sound system in the Garden is abominable, but it mattered a lot more during the Staple Singers' very professional set than when The Doors came on. The Doors originally sounded like one of the freshest, most promising things happening. Now they have released the same album under three different titles and encourage an audience that would be satisfied if they played bubble-gum music as long as up front there was their Jiiimmieeeee.

"Play 'Light My Fire.' " "Yeah, 'Light My Fire.' "

Out of the vastness of the Los Angeles Forum, its 18,000 seats filled on a recent Saturday night with the cream of L.A.'s teenybopper set, came the insolent cry. The Doors didn't want to do their 1967 hit; not only had they just finished their first number, but on stage with them and their thirty-two amplifiers were a string sextet and a brass section ready to perform new Doors music.

They got through a few more numbers, but then, with the yelling getting louder, they acquiesced. A roar of cheers and instantly the arena was aglow with sparklers lit in literal tribute. The song over, and the kids shouting for one more once, lead singer Jim Morrison, in a loose black shirt and clinging black leather pants, came to the edge of the stage.

"Hey, man," he said, his voice booming from speakers on the ceiling. "Cut out that * * * *." The crowd giggled.

"What are you all doing here? " he went on. No response.

"You want music?" A rousing yeah.

"Well, man, we can play music all night, but that's not what you *really* want, you want something more, something greater than you've ever seen, right?"

"We want Mick Jagger," someone shouted. " 'Light My Fire,' " said someone else to laughter.

It was a direct affront, but The Doors hadn't really seen it coming. That afternoon before the concert, Morrison had said, "We're into what these kids are into." Driving home from rehearsal in his Mustang Shelby Cobra GT 500, he swept his arm wide to take in the low houses that stretched miles from the freeway to the Hollywood Hills. "We're into L.A. Here kids live more freely and powerfully than anywhere else, but it's also where old people come to die. Kids know both and we express both."

The teenies had belonged to The Doors; their amalgam of sensuality and asceticism, mysticism and machine-like power, had won these lushly beautiful children heart and soul, and the kids had made them the biggest American group in New Rock. Now at one of their biggest concerts, prelude to the biggest ever in Madison Square Garden next Friday, the kids dared laugh, even at Morrison. Not much, but they had begun.

But no one takes Morrison as seriously as Morrison takes Morrison.

His stage manner, he said, unlike the acts of Elvis, Otis Redding, and Mick Jagger, with whom he is often compared, has a conscious purpose. Shyly, almost sleepily soft-spoken in private, he sees his public self as a new kind of erotic poet-politician. "I'm not a new Elvis, though he's my second favorite singer—Frank Sinatra is first.

I just think I'm lucky. I've found a perfect medium to express myself in," he said during a rehearsal break, slouched tiredly in one of the Forum's violently orange seats.

"Music, writing, theater, action—I'm doing all those things. I like to write. I'm even publishing a book of my poems pretty soon, stuff I had that I realized wasn't for music. But songs are special; I find that music liberates my imagination. When I sing my songs in public, that's a dramatic act, but not just acting as in theater, but as social *act*, real action.

"Maybe you could call us erotic politicians. We're a rock 'n' roll band, a blues band, just a band, but that's not all. A Doors concert is a public meeting called by us for a special kind of dramatic discussion and entertainment. When we perform, we're participating in the creation of a world, and we celebrate that creation with the audience. It becomes the sculpture of bodies in action.

"That's politics, but our power is sexual. We make concerts sexual politics. The sex starts with me, then moves out to include the charmed circle of musicians on stage. The music we make goes out to the audience and interacts with them; they go home and interact with the rest of reality, then I get it all back by interacting with *that* reality, so the whole sex thing works out to be one big ball of fire."

But, as the kids in the Forum knew, they've never really topped "Light My Fire." The abandon has got more and more cerebral, the demonic pose more strained: The new music they wanted the crowd to like at the concert was crashing abstract noise behind a Morrison poem of meandering verbosity.

After the show, Morrison said it had been "great fun," but the backstage party had a funereal air. And at times that afternoon, he showed he knew their first rush of energy was running out. Success, he said, looking beat in the orange chair, had been nice. "When we had to carry our own equipment everywhere, we had no time to be creative. Now we can focus our energies more intensely."

He squirmed a bit. "The trouble really is now that we don't see each other very much anymore. We're big time, so we go on tours, record, and in our free time, everybody splits off into their own scenes. When we record we have to get all our ideas then, we can't build them night after night like the days in the clubs. In the studio, creation is not so natural.

"I don't know what will happen. I guess we'll continue like this for a while. Then to get our vitality back, maybe we'll have to get out of the whole business. Maybe we'll all go to an island by ourselves and start creating again."

He looks like a young Medici, his head back, that throat, that throat of exquisite muscles holding the face which hardly rises in prominence from the column of throat before it is swallowed in the cherubic curls, the young prince, his heritage the wealth of the spoilers of the Orient, or the spoilers of the now more subtly called Far East. They shouted off the picadors, they crouched in their seats and growled, there in the Orange Julius stand decor of the Forum, they waited for the hero and the death.

He is so innocent, Jim Morrison, so innocent, as a child who tortures the cat to examine pain is innocent; there is only now and the urgency of feeling. He is so innocent, he is the innocent child who is not evil, who is forgiven because he is a child, he is the sexuality of child, the not female, the not male, the sensuosity of child only, the sexuality of child, not man, not woman, not guilty, at times not even able yet to walk, toppling off high stages across the country as though we should have known better than to let him climb up there, or rather, than to have set him up there and said, run, not holding his hand, letting this wild full feeling half crazed with wonderment child free upon the ledge to fall and die for our delight, or be horned to death on the sharp points of our blood-greedy eyes, dressed only in his thin bullskin pants, the child of death, the child in matador's clothing.

"Light My Fire" . . . they yelled for it, light my fire, it was Their Song, light the big fire, play with the forbidden matches, we aren't even adolescent yet, we want to light the match and burn the bed and the curtains and mummy and daddy and everything and see the beautiful flame we have never touched and only a burned child doesn't play with matches, but we don't want to be old enough to know that yet and he must sing that song for us, he, the baby bullfighter out there in the purple juice light and we will light our sparklers and he will set it all up in flames and he isn't real because he is a poster or a golden record or an idol or a picture to kiss at night under the covers, a piece of paper, a doll, he is the ultimate Barbie doll, and Barbie speaks when we pull her string, that's what she's supposed to do, and she only says what we want her to say because you see on the other end of the string is a piece of tape, that's why she is our Barbie doll and that's why he is our Jim Morrison and that's why we want him to sing "Light My Fire" and stop Stop STOP all these other strange sentences that the doll didn't say when we bought her, these new words on the tape, she has no right to new words, just do her thing which is our thing because we own her/him/the ticket/the poster/the record/the idol. He, he is made of

plastic, an animated long-playing record refusing us our favorite cut, the cut we want, the arm sliding over our favorite groove, the arm gone wild, the cuts strange, the record different, give her a lobotomy, give him a lobotomy, tear off his toy clothes, let's see what's in there, we don't mean the flesh part or the skin under the sad black bull pants, but where the tape is, you know man, like the heart, the tape, the TAPE, man, transplanted in there from the golden record, the one we bought, the one we helped to make golden—who knows but ours may have been that copy that made it a million. He is ours and he better get to "Light My Fire" quickly or we are going to throw him out of the crib.

He is innocent, he is the innocent child, he is the child, he is not good, he is not bad, children are neither. He plays with himself, not fucks, he is neither boy nor girl, he is feeling, he is the child. He is all dressed up for the party, and it's being catered by grownups and they are charging to get in, and they aren't letting us play with our doll, they have got him up there away from us and they are keeping him nine years old forever, the black bull pants are strangling his balls, never mind, children don't need balls, enough to suck your thumb, or mike, and if you piss on the stage, it's defiance like holding your breath until your face goes blue, or yelling, doing your yelling out there in the middle of the living room, only they aren't listening to the yelling but offering him gigantic electric trains that run by remote control, and echo chambers to hear the sound of his own screaming even louder, com'on baby light

my fire, and the snakes are crawling and the child is dying up there and it's five o'clock in the morning and the trail of lime and salt is already prepared, and he is there, see, he, someone, a man perhaps, someone strapped into the baby carriage by the big dyke governess of music-businesspromomedia exploitation and his mother is gone away and left him and if the governess can keep him little for just another year she's got a good thing going, and if we can see him die we can grow up, or die with him, or ignore the whole thing, or kill him ourselves, because we are all children there with our popcorn pockets full of matches and sparklers, com'on baby Light My Fire, com'on baby.

COLUMBUS (GEORGIA) LEDGER
JIM MORRISON JUST WANTS TO SING · *by Richard Robinson*

Once a rallying point for disagreeing pop fans, The Doors are now the most knocked about, maligned group on the scene.

Fans and critics are concluding that Jim Morrison and his cohorts are not really the fiery revolutionaries their image pretended. This disillusionment has led to the characterization, "Jim Morrison, the ultimate Barbie doll."

What do The Doors think of this sudden change? Not having ever thought of themselves as saviors or prophets in the first place, Morrison and the rest find it difficult to understand what all the hubbub is about. All Morrison wants to do is music and be accepted for that, not his leather pants.

To prove his negative attitude toward sex-

idol status, Morrison said he refused six Hollywood movie offers. Instead, he's made his own film, *A Feast of Friends*, for which he's currently negotiating for national distribution.

His press agents like to say that he could be the screen's next James Dean, if he wanted it, but Morrison prefers a more honest approach to the movies, the same approach he's always had to his music, whether disillusioned fans realize it or not.

The Doors scored another gold record last week for "Touch Me," which means somebody out there still loves them. Their new album will be released within a couple of months. The sound on the LP is a continuation of the present, expanded music of "Touch Me."

JAZZ & POP · *The Soft Parade*

by Patricia Kennealy

Run, do not walk—nay, *teleport* yourself—to the nearest record store and take this record home with you, 'cause The Doors can still do it and we all ought to be glad and I hope it shuts up the bad-rappers for good and all.

The Soft Parade: None of it is bad; most of it is very superior music and some of it is absolutely glorious. The first major bitch—of two—that I have against the album is that of the nine songs presented, five were released in single versions over the past eight months.

The other complaint is the orchestration. Paul Harris' arrangements are for the most part tasteful and effective, and The Doors are smart enough to *use* the backing, not just let it happen, or, worse, use *them*. The big loser on the orchestration trip, though, is Ray Manzarek. Ray, who plays an ascetic, thoughtful, profes-

sorial, and appealing organ, is very often snowed under by the brass Harris has added, and most of the time he is dastardly under-recorded.

The chief thing the orchestra does do, when it happens, is expand upon The Doors' sound until it all becomes both ends of one supremely smooth musical continuum, and the one thing it does more than anything is set off some of the best vocal work Jim Morrison has done to date.

All *right!* The record opens up with "Tell All the People"; not very auspiciously, I might add. "Do It" is prefaced by some bizarre cutting-up by what sounds like Jim and Robbie, followed by Morrison's wickedly gleeful chortles over the lead-in.

"Wild Child" is a real Doors song: hypnotic, dark, surreal, evil. Check out the bass and guitar figures. And oh yeah, "Runnin' Blue": wow, Robbie KRIEGER on chorus vocal! It's things like this make you properly appreciate Jim Morrison . . .

But the real beauty of *The Soft Parade* (album) lies in "Shaman's Blues" and "The Soft Parade" (song)—and, to a lesser extent, "Runnin' Blue." None of these songs sounds like anything The Doors have done before: they are all technically sophisticated, well balanced, and definitely positive in statement, and I hope like hell that they are indicative of the new direction The Doors appear to be taking: because if that is the case, gonna be a lot of doomsayers standin' round with their faces hanging out, and that would please me mightily. On that hypothesis, I will proceed.

"Shaman's Blues," then, is a Morrison-composed, scatty-sounding amalgam of jazz and blues that its author sings most convincingly. This song involves a totally new rhythmic approach for The Doors: free, choppy, much stretching and bending of measures, and a *lot* of jazzy licks, vocal as well as instrumental (especially in the backup sax runs).

And "The Soft Parade." AND IT DOESN'T SOUND ANYTHING LIKE THEIR FIRST ALBUM.

The song is built on tidal shifts of music and kinetics, declamatory poem trips: sections strung together like contrasting beads of melody and surreality. The Doors play some very original studio games with "The Soft Parade": Ray triple-tracked on piano, organ, and harpsichord or marimba or possibly both—the Manzarek way with keyboards is so beautifully involuted it's hard to tell just what is happening. Morrison comes in for some unison and harmonic doubletracking later in the piece: the effect is startling, it sounds as though he's ten feet tall, and later still it gets into a pattern of four-track vocal, tape delays of half a beat, all staggered, separated, stereo whiplashed and reverb'd into a God-of-Doom finish.

Lyrically, the record is an even split between Morrison and Krieger, with one collaboration between the two ("Do It"); Morrison has let it be known that individual writer credits are now being stated because the unity of the group is no longer so much in danger and "I thought it was time people knew who was saying what." Well, now we know: I am not going to be so ill-advised as to attempt to draw any parallels, analogies or other comparisons between Jim's and Robbie's respective songwriting heads. All I will say is that I am glad to know Robbie wrote "Touch Me," and Jim "Shaman's Blues."

"The Soft Parade has now begun . . .": come on.

PART II
LIZZE JAMES INTERVIEW WITH JIM MORRISON

Lizze James: In your early, first-album stuff, there's a definite feeling of an apocalyptic vision—"break on through"—a transcendence. Do you see this as a still existing possibility?

Jim Morrison: It's different now. (Pause) It used to seem possible to generate a movement—people rising up and joining together in a mass protest—refusing to be repressed any longer—like, they'd all put their strength together to break what Blake calls "the mind-forged manacles." . . . The love-street times are dead. Sure, it's possible for there to be a transcendence—but not on a mass level, not a universal rebellion. Now it has to take place on an individual level—every man for himself, as they say. Save yourself. Violence isn't always evil. What's evil is the infatuation with violence.

Lizze: What causes that?

Jim: If natural energy and impulses are too severely suppressed for too long, they become violent. It's natural for something that's been held under pressure to become violent in its release . . . a person who is too severely suppressed experiences so much pleasure in those violent releases . . . they're probably rare and brief. So he becomes infatuated with violence.

Lizze: But then—the real source of evil isn't the violence—or the infatuation with it—but the repressive forces.

Jim: That's true—but in some cases, a person's infatuation with violence involves a secret complicity with his oppressors. People seek tyrants. They worship and support them. They cooperate with restrictions and rules, and they become enchanted with the violence involved in their brief, token rebellions.

Lizze: But why is that?

Jim: Tradition, maybe—the sins of the fathers. America was conceived in violence. Americans are attracted to violence. They attach themselves to processed violence, out of cans. They're TV-hypnotized—TV is the invisible protective shield against bare reality. Twentieth-century culture's disease is the inability to feel their reality. People cluster to TV, soap operas, movies, theater, pop idols, and they have wild emotion over symbols. But in the reality of their own lives, they're emotionally dead.

Lizze: But why? What makes us run away from our own feelings?

Jim: We fear violence less than our own feelings. Personal, private, solitary pain is more terrifying than what anyone else can inflict.

Lizze: I don't really understand.

Jim: Pain is meant to wake us up. People try to hide their pain. But they're wrong. Pain is something to carry, like a radio. You feel your strength in the experience of pain. It's all in how you carry it. That's what matters. (Pause) Pain is a feeling—your feelings are a part of you. Your own reality. If you feel ashamed of them, and hide them, you're letting society destroy your reality. You should stand up for your right to feel your pain.

Lizze: Do you still see yourself as the shaman? I mean, lots of Doors fanatics look to you to lead them to salvation. Do you accept that role?

Jim: I'm not sure it's salvation that people are after, or want me to lead them to. The shaman is a healer—like the witch-doctor. I don't see people turning to me for that. I don't see myself as a savior.

Lizze: What do you see them turning to you for, then?

Jim: The shaman is similar to the scapegoat. I see the role of the artist as shaman and scapegoat. People project their fantasies onto him and their fantasies come alive. People can destroy their fantasies by destroying him. I obey the impulses everyone has, but won't admit to. By attacking me, punishing me, they can feel relieved of those impulses.

Lizze: Is that what you meant before, about people having a lot of wild emotions over symbols—pop idols, for instance?

Jim: That's right. People are afraid of themselves—of their own reality—their feelings most of all. People talk about how great love is, but that's bullshit. Love hurts. Feelings are disturbing. People are taught that pain is evil and dangerous. How can they deal with love if they're afraid to feel?

Lizze: Is that why you said, "My only friend, the End" . . . ?

Jim: Sometimes the pain is too much to examine, or even tolerate. . . . That doesn't make it evil, though—or necessarily dangerous. But people fear death even more than pain. It's strange that they fear death. Life hurts a lot more than death. At the point of death, the pain is over. Yeah—I guess it is a friend. . . .

Lizze: People see sex as the great liberator—the ultimate freedom. Aren't a lot of your songs pointing the way to freedom through sex?

Jim: Sex can be a liberation. But it can also be an entrapment.

Lizze: What makes the difference?

Jim: It's all a question of how much a person listens to his body— his feelings. Most people are too busy covering up their feelings to listen to them.

Lizze: Isn't sex a way to amplify feelings?

Jim: Sex is full of lies. The body tries to tell the truth. But it's usually too battered with rules to be heard, and bound with pretenses so it can hardly move. We cripple ourselves with lies.

Lizze: How can we break through the rules and lies?

Jim: By listening to your body—opening up your senses. Blake said that the body was the soul's prison unless the five senses are fully developed and open. He considered the senses the "windows of the soul." When sex involves all the senses intensely, it can be like a mystical experience. . . .

Lizze: In some of your songs, you present sex as an escape—a refuge or sanctuary—like "Crystal Ship" or "Soft Parade" or "Soul Kitchen." I've always been fascinated by the way your lyrics suggest parallels between sex and death— "Moonlight Drive" is a beautiful example. But isn't this an ultimate rejection of the body?

Jim: Not at all—it's the opposite. If you reject your body, it becomes your prison cell. It's a paradox—to transcend the limitations of the body, you have to immerse yourself in it— you have to be totally open to your senses. . . . It isn't so easy to accept your body totally—we're taught that the body is something to control, dominate—natural processes like pissing and shitting are considered dirty. . . . Puritanical attitudes die slowly. How can sex be a liberation if you don't really want to touch your body—if you're trying to escape from it?

"I am interested in anything about revolt, disorder, chaos—especially activity that seems to have no meaning. It seems to me to be the road toward freedom. . . . Rather than starting inside, I start outside and reach the mental through the physical."

— JIM MORRISON

THE MIAMI HERALD
ROCK GROUP FAILS TO STIR A RIOT · by Larry Mahoney

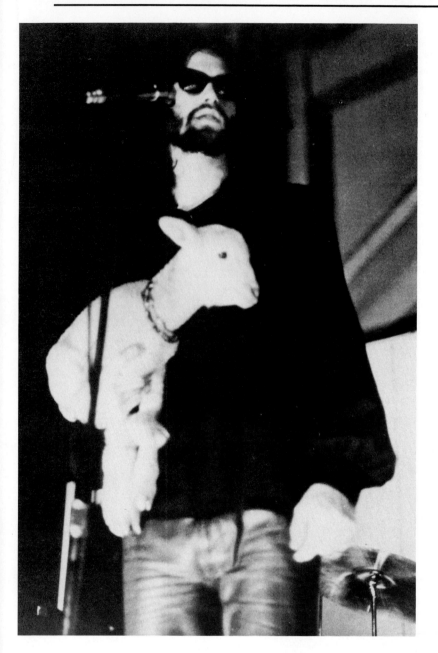

It was the night of the riot that did not happen.

The Doors, a theatrical rock group, and singer Jim Morrison pulled out all stops in an abortive effort to provoke chaos among a huge crowd of Miami young people packed into the Dinner Key Auditorium at $6 a head.

The hypnotically erotic Morrison, flouting the laws of obscenity, indecent exposure, and incitement to riot, could only stir a minor mob scene toward the end of his Saturday night performance.

There were numerous off-duty policemen present but nobody tried to arrest Morrison. Sunday, after the singer had left town, Miami police were drawing up warrants for his arrest.

Many of the nearly 12,000 youths said they found the bearded singer's exhibition disgusting. Included in the audience were hundreds of unescorted junior and senior high girls.

The Dinner Key exhibition lasted one hour and five minutes. For this, The Doors were paid $25,000. Morrison sang only one song, and that off-key. For the remainder, he grunted and groaned, gyrated and gestured, in a manner that made Elvis Presley's style seem more staid than a Presbyterian preacher's.

His words were inflammatory in a tightly packed crowd bigger than those that turn out for a Miami prep football game.

"You're all a bunch of slaves," Morrison screamed into the microphone. "What're you going to do about it?"

Other proclamations:

"Man, I'd like to see a little nakedness around here. Grab your friend and love him!"

"There are no laws. There are no rules!"

It was not meant to be pretty. Morrison appeared to masturbate in full view of his audience, screamed obscenities, and exposed himself. He also got violent, slugged several Thee Image officials, and threw one of them off the stage before he himself was hurled into the crowd.

The exhibition went on before the eyes of thirty-one off-duty City of Miami policemen, most of them uniformed. Morrison, as he does in most of his shows, stole the hat of one of the policemen. The officer wandered about on stage during the climax of the show trying to get it back. He was paid for the loss, Collier said.

Five arrests were made in and around the auditorium during the show, including one of a young man who was writhing on the floor in an apparent narcotics stupor. Other arrests were for calling police "pigs," impersonating a constable, and leaning on the hood of a moving auto.

At no time was any effort made by the police to arrest Morrison, even when the mob scene on the bandstand got out of hand. Nor was a report made to headquarters on what had happened. The officers inside were all hired by Thee Image at $4.50 an hour. The city ordered the security forces to be hired, Collier said.

Morrison, who left Miami Sunday, may yet be arrested for the exhibition, Acting Police Chief Paul M. Denham said Sunday.

"I've issued orders that as soon as we can find a policeman who witnessed it that we will take out a warrant for him," Denham said. "It is our intention to follow it up."

Ken Collier was asked why he brought to Miami a group with the reputation of creating riots. He answered: "The Doors turned down a written proposal from the University of Miami to play Miami so they could get more money playing for Thee Image.

"In a poll taken by the *University of Miami Hurricane*, the students overwhelmingly chose The Doors as the group they would most like the university to obtain for them, and it would have been a concert in the Convention Hall of Miami Beach open to all age groups."

Ken Collier was a pleased man Sunday, pleased with the police, the young people who paid him $6 apiece, and pleased that Miami had missed what certainly could have been a nasty riot. Collier felt he had risked and won.

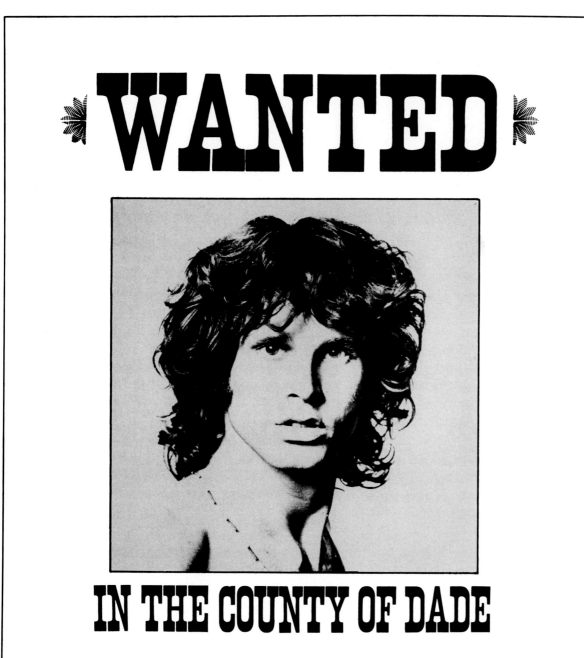

WANTED

IN THE COUNTY OF DADE

For: Lewd and Lascivious Behavior in Public by Exposing His Private Parts and by Simulating Masturbation and Oral Copulation, A Felony.

The Miami Police Department today issued warrants for the arrest of Jim Morrison, top banana of a rock music group called The Doors, for an obscene performance before 10,000 teenagers in Dinner Key Auditorium Saturday night.

Acting Chief Paul Denham said the warrants charged indecent exposure and disorderly conduct by profanity. The self-styled "King of the Orgasmic Rock" reportedly simulated masturbation and unzipped his pants during the blue-language performance.

The state attorney's office also was reported preparing charges against Morrison, including lewd and lascivious conduct, public intoxication, and indecent exposure.

There was also consideration of charging Morrison with inciting to riot. Denham said the show ended with an on-stage melee.

An assistant state attorney took evidence from an office boy in his own office who attended the show. He also questioned a Miami policeman and a policewoman who were there.

The Miami police warrants were issued after departmental investigation. Some of the thirty off-duty officers present were questioned, as were teenagers who volunteered their information. One youth submitted a tape recording of the proceedings.

Morrison and the group left for a Caribbean island Sunday.

THE VILLAGE VOICE
IT'S HARD TO LIGHT A FIRE IN MIAMI · by Stephanie Harrington

It must have been rather like the *Titanic*. Unless you were there you couldn't know exactly what happened, and the survivors were so dazed that all reports didn't fully jibe. So maybe Jim Morrison didn't really drop his pants in front of 8,000 teenagers at a Doors concert at the municipally owned Miami Dinner Key Civic Auditorium on March 1.

The general consensus is that what emboldened Morrison to give the performance that landed him on an island retreat was in fact that he was stoned—and not, children, on pot, acid, or speed, but that quaint stuff called booze that Janis Joplin so recently rescued from the far reaches of camp. (Ken Collier, one of the concert's sponsors, claims that Morrison's contract stipulated that the star's dressing room be supplied with two six-packs of beer.) It also seems that another quaint affliction thought to affect only those over thirty was involved. To wit: the profit motive.

But like the gospel, the versions of what the Master actually did and why are various. For instance, Collier, a partner in Thee Image (Miami Beach's answer to the Fillmore), which staged The Doors' happening, says he did not see Morrison actually drop his pants. (Another eyewitness says he did.) And while he does admit that there was a money hassle between Thee Image and the agents, managers, and other members of The Doors' palace guard, Collier disputes one published story. According to this story, The Doors were angry because they computed their $25,000 fee (a percentage of the house) for the hour-long concert on the understanding that the auditorium was "scaled for a $42,000 maximum" and that Thee Image later upped the scale without upping The Doors' percentage. Collier insists that there was no percentage deal, that The Doors were simply offered and agreed to take a flat fee of $25,000.

Hostilities raged right up to show time, so Collier, as he tells it, took the precaution of introducing The Doors with an admonition to the audience to keep its cool, raising his hand in the standard peace gesture as he gave way to Morrison.

But Morrison came on stage saying he didn't want to talk about peace or war or love, but about having a good time. Which sounded okay to Collier, who did not then understand how much of a good time Morrison was contemplating. And it didn't exactly swing at the start. In fact the one point on which all versions of the gospel agree is that until its (so to speak) climax, the program was pretty dreary, consisting mainly of a not impressively coherent Morrison ("The Doors could barely find the microphone," complained one erstwhile teenage fan who was there) reciting bits of poetry (his own, presumably) and fooling around with snatches of songs like "The End," "The Snake," "Touch Me," and "Light My Fire." But evidently neither the Freudian symbolism nor the invitation produced sufficient response for Morrison who then proceeded to strike his own match.

"I saw him reach into his pants and fondle himself," says Collier, "so I rushed up and took the mike away from him and said, 'This is Miami and it's not going to happen here,'" again warding off the evil eye with the peace symbol. The wave of children who at that moment had been surging forward in answer to Morrison's urging that they come up and dance (where, since every inch of space was occupied, is one of those puzzling questions of rock metaphysics) then receded, only to surge forward again when Morrison "recaptured the mike." Like two moon men Collier and Morrison proceeded to hypnotize the sea of youth before them, the one drawing the waves up, the other causing them to fall back.

"And all this time," says Collier, "I'm wondering what the hell to do. Have the cops drag him away? No, that would cause a riot."

As Collier was thus lost in thought, Morrison, apparently having come to a conclusion of his own, pushed Collier's brother Jim (also a partner in Thee Image) off the stage. Collier, thinking fast, retaliated by unplugging the instruments and kicking in the drums, while his wife, somewhere in the balcony, managed to turn the house lights on as one Larry Pizzi, manager of Thee Image and a black belt in karate, came up from behind and flipped Morrison into the crowd, into which he sank, bobbed up again, and beat a retreat, apparently unnoticed, through the by then literally rocky sea of kids. Then, at what Collier calls "the very Götterdämmerung end of it," like the phantom of the opera, the vision of the unscarred Morrison appeared briefly in the balcony.

The police, meanwhile, faked everybody out by behaving like very models of a progressive, humanitarian force. In fact they seemed to be the only ones who responded to Collier's invocation of the peace signs and symbols. (The kids, too, kept remarkably calm despite what Collier says were invitations by Morrison to get with each other, take off their clothes, have the revolution now, etc.) They, having sized up the overwhelming odds against them and the potential hysteria of the scene, wisely kept their cool. The police didn't even get around to drawing up the warrants against Morrison until he had already skipped town.

"We are aiming at no less than to go back to the human or inhuman sources of the theatre and revive it totally. Everything which forms part of the opacity and magnetic fascination of dreams, all this, these dark layers of consciousness . . . we want to see it triumph on stage, at the risk of losing ourselves and exposing ourselves to the ridicule of terrible failure. . . . We see the theatre as a truly magical enterprise. We address ourselves not to the eyes, not to the direct emotion of the mind; what we are trying to create is a certain psychological emotion in which the most secret recesses of the heart will be brought into the open."

— ANTONIN ARTAUD

"I was less theatrical, less artificial when I first began performing. But now the audiences we play to are much larger and the rooms are bigger, it's necessary to project more—to exaggerate—almost to the point of grotesqueness."

— JIM MORRISON

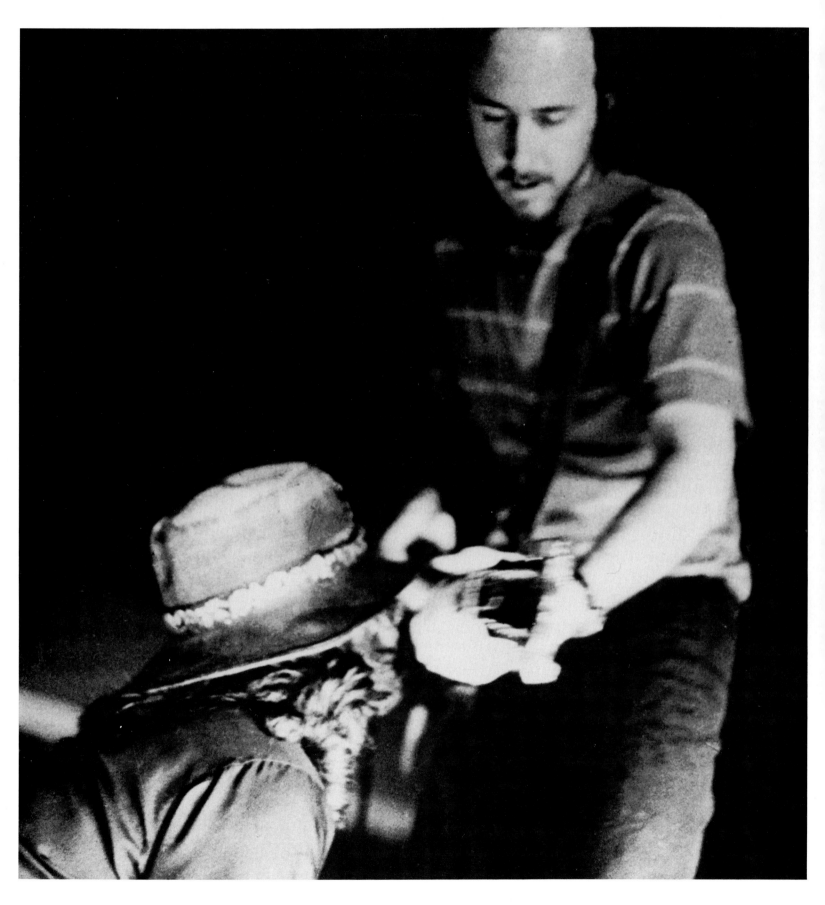

FBI REPORT ON MIAMI CONCERT
(Available by Freedom of Information Act)

On March 3, 1969, ____(Name)____ reported that Jim Morrison, a rock and roll singer, appeared at the Dinner Key Auditorium, Miami, Florida, on March 1, 1969. Morrison, a white male, age 25, born in Cocoa Beach, Florida, and who once attended Florida State University, reportedly pulled all stops in an effort to provide chaos among a huge crowd. Morrison's program lasted one hour, during which time he sang one song and for the remainder he grunted, groaned, gyrated and gestured along with inflammatory remarks. He screamed obscenities and exposed himself, which resulted in a number of the people onstage being hit and slugged and thrown to the floor. There were 31 off-duty Miami Police Officers, hired by the sponsors, who observed most of the action but failed to make any arrests, as to do so might possibly incite a riot. ____(Name)____ advised that he is conducting an investigation and warrants will be obtained for Morrison's arrest on misdemeanor charges. In addition, the matter will be discussed with the Florida State Attorney's office to determine if Morrison can be charged with a felony.

MIAMI NEWS REPORTER
FUGITIVE "DOOR" SURRENDERS · by Ian Glass

Rock singer Jim Morrison surrendered to the FBI in Los Angeles last night on a charge arising out of a controversial appearance he made at Miami's Dinner Key Auditorium a month ago.

A fugitive warrant had been issued on the twenty-five-year-old Morrison, charging him with flight to avoid prosecution.

The long-haired singer, who calls himself "The King of Orgasmic Rock," made a brief appearance before a U.S. commissioner. He was freed on bail.

An extradition hearing was set for April 14. Morrison indicated he will fight any move to have him returned to Florida.

Six warrants, including one for a felony, have been issued by the State Attorney's office here.

The felony charge is "lewd and lascivious behavior." The misdemeanor charges are two counts of indecent exposure, two counts of open public profanity, and one of public drunkenness.

The combined maximum prison sentence on the six charges could be more than three years in Raiford.

Morrison's group, The Doors, appeared before an audience of 12,000 young rock music fans—many of them girls.

From the beginning of his sixty-five-minute appearance, former Florida State University student Morrison went wild.

He screamed obscenities, exposed himself, and appeared to masturbate. He then assaulted officials of Thee Image, a local rock concert hall that sponsored the show.

The audience had paid $6 and $7 for tickets to the performance. A dozen police officers did not arrest him during the performance—they had their hands full trying to cope with another 2,000 fans trying to get into the auditorium.

LOS ANGELES TIMES
ROCK SINGER RELEASED ON $5,000 BOND

Jim Morrison, twenty-five, lead singer of the rock group The Doors, was free on $5,000 bond Friday after surrendering to the FBI here on a Miami lewd and lascivious conduct charge.

The FBI said Morrison gave up to a U.S. commissioner Thursday and was released on bond.

The charge stems from a March 1 appearance by the rock group in Florida. After the appearance Morrison was charged with public intoxication, open and public profanity, and indecent exposure. The FBI said he had also been charged with unlawful flight to avoid arrest.

THE MIAMI NEWS
MORRISON NABBED IN PHOENIX

THE ARIZONA REPUBLIC
ROCK SINGER WINS SENTENCING DELAY

Lead singer Jim Morrison of The Doors, who ran into trouble in Miami in March, was arrested here last night after arriving aboard a commercial jet from Los Angeles.

Morrison and a companion, Thomas Baker, were booked for investigation of charges of drunk and disorderly conduct and interference with flight crew members, a federal offense.

Police said the two used vulgar language on a Continental Airlines plane and threw glasses across the aircraft while it was in flight.

Their hearing was scheduled later today before a Phoenix magistrate.

The two reportedly came to Phoenix to see a performance by the Rolling Stones.

Meanwhile, Morrison is to appear Friday in Los Angeles for extradition to Florida, where he was charged with lewd and lascivious conduct and public drunkenness during a performance at Miami's Dinner Key Auditorium.

Morrison appeared here Monday and pleaded innocent to the charges.

Rock singer James Morrison, convicted of assaulting an airline stewardess last November, yesterday won a delay in sentencing after his attorney told a federal judge a key prosecution witness will change her testimony.

Morrison, lead singer for The Doors, was scheduled to be sentenced yesterday by U.S. District Court Judge William P. Copple for assaulting stewardess Shirley Ann Mason November 11 on a Los Angeles–Phoenix flight.

Copple rescheduled the sentencing to noon April 20. Copple convicted Morrison at the end of a one-day, nonjury trial March 26. Thomas F. Baker, twenty-seven, a film-maker charged along with Morrison, was acquitted.

Morrison's attorney, Craig Mehrens, told Copple that one of the three stewardesses on the flight had informed Mehrens she misidentified Morrison as the one who assaulted Miss Mason. But Mehrens did not reveal the name of the stewardess.

Mehrens told the court the stewardess is will-

ing to supply an affidavit changing her testimony, but since she lives in Houston, additional time would be needed.

Both Morrison and Baker were charged in a two-count indictment involving two of the three stewardesses on the flight. Testimony disclosed both were drunk when they came aboard the plane, and that they were served additional drinks.

Morrison allegedly started grabbing Miss Mason by the arm every time she walked down the aisle. Even after being told to keep his hands to himself, he continued to do it, according to trial testimony.

A LETTER FROM THE DOORS

On April 20 Jim Morrison of THE DOORS was acquitted in Phoenix, Arizona, on a charge of "simple assault" of an airline stewardess. Sherry Mason, the key witness in the trial, reversed her testimony due to her inability to identify Jim as the culprit, mistaking seating arrangements and persons involved. On the basis of conflict of testimony, U.S. District Court Judge William P. Copple threw the case out of court and Jim was released free of all charges, *not guilty*. As usual, the events surrounding the original incident were highly exaggerated.

— *Danny Sugerman*

THE MIAMI HERALD
JUDGE TO RULE ON "DOORS" INJUNCTION

CLEVELAND—A U.S. district court judge is expected to rule this week on a suit seeking an injunction to permit a singing group to perform here March 30.

Following a three-day hearing, Judge Timothy S. Hogan said he would take under advisement a suit filed by attorneys for "The Doors," a folk-rock group, and their promoters. Hogan said he would make a decision early this week.

The group was scheduled to perform in concert at the Music Hall, but its performance was canceled by the Music Hall Association following reports of an appearance by the group in Miami March 1.

The leader of the group, Jim Morrison, faces six charges in Miami, including inciting to riot and indecent exposure, as a result of the show performed before some 10,000 persons.

Local attorney Allen Brown, who filed the suit, claimed his clients were deprived of their rights of freedom of expression and their civil rights through prior censorship.

The suit asks $1,020,000 in damages from the five defendants on behalf of the promoters, Belkin Productions of Cleveland and Squack Productions of Cincinnati.

THE MIAMI NEWS
DOORS' MORRISON IN COURT AS JURY SELECTION BEGINS · *by Ian Glass*

The criminal court jury due to be picked today to hear the indecency trial of Jim Morrison, who calls himself "The King of Orgasmic Rock," may get to see some adult movies free of charge.

Before the trial started, the twenty-five-year-old singer's California lawyer, Max Fink, said he would seek permission of Judge Murray Goodman to show a half dozen movies, including *I Am Curious, Yellow,* to illustrate "what present community standards are. I am not even going to call on the X-rated movies."

Fink, who is sixty-two, said, "We have to accept the generation gap. People like Morrison's group, The Doors, are protesting the problems created by their forebears." Fink said he would base his defense on Morrison's right to freedom of expression.

Fink said he will ask of the jury members only that they are well read and aware of the new, different social order. He pointed out the irony of the trial being held here—"considering Miami Beach is one of the most immoral cities in the U.S."

Fink said he expected the trial to last six to ten weeks and said he can call up to a hundred witnesses.

Mike Gershman, press agent for The Doors, who was listening, shuddered. The others—Ray Manzarek, Robbie Krieger, and John Densmore—are due to start a European tour August 28. They earn between $15,000 and $25,000 a performance.

Assistant state attorneys Terence Mc-Williams and Leonard Rivkind, who are prosecuting, say they are ready to call on up to fifty-six witnesses.

Morrison, who is free on $5,000 bond, wore a comparatively subdued white shirt and black slacks today. He was accompanied by the other members of the group.

ROCK
MORRISON'S MIAMI TRIAL: IF ALL ELSE FAILS YOU CAN PETITION THE LORD WITH PRAYER · *by Mike Gershman*

There just are no summertime blues to compare with those felt here in Miami. We're here—me, Jim, John,

Ray, and Robbie, waiting—four Doors and a publicist—waiting for the big trial.

The trial was supposed to start Monday, August 3, but was pushed back to the tenth. Then Judge Murray Goodman got his calendar all screwed up and there was another delay.

Monday, 10 A.M.—We all go down to court with Max Fink, The Doors' L.A. attorney, David Tardiff, his associate, and Robert Josefsberg, The Doors' Miami attorney. The TV cameras, radio stations, and reporters are the only ties to a former reality/illusion we can recognize. The interviewing and picture taking begin, while a hundred feet away Murf the Surf is awaiting trial on yet another robbery charge. It is absolutely unreal.

We talk about heroes and the lack of them in our world today. "While I was in Europe getting ready for the trial," Morrison says, "I saw this documentary about a guy who entered an around-the-world boat race. About the second day out he decided to just sit around and drink beer and send

in these great phony reports that he was really getting it on. He was in competition with another guy and he figured this other guy would beat him anyway, so he just sat there with some beer, the Bible, and a book on Einstein's Theory of Relativity, radioing back false reports of where he was. Well, the other guy he was racing against gets himself all fouled up and drops out of the race. So this English guy just can't face it. Here everybody is declaring him the winner and it's gonna take him another three weeks at least just to catch up. He can't face it, so he kills himself by jumping off his boat. A real tragedy." (If you're interested in the story, read "The Last Strange Voyage of Donald Crowhurst.")

Back to the courtroom. Nothing much is happening here Monday morning. The interviewing over, we're just sitting around. Rumors leak out of the judge's chambers that are just incredible. First the word is the jury will be selected right away. Then, because Goodman has scheduled another case for the same time, and it's a case that's already been

postponed three times, this larceny case takes precedence. There is grumbling and some paranoia, but it subsides quickly. Next a long wait.

John runs over: "Did you hear that? They're going to postpone this thing until November. What a drag." Everybody proceeds to freak out until five minutes later, when Bob Josefsberg corrects the misunderstanding. "We get started Wednesday at one o'clock. You can all go back and take the rest of today and tomorrow off."

Wednesday, one o'clock—the Big Day. As I arrive, a reporter from the local ABC station asks for an interview with Morrison. I tell him that Jim is in no mood to be interviewed. Can't he at least be human in the performance of his job, I ask him. He looks shamefaced, apologizes, and then interviews me instead. I make my TV debut shitting in my pants.

Court starts. The Doors' lawyers ask for a dismissal on the grounds that the charges are unconstitutional under the First Amendment, which guarantees free speech. They know the judge will deny the motion, the prosecution knows it, everybody in court knows it, but it's gotta happen.

Then we get down to the incredibly dull job of picking jurors. In Florida the court is six people. Max Fink tried to have a twelve-person jury earlier in the case and was denied. Jurors are picked from the voter registration lists. Both the prosecution and the defense have six peremptory challenges, which means they can arbitrarily excuse six jurors apiece. The judge can also excuse jurors for a variety of reasons.

The day's proceedings over with, Chief Prosecutor Terence McWilliams, a young man obviously under thirty, walks over shamefacedly to talk with Morrison, saying, "Can I have a copy of the new album? I have all the others." It becomes more and more apparent that he hates the job he has to do and is trying to apologize. Morrison graciously accepts and we recess until Friday at 10 A.M.

The case will be tried every other day. At this point, it looks as if The Doors may have to cancel their European tour, which was supposed to start with an appearance at the Isle of Wight on the twenty-ninth. The Doors are not very happy about this. Their attorneys are freaked out over the fact that the trial will be conducted every other day. Apparently this is a first. However, Morrison takes the whole thing in stride. Since he showed in Miami, he has been on his best behavior.

Judge Goodman, who was originally appointed to fill a vacancy on the court, comes up for his first election September 8. There is no way he can let the jury acquit Morrison and win his election. Also, Josefsberg, The Doors' Miami attorney, was offered the judgeship that Goodman now sits in. Both men know it, and Goodman is the slightest bit antagonistic toward Josefsberg all through the trial.

THE MIAMI HERALD
"MORRISON JUST TUCKED SHIRT" (HAW!) · *by Herb Kelly*

Goodness, gracious, how poor, innocent Jim Morrison has been maligned. It took his booking agency, Ashley Famous, eighteen days to think up this one as an excuse for his obscene performance at Dinner Key Auditorium March 1.

Morrison did not fondle himself on stage, the agency said, he was tucking in his shirt. "And how can you do that without putting your hands in your pants?" his agents ask.

For the information of Ashley Famous, a guy can tuck in his shirt without exposing himself. I talked with a fellow who was sitting up front and he verified the exposure. Anyhow, the disgusting Miami performance of The Doors has cost the group more than $100,000. Seven dates already have been canceled by promoters in Philadelphia, Providence, R.I., Toronto, Pittsburgh, Cincinnati, Cleveland, and Detroit. They wouldn't touch the crummy group with a mile-long pole.

THE MIAMI NEWS
JIM MORRISON PLEADS INNOCENT HERE · *by Barbara Malone*

Rock singer Jim Morrison pleaded not guilty at his arraignment in Dade Criminal Court today on a host of charges stemming from a wild performance at Dinner Key Auditorium here last March 1.

Morrison, vocalist with The Doors and known as "King of Orgasmic Rock," is charged with lewd and lascivious behavior, indecent exposure, open profanity, and drunkenness.

The twenty-five-year-old singer flew in from Los Angeles to appear today. He gave his address to the court clerk as 8512 Santa Monica Boulevard, Los Angeles.

Attired in a tan suede jacket with sheepskin lining, Morrison looked like a ranch hand in search of a barber. His brown, curly, shoulder-length hair was neatly combed.

He was clean-shaven in contrast to his usual singing appearance with a scraggly beard. He wore a navy-blue shirt with striped blue-and-white pants that dropped over brown boots.

An unidentified friend accompanying Morrison was far more flamboyantly attired in tapestry coat and rust-colored bell bottoms.

Defense Attorney Robert Josefsberg told Judge Murray Goodman that he didn't want to decide today on waiving a jury trial. But a jury trial appeared inevitable.

THE MIAMI HERALD
SINGER EXPOSED SELF, 2 SPECTATORS TESTIFY · by Paul Levine

Two young witnesses testified Monday they saw Doors singer Jim Morrison pull down his bell-bottom pants and expose himself during his appearance at Dinner Key Auditorium seventeen months ago.

The pair, Colleen Clary, seventeen, and her boyfriend, Carl Huffstutlear, twenty, both of Hallandale, spent a great deal of time on the witness stand parrying questions from defense lawyers.

Morrison is charged with one felony, lewd and lascivious behavior, and three misdemeanors, indecent exposure, profanity, and drunkenness.

Miss Clary, visibly embarrassed by the questioning, testified under direct examination that she saw Morrison roll down his tight pants to a point, midway between his waist and his knees.

Morrison then placed his hand on his exposed genitals, Miss Clary said.

Miss Clary, a drugstore cashier who wore her blond hair in a ponytail, said Morrison exposed himself for about ten seconds.

Under intensive cross-examination, the girl, wearing a pink mini-dress and white shoes, broke out in tears, forcing Criminal Court Judge Murray Goodman to call a hasty recess.

Co-defense counsel Max Fink referred to sworn statements Miss Clary gave prior to the trial, and attempted to show to the jury that they conflicted with answers the girl gave Monday.

In one statement, the girl said she had tickets for the concert. On the witness stand Monday, she said her brother-in-law, Bernard Sullivan, a Miami policeman, had admitted her and the boyfriend free of charge.

When asked what unusual words Morrison used on the stage, she said, "the one that starts with 'f.' "

Huffstutlear, the boyfriend, gave similar testimony. Fink also struck hard at any inconsistencies between his testimony Monday and a sworn statement given two months ago. At one point in the statement, Huffstutlear said he had a "vague memory" of the incident. On the witness stand, he said his memory was not vague.

Under direct examination, Huffstutlear said he was embarrassed for his girlfriend. But, in response to a question from Fink, the youth admitted taking the girl to see the documentary film *Woodstock*, though he said he knew it featured nudity.

In the defense's opening statement Monday, Fink told the three-man, three-woman jury that he would like to take them to see the film about the massive rock fest in New York State. It will be up to Judge Goodman whether the jurors will be allowed to see the film as part of the defense presentation.

Following the prosecution's opening statement, co-defense lawyer Robert Josefsberg moved for a mistrial, claiming that prosecutor Terry McWilliams had accused Morrison of inciting to riot, though the performer is not charged with that offense. McWilliams had told the jury that Morrison called for a revolution among the spectators. Goodman denied the motion that would have called for a new trial.

In the opening statement of the defense, Fink said the charges were the result of political pressure.

"There were twenty-six officers present in uniform and nobody arrested Mr. Morrison," Fink said. "Nobody claimed there was a crime then, because there was no crime."

ROCK
APATHY FOR THE DEVIL · by Mike Gershman

Nobody really cares what happens to Jim Morrison in Miami.

This dawned on me the other day while we were waiting for the trial to start. The groupies are there in court mainly to be "on the scene." After all, what they're seeing makes great conversation, doesn't it? The press acts as if the whole thing were going on behind a glass wall. They could give less of a shit whether or not Morrison goes to jail for five years. They're in court to do a job and that's that.

What is behind this apathy for the devil who supposedly corrupted Miami youth beyond recall? I think it has to do with Morrison's head. He is so used to relating to people on a mythic level—as shaman, sex symbol or poet-philosopher—that he finally has become a living legend. You can sense this when reporters interview him. They approach the whole thing as if they were entering a church. The questions are so respectful as to be meaningless. The attitude of sacredness that surrounds this twenty-five-year-old man is nothing short of astonishing.

I got my first flash on this score when prosecutor Terry McWilliams read the charges to Morrison. He walked from his side of the court deliberately, stopped, paused, and then started reading from the complaint. " . . . lewdly and lasciviously exposed his penis . . . simulated masturbation and oral copulation . . . exposed his penis in a vulgar or indecent manner with intent to be observed . . . used profane language . . . performed under the influence of intoxicating drugs or liquor." When he finished, he still stood there as if it would be disrespectful to leave so quickly. Then he looked at Morrison as if he were seeing Christ.

The next day of trial a very attractive lady cop named Betty Racine testified that Morrison pulled his pants down, said, "Do you want to see my cock?," and pulled his pants back up again. Unfortunately, her deposition of eleven months ago shows she heard or saw nothing of the sort when originally questioned. A photographer named Jeff Simon said he was five feet from the stage the entire time and saw nothing. His 160 photographs likewise revealed no exposure.

The real excitement of the day came when the prosecution tried to enter a misleading negative as evidence when 8 × 10 prints were available. Morrison's local attorney, Robert Josefsberg, was furious and approached the bench. Said Judge Goodman, "Don't get upset. They made a nice try and it didn't work." The judge's cavalier attitude infuriated Josefsberg even more and he was heard mumbling about judicial ethics the rest of the day. Goodman is either stupid or insane. Certainly, no intelligent judge could compliment the prosecution on a nice try at introducing misleading evidence.

The essential hypocrisy of the whole trial came to light last Thursday when the state's star witness, Robert Jennings, testified. First of all, he's six foot nine, has a red beard and freckles, obviously is no stranger to dope, and—WORKS IN THE PROSECUTOR'S OFFICE. Didja ever? Not only that, but he's the guy who signed the original complaint against Morrison—thirty-nine days after the concert. You see, to extradite someone from another state, you have to formally charge them with having committed a felony offense. Since nobody else in the city of Miami felt up to it, Jennings signed the complaint charging Morrison with lewd and lascivious behavior. This started the extradition riff which wound up taking eleven months.

Jennings testified that Morrison put his hand in his pants and rubbed it up and down, put the microphone in his pants and later exposed himself, poured wine over somebody's head, and so on. He was a very convincing witness and there was gloom on the defense side of the courtroom momentarily. Max Fink then began to tear Jennings apart. He mentioned a conversation with another attorney in which Jennings said, "I don't see why they want me to testify. What do they want from me?" There were several other inconsistencies which helped destroy Jennings' testimony. The crusher came when Jennings' best friend, James Wood, testified that he sat next to Jennings the whole concert and saw no exposure, no simulated oral copulation, etc., etc.

All of this provided only momentary satisfaction.

Judge Goodman then dropped the bomb of the day by ruling that the defense could not take the jury to see *Woodstock, Mash, Hair,* or read excerpts from controversial best-sellers like *The Sensuous Woman* or *Portnoy's Complaint.* Since the defense's case rests on the fact that these books, movies, and plays use words like "fuck" and display nudity and open love-making, this was quite a blow. The judge's ruling is so obviously wrong that other attorneys not connected with either side said that on appeal, the case would be reversed and Morrison acquitted or retried. This was little satisfaction at the moment. Max Fink asked that the jury be excused and then delivered a blistering argument about the court's ruling. The audience responded quite warmly but Goodman remained unmoved.

ROCK
MORRISON: NO NEWS IS BAD NEWS · by Mike Gershman

The utter senselessness of Jim Morrison's Miami trial for lewdness, exposure, profanity, and drunkenness was underlined by last week's lack of activities.

Nothing happened.

The prosecution wound up its flimsy case with more police witnesses. To sum up, they have no still photographs or moving pictures of the concert showing Morrison exposed or simulating oral copulation with Robbie Krieger. They have a tape of the concert with various obscenities but there is no crowd reaction to indicate any exposure or other astounding behavior. Their eyewitnesses differ markedly in their stories. Some say the concert lasted twenty minutes and Morrison exposed himself after fifteen. The tape is an hour and five minutes long. One cop says Morrison bent over Krieger in a "copulatory manner," another says it was the other way around. Several prosecution witnesses located within ten feet of the stage all night report seeing nothing. A local attorney said, "If I were a prosecutor, I would be embarrassed by having to present this case."

The defense case started with seven kids who went to the concert, had a great time, and saw nothing like what the prosecution charges. The cross-examination was even more lackluster. More and more it becomes evident that prosecutor Terence McWilliams would rather be pruning his rose garden than trying this case.

All this nonsense is taking its toll on our happy little band. No one can really get worked up about the sham of the trial, the shallowness of the press, the insipidity of the groupies. When you're asked for the fifteenth time (with standard accompanying leer) if you want to get turned on, the yeses get more and more mechanical. The groupies have good intentions, but their utter disregard for the real issues of the case grate more and more on all concerned. The lawyers who were once all worked up about defending Morrison find themselves faced with shapeless opponents, the prosecution having provided no real contest of facts, logic or justice.

We're all waiting for . . . the sun? . . . Godot? . . . The End? Something. Anything.

THE MIAMI HERALD
SINGER JIM MORRISON GUILTY OF INDECENCY · *by Colin Dangaard*

James Morrison, twenty-six, the shaggy-haired, bearded, self-styled "King of Orgasmic Rock," was found guilty Sunday of two indecency charges arising from his controversial show on March 1, 1969, at the Dinner Key Auditorium.

But the three-man, three-woman jury found Morrison, leader of a rock group called The Doors, not guilty on two other charges, including the most serious allegation.

The jury, which began its deliberations Saturday and finished with an hour-and-a-half meeting Sunday, decided Morrison was guilty of: vulgar and indecent exposure, and vulgar and indecent language.

Morrison, the jury said, was not guilty of: gross lewdness and lascivious behavior (the only felony charge), and drunkenness.

Criminal Court Judge Murray Goodman, after a meeting in chambers with prosecutor Terry McWilliams and defense attorneys Robert Josefsberg and Max Fink, raised Morrison's bond from $5,000 to $50,000.

Morrison said he would appeal the jury's decision, although legal costs had so far amounted to a "fortune."

"This trial and its outcome won't change my style," he said, "because I maintain that I did not do anything wrong."

The Doors plan more concerts but nobody at this stage is saying just where.

Morrison did say, however, he'd like to do a tour in some place like Australia for a change, appearing in small-town parish-church-type halls rather than big auditoriums.

During his trial, Morrison spent much time taking notes. He plans to write an "essay or something" about his impressions.

"I might even put some of it in a song . . . but trouble is, the outcome wasn't clear-cut enough for that."

BERGEN (NEW JERSEY) RECORD
"KING OF ROCK" IS CONVICTED OF INDECENCY

Shaggy-haired James Morrison, lead singer of The Doors, has been convicted of indecent exposure and profanity during a 1969 performance before a large audience of teenagers.

A jury of three men and three women returned the verdict against the self-proclaimed "King of Orgasmic Rock" after a sixteen-day trial. Maximum sentence is eight months in jail and a $525 fine.

The bearded singer declared, "This trial and its outcome won't change my style because I maintain that I did not do anything wrong."

Witnesses said Morrison dropped his trousers during the performance. "I was shocked and it was disgusting," Colleen Clary, seventeen, told the court.

The singer's performance sparked several campaigns against indecency, including an Orange Bowl rally by 30,000 persons.

Morrison was freed on $50,000 bail until sentencing October 23.

CREEM
MIAMI ONE SENTENCED · by Danny Sugerman

Jim Morrison was sentenced October 30. It was expected that Jim would receive the maximum sentencing, but the judge got goodhearted and whacked off two months and sentenced Jim to six months with a $500 fine.

But Jim won't be serving his time for a while yet. The appeal has already started in the higher courts, and till it goes through, Jim Morrison is relatively a free man! Appeals sometimes may take up to two years to go through and when it does go through, chances are very good that Jim won't be sentenced at all, considering all the flaws in the first trial. Or, if it does, the penalty will be very minimal.

Controversial Jim hasn't appeared very worried or concerned about the outcome since he has returned to Los Angeles. He's been staying with a friend in a hotel suite on the Sunset Strip, relaxing and recording and taking care of some business that was neglected while he was away.

The trial did take its toll on Jim, and for that matter on the rest of the band, as well. Their European tour was canceled by Judge Goodman because he didn't want Jim to miss any court sessions. The tour was planned to start immediately after their Isle of Wight performance. Also, many of their concerts in the States were canceled. Plane tickets to Miami alone cost a small fortune, not to mention the lawyer fees. (Max Fink, Jim's lawyer, should be congratulated for doing an excellent job, on a most difficult, yet trivial, case.)

The law has always held an interest, although a disgusted interest, for Jim. This trial gave him a chance to find out how the law and the upholding of the Constitution was carried out. Jim took notes throughout the entire episode, and there is a good chance that his views may be out in book form shortly.

ASSOCIATED PRESS REPORT
DECENCY RALLY DRAWS 30,000 IN MIAMI BOWL

Some 30,000 hand-clapping people, some waving signs saying: "Down with Obscenity," rallied in the Orange Bowl today to support a teenagers' crusade for decency in entertainment.

Teenagers organized the rally after Jim Morrison, lead singer of The Doors, was charged with indecent exposure during a Miami concert on March 1. Six warrants were soon issued for Morrison's arrest.

LETTER FROM THE PRESIDENT
(From Richard Nixon to Mike Levesque, organizer of the Decency Rally)

I was extremely interested to learn about the admirable initiative undertaken by you and the 30,000 other young people at the Miami Teenage Rally for Decency held last Sunday.

This very positive approach, which focused attention on a number of critical problems confronting society, strengthens my belief that the younger generation is our greatest natural resource and therefore of tremendous hope for the future.

I hope that you will express my appreciation to everyone involved, and my congratulations on the success of their efforts.

SALT LAKE CITY TRIBUNE
"DOORS" WON'T OPEN / CONCERT CANCELED

Salt Palace officials today ruled the performance of an "acid rock" group known as The Doors was both "uncontrollable and unsuitable for Salt Lake area audiences."

McCown E. Hunt, chairman of the board of directors for the Salt Palace, announced the scheduled concert for Saturday night was canceled and that the Palace would refund $18,000 cash in advance tickets sold to the public for prices ranging from $3 each to $5.50

Hunt said the decision to cancel the performance was made by Salt Palace manager Earl Duryea, who flew at Salt Lake County expense,

back to Boston to view the group in an effort to determine whether they were suitable for northern Utah audiences.

Duryea viewed The Doors twice, Hunt said, and early Saturday telephoned officials in Salt Lake City that he felt the performance "was uncontrollable." The act was "therefore unsuitable for local performance," Duryea said.

Hunt said the contract cancellation provision had been written into terms of the agreement before a representative for The Doors signed it.

"We're setting up for the refunds now, but we can't make them until Monday," Hunt said.

TOP POPS
"THEY CAN KEEP THEIR DIRTY HABITS TO THEMSELVES" · by Jerry Hopkins

Three more Doors concerts have been canceled—thanks to city authorities in St. Louis and Honolulu who think the group's vocalist Jim Morrison is "obscene."

The Doors had been scheduled to appear in St. Louis on June 13 and in Honolulu, July 3 and 4, but in the first city the city council stepped in and in Hawaii, Honolulu's mayor made his feelings known. Thumbs down on The Doors both places.

In the two cities it was determined that because Morrison had been charged with public drunkenness and exhibitionism, among other things, well . . . The Doors could just keep their dirty old habits to themselves. This, despite city attorneys advising the coun-

cil in St. Louis that the council had no legal right to make such a ruling.

The St. Louis show was to have been the first performance by the Elektra group since the charges, still untried, were filed in Miami the first week in March. The Doors went on to Chicago, performing there June 14. Both Chicago shows were sold out.

From Chicago the band went to Minneapolis for an additional show, then were set to appear in Mexico City's largest bullring, the Plaza Monumental, July 28. In addition, the group also will be appearing at the Aquarius Theater in Los Angeles (the West Coast home of *Hair*) in July . . . and current plans call for another seven concerts in the U.S. in August.

6

MORRISON HOTEL
ABSOLUTELY LIVE

February, 1970

VARIETY
THE DOORS TRIUMPH IN MEXICO, BUT NOT ON THE EXPECTED SCALE · by Pat Alisau

The Doors were received enthusiastically by Mexican youth, but not by the city officials or the Mexican press.

The Doors were brought down to open up Mexico for future presentations by other top rock groups, according to Mexican promoter Mario Olmos. It had been reported before their arrival that they had been granted permission by president Gustavo Kiaz Ordaz to perform in Mexico City's Plaza Monumental bullring where the poorer classes of people would be able to afford the price of admission. But it didn't work out that way.

Instead, The Doors found themselves confined to performing during their four-night stay at the Forum Club and to a select crowd that could afford the 200 pesos ($16) cover charge.

Attempts were made to get permits for the group to perform at the Mexican arena, the National Auditorium, and even in a security-tight closed performance for the students at Mexico's National University, but permission was not granted.

Mayor Corona Del Rosal was afraid that a large public appearance by The Doors would spark some kind of riot or demonstration by students who have been in a state of agitation during the past year. Plans that had been announced for benefit shows, videotape concerts, and a photo art display did not materialize either.

The Mexican press was not too kind to The Doors either. *El Heraldo* was quoted as calling the group "hippies" and referring to them as undesirables.

The group was also denied accommodations in several of the large hotels and ended up staying in a smaller private hotel in one of the residential sections.

There was no doubt that The Doors were a sensation at the Forum, where they played to record-breaking audiences nightly. With a selection of recorded songs, some that have not been released, and improvisations, they literally rocked the rafters loose. Jim Morrison, singing from the gut, completely losing himself as he does when he performs, had the audience totally absorbed, alternately screaming, chanting, and completely silent.

VARIETY
MEXICO CITY SHUTS PLAZA ON DOORS SO THEY PLAY 4 NIGHTS AT FORUM CAFÉ

Concert by The Doors scheduled for June 28 in Plaza Monumental bullring here was canceled at the last moment when it was recalled that the date also marked the first anniversary of the 1968 student revolt in this city. It was feared that the crowds of youths who would turn out for the rock event might serve as a catalyst for some elements to touch off a demonstration commemorating the anniversary.

From **NO ONE HERE GETS OUT ALIVE**

THE DOORS IN MEXICO · by Jerry Hopkins and Danny Sugerman

It was with mixed feelings that The Doors anticipated the shows in Mexico City scheduled for the end of the month in the Plaza Monumental, the city's largest bullring. Again it meant playing to a large outdoor audience (forty-eight thousand), but The Doors felt the prestige of the show was more important than aesthetic reward, and because tickets were to be priced from 40 cents to $1, they believed they would not be excluding the poor. It was also planned that the band would perform a United Nations or Red Cross benefit at the Camino Real Hotel as well as in an expensive supper club.

But the promoter in Mexico City, a young bearded interior decorator named Mario Olmos, was unable to get all the necessary permissions, so he went to Javier Castro, a twenty-six-year-old singer who owned the Forum, a one-thousand-seat supper club that was roughly equivalent in decor and clientele to the Copacabana in New York. He told Javier he could deliver The Doors for four nights at $5,000 a night. Together they found a friend who provided a $20,000 cashier's check to take to The Doors as a guarantee, and the next morning Mexico City newspapers carried a full-page ad heralding the appearance of The Doors at the Forum that weekend.

The Doors had not been consulted on these plans and they were furious when Mario and Javier entered their offices with the newspaper ad and check in their hands, wild promises on their lips. The office that night was dimly lit, the desk of manager Bill Siddons was littered with empty beer bottles and posters and Forum newspaper ads. Members of the band were sitting around with long faces, talking about how they should have called in a psychic. That idea came when a friend, Alan Ronay, and agent Leon Barnard both had reported premonitions of Jim's death. This wasn't the first time, but it seemed to be the harbinger of doom.

Bill Siddons never came to accept such reports comfortably. On a dozen Monday mornings in the past year Jim had been rumored dead, the victim of a weekend of self-abuse, and each time Bill had panicked, calling around frantically to find Jim, until Jim himself squelched the wild tales by arriving at the office to read his mail.

"You're supposed to be dead," Bill would say, smiling, obviously relieved.

"Oh?" Jim would reply, opening the refrigerator in Bill's office and pulling out a can of Coors. "Again? How did I go this time?"

Jim was not told about the premonitions Leon and his close friend Alan felt. The packing for Mexico resumed.

"Jeem! Jeem! Where is Jeem?" Thousands of Doors fans had come to greet the band and welcome them to Mexico.

The Doors walked through customs and into the lobby of Mexico City's airport. In his full beard Jim went unrecognized: he didn't look like the Jim Morrison who had been painted on the front wall of the Forum, and there were dissatisfied rumblings within his party. Siddons was asked to talk to Jim, which he did. But the beard stayed.

The performances were among the best they ever gave. The Doors were far more popular in Mexico than they'd thought and the response from the rich teenagers who packed the club each night fired them to unusual musical highs—although they remarked how *strange* some of the popularity seemed. It was the reaction to "The End" that puzzled them most.

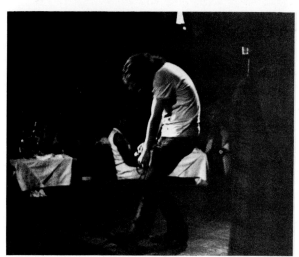

The first night Jim and the others ignored the repeated calls for that song, but the second night they acquiesced. As they approached the Oedipal section, so many in the audience began to shush each other that it sounded like a roomful of snakes.

"Father?" "Yes, son?"

Jim recoiled at the response that line elicited, as instantly every young man in the room called out *"I want to keeeeeel you!"*

Jim looked into the darkness, visibly stunned. "Mother?" he offered tentatively. "I want to . . ." and again the audience erupted.

Jim was impressed.

So popular was this song in Mexico, it has been released on an extended-play 45, and was played so often on jukeboxes that

the lyrics were barely intelligible. "Mexico is an Oedipal country," someone later told Jim. "It's all wrapped up in national *machismo* and 'Mother Church.' "

The Doors were treated as royalty, and in a week's time grew to appreciate the comfort that accompanies an extended engagement. There was time for sight-seeing and for this there were matching black and white Cadillacs, chauffeurs, and a woman named Malu, who normally served as the Forum's publicist but was now The Doors' interpreter and den mother. All were available on a twenty-four-hour basis. The motel was situated in the best residential neighborhood. They were introduced to the Mexican president's son, who was dressed in the latest Carnaby Street styles and in whose wake traveled a covey of American girls, known locally as "presidential groupies." Backstage someone appeared carrying what looked like a pound of cocaine in a large plastic bag, offering the boys as much as they wanted.

The Doors returned to their motel after the last of the five shows. The chauffeur of Jim's Cadillac sped along the broad tree-lined boulevard at eighty miles an hour, slowing to fifty for the ninety-degree turns. The speed made everyone laugh nervously.

Jim formed a gun with his finger and thumb and made the throaty sound of pistol shots. *"Andele! Andele!,"* he shouted. ("Go! Go!") The Doors thundered into the Mexican night.

POPPIN
DOORS AT SEATTLE · by Edd Jeffords

Something has happened to The Doors. Ray Manzarek knows it, several thousand people who attended the Seattle Pop Festival know, and probably so does Jim Morrison.

Once one of the vital influences in rock, The Doors apparently have been captured entirely by the ego-tripping of Morrison. Instead of giving their audiences the music that turned us all on a couple of years back, The Doors now come on like some kind of carnival sideshow, with Morrison as the geek out front.

I'm not sure what I expected of Morrison and The Doors at the Seattle Pop Festival, but I hadn't seen them perform in more than a year and was as curious as anyone about the changes they were said to have gone through.

The tension there was high. Only a chicken-wire fence separated the stage—and us—from 40,000 rock fans, fronted by a phalanx of screaming teenyboppers who had come out from Seattle for the day just to see Morrison. Black Panthers recruited by promoter Boyd Grafmyre patrolled along the fence, politely asking the jammed-in kids not to crash the stage.

"We want Morrison." "We want The Doors." "We want Morrison." Empty wine bottles and garbage cans were converted to drums which accompanied the hollow chant. Those of us in the press area felt the animal presence revealed in the primitive rhythm of the chanting audience. For the first time, we seriously began discussing an escape route in case the crowd should rush the stage.

Manzarek walked first onto the darkened stage. As he struck a single note on his keyboard the chants stopped. The crowd was waiting in silent anticipation. Few realized that Morrison, dressed in denim work coat and wearing a full beard, had been on and off the stage several times.

As John Densmore tested his drums the crowd tensed again, still waiting for the harsh-throated singer they thought they would recognize from their album covers.

Then came Morrison.

Looking old and a little wild he walked to his microphone, lovingly stroked his black moustache, smiled evilly at the fourteen-year-old girls behind me, and laughed. "This is where it's at, now," he said, still running his hands through his beard.

When he opened with "When the Music's Over," Morrison sounded almost like the singer he used to be. As the song continued, however, so did his crude asides. When he was through someone tossed a crumpled cup at him. Morrison gave his unseen assailant the finger. The crowd dug it.

The Doors ran through an obligatory five minutes of "Light My Fire," a song Morrison told an interviewer earlier this year he wouldn't perform again in public. "It stinks. We're beyond that now," he had said. His performance of the song, only a ghost of the recorded version, indicated he probably does think it stinks—and that's the way he sang it.

More than anything else, Morrison's attitude dominated the stage throughout the show. Puffing on a cigar borrowed from a stagehand, he continued on his uninterrupted ego trip, all the while abusing, insulting, and ridiculing his audience.

It was apparent that this wasn't the Morrison the young chicks had come to see. The tension on the fence behind me relaxed, and we no longer feared the teenyboppers would try to crash the stage. They didn't want him that bad.

"I read in the paper that some headshrink says people like me who perform on stage are crazy," Morrison was shouting. "I read that they didn't get enough love when they were kids . . . I didn't get enough love."

It was a personal ego thing. He combed his fingers through his long beard, then ran his hands down his chest and along his legs.

"He's got a hard on," the chick behind me whispered. It looked as if she was right.

So Morrison turned himself on in front of 40,000 people. But he still wasn't making music—only speeches.

Someone out front made an audible remark.

Morrison latched on to it, called the person a big-mouthed bastard, dared him to repeat it. "Get it all out. All the little hatreds, everything that's boiled up inside you. Let me have it," he commanded.

"Fuck you," the crowd screamed. "That's the word I wanted to hear. That's the very little word," Morrison told them.

A quiet voice from the audience said "Shuck!" Morrison laughed.

Speeches done, the band went into "Five to One." But the audience no longer was willing to follow Morrison. Obviously not getting the response he was after in his bubble-gum revolution song, he grabbed a maraca and pretended to beat off. He hugged the guitarist, Robbie Krieger, and made faces at the teenage chicks.

Manzarek shook his head. It was hard to tell if he was keeping time with the music or thinking about Morrison.

The set ended with The Doors' traditional "This Is the End." A sparkler flew from the crowd and bounced off the light show screen, as stagehands rushed to extinguish it. Morrison never noticed. He had digressed from the recognized version of his song and was parodying the old Negro blues singers.

"I'se an old blues man. I'se an old blues man, getting anything I can," he sang.

Then he slipped back into "The End," moving toward the Oedipal climax where he would say, "Mother, I want to . . ." Only the song didn't stop there. "I wanta make love, sweet, sweet love to you all night long," he sang on.

Then the set was over. Manzarek switched off the recorded bass accompaniment and left the stage. Krieger and Densmore followed. Morrison hung there, very still, bathed in a red flood, with head drooped, eyes closed and arms outstretched—Christ on the cross. After the performance he gave, it was difficult to accept his crucifixion gesture without feeling that he was doing it to himself.

I waited for him as he left the stage, flanked by several newsmen and some of his staff. "It's going to be all right," he was saying over and over. The groupies just lined the stage stairs and watched as Morrison climbed into his chartered helicopter and was lifted into the sky—a continuance, though unintellectual, of his Christ pose.

The promoter turned to me. "That's a quick way for him to make thirty thousand dollars," he said.

But Jim Morrison is in no danger of being out of work, unless he loses Manzarek or Krieger or decides to do a Joplin on his own. All he has to do is show his ass on stage in an uptight town, get arrested, and become a cult hero to millions of teeny-boppers who don't seem to mind being insulted and laughed at.

But some of us still like music, Jim.

CHICAGO DAILY NEWS
DOORS PLAY IT COOL · by James Spurlock

Jim Morrison didn't "do it."

The rock singer of The Doors, whose allegedly obscene performance last March in Miami still has him in legal troubles, came to Chicago for two shows at the Auditorium Theater Saturday night, and he didn't do it.

But he did a lot of other things.

Like, Jim comes out on stage for the first set and, oh wow, he's got a beard. Not one of those tame ones that cries out against the very idea behind a beard, but a woolly wild one. Outasite!

The first set, Jim gives a little of the image that has been manufactured around him. He's singing about following him down, and you're all set with those images of here stands a broken man.

The Doors do two encores, one a planned one of "Light My Fire" and the other a blues rendition in which (Jim) sings, "I'm only twenty-five but I'm an old blues man . . ." and angry thoughts run through your mind about how he is one all right and they really crucified him.

But down in the dressing room, it doesn't seem to be like that at all.

Jim's sitting up on the table drinking a beer and smoking a cigar, and The Doors are eating take-out chicken.

There are to be no questions about Miami, so it starts off with a question about The Doors' Rock Theater concept.

But Morrison says, "We started with music, then we went into theater but it was so shitty we went back to music. Actually, we are going back to where we started, which was just being a rock group."

Where does your sexual appeal stem from?

"Actually I haven't really had too much success with chicks. Really," says Morrison with a shaman smile. "I don't know what it is. I can hardly get a date, man." In the background, the other Doors can be heard making like violins.

And just about the time Jim is laying on you some more about his problems with trying to get chicks, a messenger comes in with a note from a chick from Milwaukee that says she will be at the hotel.

For the second set, Morrison, dressed all in brown, swings into action. He even rolls around on the floor. Sandwiched between the jumping around and the screeching, however, is his different side—his funny side. His side remarks have a lot of the audience laughing, instead of sitting on the edges of their seats waiting for him to "do it."

This set lasts for two hours, and The Doors still end up doing a "Light My Fire" encore at 2 A.M. after Ray comes to the fore of the stage and says, "It's good to be home."

"See you guys later," Morrison says, and he walks off the stage.

SAN FRANCISCO HERALD EXAMINER
"DOORS" STAGE A MUSICAL CIRCUS · by Philip Elwood

Winterland had a four-ring musical circus (with plenty of sideshows) going on last night that would fit comfortably into the "greatest show on earth" designation.

The big star that 5,000 fans came to observe was Jim Morrison, the orgasmic singer, poet, screamer, poseur, focal point of The Doors, a rock trio plus Morrison, who are about five years old now.

Morrison and his colleagues, it seemed to me last night, have set out to assure us all that they still are capable of outstanding musical performance regardless of a sag in their popularity recently, and in spite of the considerable clamor raised around the country because of Morrison's

shocking and ungentlemanly stage conduct on occasion.

Morrison last night didn't fool around—he came on full steam at midnight and was still going strong well after one, when we departed. He throws out his excellent lyrics in tones ranging from strained whispers to bellowing, mike-swallowing roars.

He does not just sing, he puts on a full dramatic performance, which includes actions and stances quite valid within the scope of the musical presentation. He sings, for instance, "When the music's over, turn out the lights . . ." with such crescendo and dynamic force that one expects a dazzling ball of fire to light up the sky when the ten-minute tune ends.

"Let's get it all together . . . one, more, time . . ." or "Rollll, rollll, oh rollll, all night . . ."—Morrison stretches out syllables, often making them theatrical incantations. A magnificent performer, no doubt.

As usual, The Doors' guitarist Robbie Krieger (although wildly loud) was outstanding in the Morrison accompaniment.

LOS ANGELES FREE PRESS
LONG BEACH OPEN DOORS CONCERT · *by Judith Sims*

Albert King strode on, exhorted the audience to say, "Yeah!" which they did, and then they had to say, "Yeah!" again, filling the aisles, crowding the front, clapping along. I saw three black people in the audience, but the young white girls in long dresses and bare feet pretended to be spade, and it didn't really matter because Albert seemed to be enjoying himself enormously. He left the stage with arms wide, a peace sign on each hand. About two minutes later the cheering and stomping brought him back for a nice long encore.

Lights down. "Please bear with us while we make a five-minute sound check." With the dim-

ming of the lights came the forward surge. ("He's there, I see him!" from a girl in fringe, a frantic whisper.) ("He's so bitchin' " agreed her friend in wool shawl.)

Lights up, Jim Morrison, center stage, unleashed a hoarse scream and followed with a new song, "Roadhouse Blues," a loping song, almost good-timey. He stood there and sang it, no leaping or prancing. His left hand over his left ear, right hand grasping the microphone—the Morrison stance. No leather, no beard, medium hair.

For nearly two hours The Doors played MUSIC. When the instrumental breaks came, Morrison turned his back to us, bending close to the drums, shaking maracas. He didn't even ask the audience for a cigarette. He sang, sang very well despite a voice all cracked and husky from four sets in San Francisco. They played "When the Music's Over," did a medley of "Alabama Song" and "Back Door Man" and "Soul Kitchen," ran through some songs on the new album like "Peace Frog," "Maggie Magill," "Ship of Fools," "Spy in the House of Love," and "Freedom Man" (which I think they call "Universal Mind"). With only one exception—an incredibly insipid love song called "Blue Sunday"—the new songs recapture that rhythmic lilt of their first album, and the performance has come full circle, too. Low key, straightforward, no nonsense, except an occasional scream and one galloping prance across the stage which was too controlled to be irrational.

They closed with "Light My Fire," but they didn't really. They came back and announced they would stay all night if we wanted. We wanted.

A few minutes later the audience took advantage of the between-song silence to shout requests. "OK," Morrison said, "which song do you want to hear?" There was a full-throated roar. "Hey, this is impossible, I can't hear anything," Morrison complained, as if he was genuinely surprised that he didn't hear one clear bell-like voice with one simple request coming from 15,000 people. Finally he settled the dispute "demo-cratically, by vote." The old applause meter in his head indicated that we favored "Crystal Ship" more than "Touch Me," so he started "Crystal Ship."

Several tunes later Morrison announced a song "that traditionally finalizes things," and the opening notes of "The End" started up.

A more relaxed Doors concert I've never seen. There was only one moment of tension, and that was handled briefly and casually. A heckler near the stage kept bugging Morrison, demanding Albert King. "Yeah, we'd like to hear him too, but he's gone, so you're stuck with us." The heckler didn't shut up. "You know, sometimes I wish this weren't a democracy," Morrison mused, "because if it wasn't, we could take this guy out somewhere and beat the shit out of him." The audience cheered.

When it was all over, there was further testimony to the New Doors—a press party in the bowels of the arena, food and drink on long tables with white tablecloths and all four Doors circulating amongst the people. I couldn't recall any instance in the past three years when The Doors had allowed themselves to get that close, to be that unprotected with that many people.

"This was a test run for us," John Densmore noted. "There were plainclothes detectives and vice squad all over the place, but Jim didn't say fuck so I guess we're OK."

Better than ever, I'd say.

JAZZ & POP • *Morrison Hotel*
by Bruce Harris

Morrison Hotel, The Doors' fifth album, is not what it seems. And anyone who tells you it's The Doors' return to that "good old rock 'n' roll" has either confused Fabian with Walt Whitman or has just been listening to the Moody Blues for too long.

No, The Doors have revived, even resurrected, a lot of lost arts in *Morrison Hotel*, which lyrically encompasses everything from poetry to parable, but in their hands, rock 'n' roll and all its magic have always been full of life and have never needed any special care.

Poet, singer, shaman, high priest, prophet, politician, Messiah, Father, Son, and Holy Ghost.

Jim Morrison.

Film-maker, actor, writer, director, composer, and all-around, kiss-'em-on-the-lips rockandrollstar.

Teenage idol.

Sex symbol.
Superstud.
Superstar.
Jesus Christ.
Oh, well.

Jim Morrison is a masterful songwriter, a provocative and inventive lyricist, a worthy composer, and a motherfucker of a singer.

The best way to discover The Doors is to investigate the critical reaction against them. The people who dislike The Doors the most, in their attempts to demonstrate what's wrong with The Doors, never fail to point out just what it is that makes The Doors so great. Critics raving about The Doors often get so carried away that they have to be . . . well, carried away. The best picture of The Doors' brand of insanity is best drawn by the sane man who hates them. Only he can truly do justice to the group.

The critic arguing with the concept of Morrison as leader has tried to restrict Morrison to only one of his many social functions. Morrison's performance, for instance, tends to be far more religious than it is political: Morrison has always been more a prophet than a pied piper, and if he cannot teach us how to live, he can at least teach us how *not* to live: "*Cancel* my subscription to the Resurrection" and "You *cannot* petition the Lord with prayer." (Italics added.) After you've canceled your subscription to the Resurrection, it's entirely up to you whether you will find "sanctuary" and "soft asylum," or will remain "lost in a prison of your own devise." Morrison has not so much attempted to destroy religion as he has attempted to replace it.

All Doors albums have been deeply autobiographical, especially the unjustly criticized *Soft Parade* LP, which was really on the whole an awful lot better than an awful lot of awful people wanted to have to admit. More than any other of the group's albums, *The Soft Parade* is most specifically an album about The Doors and their meanings in our society.

Morrison Hotel, for all its flurries of autobiography, is really more directly an album about America. But like *The Soft Parade* it is about you and me only by inference. Most of what has already been written about the album has been about the music, about how it is a return to the tight fury of early Doors music, of how it abounds with funk and guts and earth-energy. All this is true, and there can be little doubt that *Morrison Hotel* is one of the major musical events of Rock '70.

SALLI STEVENSON INTERVIEW WITH JIM MORRISON

Salli Stevenson: Did you ever have a pet snake?
Jim Morrison: No.

Stevenson: Oh, you missed something. They're great. They're fantastic.
Morrison: I like lizards. . . . Snakes, they're beautiful but I can't really get too near them. They make me nervous.

Stevenson: What was your state of mind when you went into the trial?
Morrison::   I think I was just fed up with the image that had been created around me in which I sometimes consciously and most of the time unconsciously cooperated with it. It just got too much for me to really stomach and so I just kind of put an end to it in one glorious evening.

Stevenson: What is the end result of that going to be?
Morrison: Well, I go back. I had a trial of about six weeks. It was very interesting and the felony rap was dismissed and I'm still stuck with two misdemeanors which could add up to about eight months in jail but I maintain that I'm . . . I'm admitting the charge of the public profanity but I'm denying the exposure charge, and so we're going to appeal that for as long as it takes to get it dismissed. It may take another year or two.

Stevenson: What exactly did you do in the "glorious evening"? Or would it hurt your case if I were to print it?
Morrison: Oh, I basically think it was more of a political than a sexual scandal. I think they picked up on the erotic aspect because there would really have been no political charge they could have brought against me. It was too amorphous.

I think it was, really, it was a life-style that was on trial more than any specific incident. I guess that what it boiled down to was that I told the audience that they were a bunch of fucking idiots to be members of an audience, you know. What are they doing there anyway, you know, and that was . . . I think the basic message was that you realize that you're not really here to listen to a bunch of songs by some very good musicians but you're here, you know, you're here for something else and you might as well admit it and do something about it.

Stevenson: A lot of people have said The Doors have declined.

Morrison: The music has gotten progressively better, tighter, more professional, more interesting but I think that people resent the fact that, well . . . three years ago there was a great renaissance of spirit and emotion and revolutionary sentiment, and when things didn't change overnight I think people resented the fact that we were just still around doing good music.

Stevenson: Do you consider yourself more of a hero or an idol?

Morrison: A hero is someone who rebels or seems to rebel against the facts of existence and seems to conquer them, but obviously that can only work at moments. It can't be a lasting thing. But that's not saying that people shouldn't keep trying to rebel against the facts of existence. Who knows, someday we might conquer death and disease and war.

Stevenson: But you, yourself, do you think of yourself as a hero?

Morrison: I think of myself as an intelligent, sensitive human being with the soul of a clown which always forces me to blow it at the most important moments.

Stevenson: If you had the whole thing to do over, where would you go and what would you do? Would you become Jim Morrison of The Doors, would you go into the film? What would you do?

Morrison: I'm not denying that I've had a good time these last three or four years and met a lot of interesting people and seen a lot of things in a short space of time that I probably wouldn't of run into in twenty years of living, so I can't . . . I can't say that I regret it. If I had to do it over again, I think I would have gone more for the quiet, an undemonstrative little artist plodding away in his own garden trip.

Stevenson: What is happening to music right now, I mean in regard to everything that has happened with the deaths of Al Wilson, Janis Joplin, and Jimi Hendrix? Where do you feel music is going and why do you think they're burning themselves out?

Morrison: I guess that great creative burst of energy that happened three or four years ago was hard to sustain and for the sensitive, I guess they might be dissatisfied with anything you know except "the heights." When reality stops fulfilling their inner vision, I guess they get depressed but that's . . . that's not my theory on why people die.

Stevenson: What is your theory?

Morrison: They . . . sometimes it could be an accident . . . sometimes it could be suicide, sometimes it could be murder. There are a lot of ways people die. I don't really know.

Stevenson: *How do you think you'll die?*

Morrison: I hope at the age of about 120 with a sense of humor and a nice comfortable bed. I wouldn't want anybody around. I'd just want to quietly drift off, but I'm still holding out for . . . I think science has a chance in our lifetime to conquer death. I think it's very possible.

Stevenson: *If it did, what would happen to the spirit world?*

Morrison: Well, they'd just have to fend for themselves. Leave us poor immortals alone.

Stevenson: *What about the state of America? Where do you think that's going?*

Morrison: I can't decide whether to try and be a citizen of the world or to identify with a particular country, but I guess you really have no choice. I think whatever happens, that America is the arena right now. It's the center of action even with . . . It will take strong fluid people to survive in a climate like ours, but I'm sure people will do it.

Stevenson: *What is the climate in your opinion?*

Morrison: I think for many people, especially city dwellers, it's a state of constant paranoia. Paranoia is defined as an irrational fear, but what if the paranoia is real? Then you just cope with it second by second.

Stevenson: *If you spend eight months in jail, Jim, what is going to happen to the group during that period of time?*

Morrison: You would have to ask them, but I would hope that they would go on and create an instrumental sound of their own, that didn't depend on lyrics, which aren't really that necessary in music anyway.

Stevenson: *If the sentence comes up, is it definitely decided that you are going to be going back to jail or will there be a fine, or what?*

Morrison: The maximum would be eight months in jail and a fine; however, whatever the sentence would be, we would still go ahead and appeal the conviction . . . we'll appeal it and then take it to a higher court. So I wouldn't go to jail immediately. I don't think so.

Stevenson: *I would hope not.*

Morrison: Me too.

Stevenson: *What about the police?*

Morrison: Police are different in every town and every country. The cops in the L.A. area are different than in most towns, they are idealists and they're almost fanatical in believing in the rightness of their cause, of their profession. They have a whole philosophy behind their tyranny. Whereas in most places the police are doing a job, in L.A. I've noticed a real sense of righteousness about what they're doing, which is kind of scary.

Stevenson: *What do you think of groups like the Stooges and Alice Cooper?*

Morrison: I like people who shake other people up and kind of make them uncomfortable. A young friend of mine thinks Iggy is great.

Stevenson: *Wasn't this the whole theory eventually of what your press turned you into, somebody who was an earthshaker, who shook everybody up?*

Morrison: The press always does that to you.

Stevenson: *But it's more the image than the person performing up there.*

Morrison: Actually I always liked all the things I read. You know, of course, it was about me. Usually you are most interested in yourself and people you know. But they were concentrating on my progenitive organ too much and weren't paying attention to the fact that I was a fairly healthy young male specimen who also had other than your usual arms and legs and ribs and thorax and eyes and nose and all that but a cerebellum. . . . Just your completely equipped human being with the head and there are other things, too, I mean . . .

Stevenson: *Sensitivity.*

Morrison: The full equipment.

Stevenson: *What do you think about love?*

Morrison: Well, love is one of the handful of devices we have to avoid the void, so to speak.

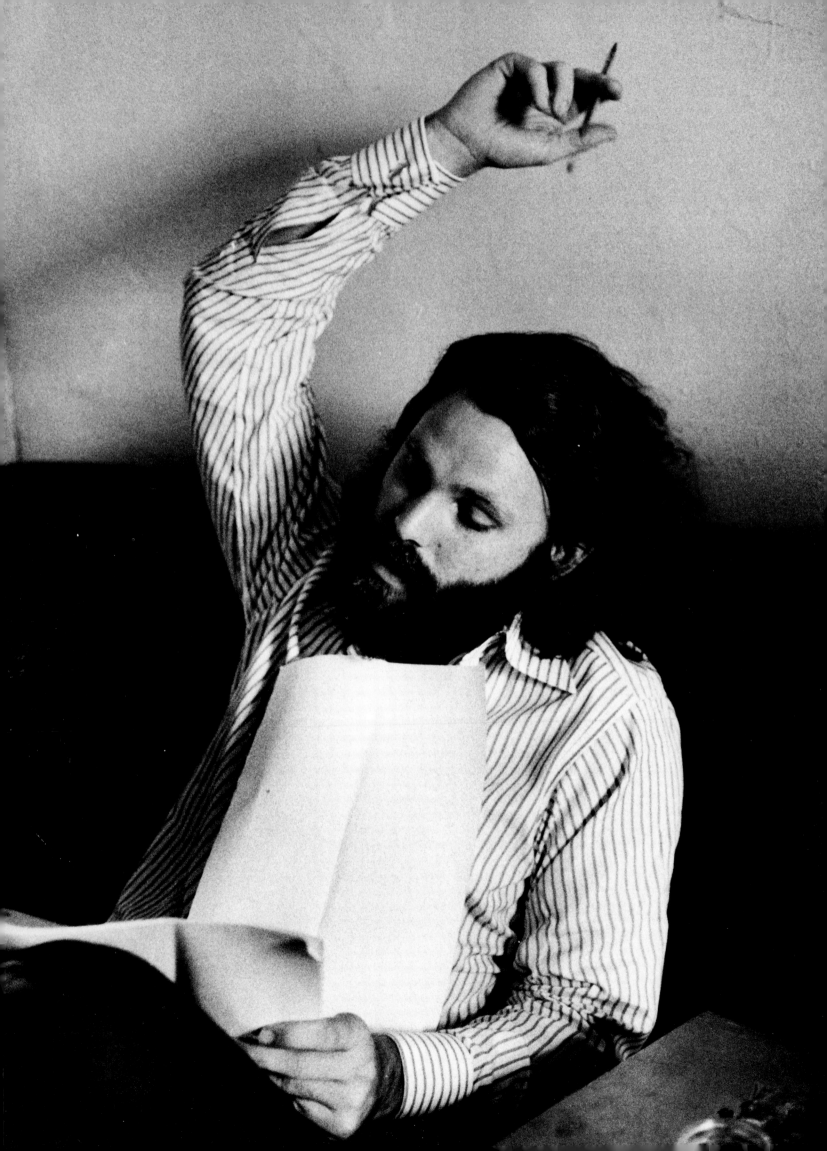

JAZZ & POP
THE DOORS IN NEW YORK · by Patricia Kennealy

"YEAHHH, we're really gonna git it on t'night." Jim Morrison leered encouragingly from the stage of the Felt Forum. The audience, apparently not too willing to suspend disbelief, merely giggled and emitted a few polite catcalls, but by the time the evening was over, they were thronging the stage area, arms upstretched, Touch Me, Touch Me, as though the white-shirted Morrison were a piece of the True Cross.

Not that it mattered. The Doors were in town again, for The Second Annual January New York Doors Concert, though this time, wisely, they had chosen not to perform in Madison Square Garden's vasty main arena, but in the 4,000-seat downstairs Felt Forum: a crescent-shaped, acoustically cheerful auditorium; and they were recording the entire proceedings.

Anyone who thinks The Doors are dead should have been tied to the orchestra railing and made to listen to all four shows that the group did; The Doors are rusty, they may even be jaded, but they are not dead. They are just someplace different. Though Morrison received approximately the same reaction he has been receiving for the past few years (i.e., vocal adoration/vituperation, flung tokens of affection such as bras, panties, rings, and lighted cigarettes), one had the impression he would have been equally happy, nay, happier still, had the audience sat quiet and listened to what The Doors were doing.

The evening after the concert, The Doors hosted a party in the penthouse suite of the New York Hilton; falling somewhere between a Hieronymus Bosch engraving, the party from *Blow-Up*, and a college Homecoming mixer, it was suitably decadent, a thumping success, and everybody from New York had a lot of fun. Ah, but if the party had been the concerts, though . . .

THE VILLAGE VOICE
STRANGE DAYS · by Jim Nash

The Hilton penthouse is something grotesquely yanked out of one of those films about high society that Hollywood used to crank out in the Depression era. The suite of rooms is totally plastic, just the right setting for the beautiful people in their mime costumes.

They had all come to a party honoring Jim Morrison and The Doors, especially Morrison who had brought the theater of the absurd to rock 'n' roll. Morrison, so long the sex symbol of so many teenyboppers and Eighth Street freaks, and he had become a legend in his own time. Coming on stage in tight-fitting leather slacks, shirtless, with shoulder-length hair, he turned on the freaks.

Only three years had passed since Paul Rothchild first hustled the group at the then super-in Ondine on the Upper East Side. Pop was dominated then by the Top 40 stations and FM was dominated by the classicists. There was no underground. The best-selling album had barely begun to happen. Jim Morrison became the darling of Elektra. He built a fortune for Elektra president Jac Holzman and producer Rothchild.

But Holzman has not played hundreds of one-nighters since, and Rothchild has not been mobbed by thousands of fans. They have been able to maintain their minds. A lot has happened since The Doors started out, and the character of rock has altered drastically. Jim Morrison has changed since those early days. He no longer has

bright eyes and he can't seem to get enthusiastic about those crowds that still cling to him. He has become a shadow of himself, with his face grown chubby, his body showing flab, his once shoulder-length hair receding into his forehead.

The pretty people still gather around him, though, just to say that they have touched him. They walked up to him at the Hilton, kissed him, held him, lied to him, just as they lie to themselves.

Every time one of them mentioned the music to him, I could feel him wince, as if it were another jab to his belly, another reminder of what once had been. He was the punch-drunk champ, remembering that once he had been all right, but unable to recall a time for that memory. High school girls in Kansas still worship Jim Morrison, but looking at him across that hotel room, I could smell death, could see the destruction of a man.

We spoke for a few moments. Spoke about film. Fellini was in town and Morrison is into film-making. He has experimented with two shorts and is working on more. He asked me if I had seen the new Fellini film and when I told him I had not he was disappointed. We promised to speak again, but the beautiful people were at his side and he seemed to belong to them.

The party was filled with crashers and curiosity seekers. The freeloaders had got wind of it. I don't think Morrison ever saw them.

I watched as a Warhol superstar sidled up to him. She was grotesquely ugly in painted face, shoe-polish black hair, flabby tits showing through her tight-fitting leopard mini-dress. She handed him a drink and it looked like something out of the seduction scene in *La Dolce Vita*.

I got my coat and began to leave, bumping into Danny Fields, the Max's freak who discovered David Peel and left Elektra a long time back. Danny looked glazed and shallow. He too has yellowed with the years. He walked directly toward the crowd of Warhol freaks, who had now made Morrison their private property. They made room for him and soon Morrison was surrounded.

I rode down in the elevator with a pudgy man who described himself as head of publicity at Elektra. "The Doors are the greatest band in rock," he told me jubilantly. I just nodded. I couldn't answer.

LOS ANGELES FREE PRESS
STAGE DOORS · *by Harvey Perr*

The art of The Doors is, more and more, removed from those standards of art by which rock music is measured. It is, therefore, understandable that The Doors keep getting the worst imaginable reviews from those who put them on some sort of rock pedestal in the first place. It is also understandable that The Doors are still around and are likely to remain forever, despite all that crap, their art surviving all their critics.

The trouble is that The Doors have not conformed to fashion and have not, as almost every other major rock group has done, made a fetish of growing, changing, developing, and reverting to form. They have, instead, played out their own fantasies at their own pace in their own way, saying the hell with everything else. The result was a subtler, deeper growth than that of almost all of their contemporaries. But, as I said, it is not as a rock group that these changes have taken place; it has become increasingly clear that their art is the art of restlessness and rebellion, the art of getting through that restlessness and that rebellion by personal investment, by the piling up of obsessive, compulsive images; the art, finally, of poetry and drama, where the personal and the obsessive are the shrines at whose feet true artists always worship.

So, it's a matter of little importance if there has been no real change between "Light My Fire" and "Tell All the People," if their sound has become monotonously familiar, if they have chosen to continue writing variations on a theme rather than creating new themes. Commitment, not versatility, is the key to Art. And in the intensity with which The Doors have made a commitment lies the true measure of their talent, maybe even their genius.

Where The Doors have arrived, in terms of maturity, and of making some new statement about themselves and on their restless art, was there for all to see in their two appearances recently at the Aquarius Theater, where they recorded a live album. This album, I'm sure, will convince everyone that The Doors have gotten it together, because the electricity in the air, the magic that was created that evening, was a testament to the fact that whatever it was The Doors had once upon a time, when they and their world were younger, they not only had again in spades but had the added virtue of being as sublime and self-assured as they were once brash and vulgar (not vulgar in the bad sense, since the best rock 'n' roll has always had more than a trace of real vulgarity, which after all is a true American trait, and not necessarily one to be ashamed of or to avoid on artistic terms).

There was Jim Morrison, more the rabbinical student than the Sex God and looking more comfortable in the new guise. Seeming less self-conscious, but singing, if anything, better than even his greatest fans thought he could sing, and projecting truer Sex than he ever did when he writhed calculatedly, because the Sex was warmer, more secure. Not that he wasn't capable of the old theatrical excitement as he proved in one electrifying moment when he disappeared from the stage for a few minutes, then showed up suddenly in a blue flame (all right, so it was only a blue light shining on him!) above the audience's head (on the scaffold, left over from the *Hair* set), growling out "The Celebration of the Lizard."

For me, it was the personal pleasure of seeing what Morrison could really do, since the only other live appearance of The Doors that I had seen was the Hollywood Bowl concert, which was a drag. It was the excitement of seeing them live up to an image that had become all but distorted, for surely the bum-rapping The Doors have received in the past year was as out of proportion to the reality of their talent as perhaps the early praise was. That, indeed, may be the real tragedy of their public image, the fact that they were praised too much too soon and were forced almost immediately, before getting a chance to move on in their own direction, to become a commercial commodity, to have to live up to an already overblown success image.

I am glad that I resisted the first album, convinced at the time that nothing that was so instantly popular could have any real value, because, as a result of my resistance, I didn't get carried away by the hype. I think now that the first album is a fine one, perhaps the finest if an album is to be measured in its totality, but I don't think it is the only one, and every single subsequent album has had high points that far surpassed even the best things on the first album.

Perhaps the first real attraction to The Doors came with "Waiting for the Sun" because there's something about the underdog (and the harsh reviews of that album suddenly turned the heroes into underdogs) and the vulnerability of the underdog that forces one to consider and appreciate more genuinely where it is he has failed. And it was under this light that it became clear that The Doors hadn't failed at all, except in the eyes of a fickle audience, and that they were pushing toward something that may not have immediately fascinated their public but which was successful on its own terms, successful in defining what the hell The Doors were all about, if indeed they were about anything (and I, for one, think they were and are).

How can we dismiss anyone who gave us "The End" and "When the Music's Over," which have got to be in some sort of pantheon when the rock era is ultimately re-evaluated, and "The Soft Parade"? How can we fail to see the inner poetry become the dark underside of life as "Break on Through" moves to "You're Lost Little Girl," and finally does make that prophetic breakthrough with the excessively romantic, but always true to the spirit of The Doors (for isn't Revolution as much a form of Romanticism as anything else), "Touch Me"? How can Morrison be accused of singing less well just because the hostility and the sensuality has given to something richer-textured, fuller, more aggressively grim? And when Ray Manzarek's organ playing is ripped apart, isn't it because he has stubbornly insisted on refining his own unique sound (and it is uniquely his, it is part of whatever charisma The Doors have ever had, that whether you think it's bad or good, you always know it's The Doors, and that is Personal and therefore Art) instead of indulging himself in the fancy flourishes of most of his peers?

I'm not altogether sure that my own admiration of The Doors has anything to do with their music. Some of it is terrible, but I find the degree to which they give themselves to banality is more strikingly impressive than the degree to which lesser artists consciously avoid banality. It seems to me that if a group has truly reached the poetic heights, they should enjoy the luxury of making gross mistakes; too few do either one or the other. It's like Morrison's poetry; some of it is the work of a genuine poet, a Whitman of a revolution-ready 60s, and some of it is embarrass-

ingly sophomoric. There is no crime in going from one artistic extreme to another; these are, after all, human flaws, and there is no art if there is no humanity. But, again, it's not their music at all, and maybe not even the poetry or the musicianship or the charisma, neither the albums nor the Aquarius concert, all of it as strange and beautiful and exciting as it is, that really makes me admire The Doors. Instead it's the vibes I get from them because of the thing I feel they're trying to get into and get us into, a world that transcends the limited one of rock, and moves into areas of film and theater and revolution. Seeing Morrison not on stage but living his life, in those quieter public moments; seeing him at a production of Norman Mailer's *The Deer Park,* at every performance of The Living Theater (just prior to, incidentally, the Miami incident), at the opening of The Company Theater's *James Joyce Memorial Liquid Theater* (when he was still a fugitive, taking chances); always at the right place at the right time, involved furiously in the kind of art that is pertinent rather than tangential to living. That kind of person doesn't have to have poetry in him but if he does, when he does, you tend to look at it more closely, take it more seriously. In the case of Jim Morrison and The Doors, it is worth the trouble. They have approached Art, no matter how much they have offended, amused, or even thrilled the rock critics. The standards by which their art must be measured are older and deeper.

LOS ANGELES TIMES
AUDIENCE HEARS A NEW
JIM MORRISON · by Robert Hilburn

Though the concert wouldn't start for another hour, the line outside the Aquarius Theater stretched far down Sunset Boulevard. Six nights a week the theater is the home of the Hollywood company of *Hair,* the love-rock musical that has captured the imagination of those on both sides of the generation gap. On Mondays, the theater is normally closed.

But last week, just as *Hair* always plays to capacity audiences, the sold-out sign was again displayed. The special Monday night attraction was Jim Morrison, the twenty-five-year-old sex symbol of rock and lead singer of The Doors, a vigorous group whose music sends chills up parents' spines much like Elvis Presley, Morrison's reported idol, once did.

Tickets for both shows (which were being recorded for an album) had been sold out for weeks. The Doors are a hot item. Formed three years ago in Los Angeles, the group's early appearances at the Whiskey-a-Go-Go were wild, unpredictable, and exciting. It led to an Elektra recording contract.

Ever since their first album, The Doors, particularly Morrison, have been involved in controversy. Tight black leather pants became Morrison's trademark. His almost panting vocals were often punctuated with sudden body movements that excited the teenage girls and outraged others. The themes of The Doors' songs often dealt with such subjects as death, violence, fear or, above all, sex.

All this emotion and theatrics reached a peak last spring when Morrison was accused of indecent exposure during a Miami concert. The widely publicized incident led to an equally publicized "Rally for Decency" that featured Jackie Gleason, Kate Smith, and the Miami Drum and Bugle Corps. The Miami affair has continued to follow Morrison. When the group played Chicago recently, one writer started his review: "Jim Morrison didn't 'do it.' "

Well, as you may have heard by now, Morrison didn't do it last week at the Aquarius either. He looked anything but a sex symbol as he sat almost motionless on a stool at center stage. Puffing slowly on a cigar while the sound system was being tested, Morrison stroked his new, full beard and stared through tinted glasses into the auditorium darkness. He was wearing loose carpenter-like pants and a white sport shirt.

He seemed only remotely interested as the theater doors opened a little past 7:30 P.M. and the stream of fans moved inside. Two girls, who were in the first wave, were walking by the front of the stage when they realized the bearded guy above them indeed was Morrison. They finally composed themselves long enough to take a picture.

A seventeen-year-old, who sat next to me clutching a $2 ticket that she had bought from a scalper for $5, seemed puzzled by Morrison's new beard. "It ruins his looks," she said at first. A few moments later, she added: "Before he looked like a devil. Now he looks holy. It's all right. He's so exciting."

At 8:15, the concert began, Morrison cupped his hands around the microphone, closed his eyes, moved his mouth next to his hands, and began singing "Back Door Man," a gutty song from his first album. The other Doors—Robbie Krieger (who writes many of the group's songs) on guitar, Ray Manzarek on organ, and John Densmore on drums—play simple but solid rock support.

Morrison's range as a vocalist is limited, but he has a sensual intensity and deliberate phrasing that make his delivery powerful. The reaction was overwhelming at the first show. The audience seemed to sense Morrison was trying something different and it was with him.

By ridding himself of all the old symbols, Morrison was trying to demonstrate that he is more than a black leather freak, more than a rock sex symbol, more than a Miami incident. Perhaps more mature and more serious, Morrison is concerned with a higher ambition. He wants to be recognized as an artist.

Without doubt, he was an artist last Monday. If he continues in his new bag, Morrison may prove that, far from being as bad as much of his past publicity would have one believe, he is as good as his many fans have long felt that he is. He took a giant strike in that direction at the Aquarius.

TWENTY-MINUTE FANDANGOS • *Absolutely Live: The Doors*

by R. Meltzer

It takes all kinds. There's some who'll say The Doors have shot their wad. Anybody says that's gotta take me on and that means a fight. And it means a fair fight, too, Marquis of Queensberry rules. My trainer's gonna be the late great Whitey Bimstein, so the odds are I'm ahead, which means if I don't win I'll be real surprised. Besides, I've got right on my side.

In fact, George Putnam, the Denver-based group analyst extraordinaire, was flown in to give The Doors the once-over. He looked once, he looked twice, and what he finally concluded was, "Drug use isn't always best." Since their recent tastes have ranged to booze, booze, and booze, they received a clean bill of health from George. He knew they had more going for them than ever.

But the change, if there is any, can be indicated in a number of ways. For instance, are the performances just as good? Are the press parties just as good? Are the fans just as good? The answer to the last one's a damn sight easier than the rest, speaking from the standpoint of yours truly, of course. I'm just as good as I was then, and everybody else I've asked is just as good, some even better. So that leaves two very important questions unanswered.

The press parties are not as good as they were. That's an apparent strike-one against the boys, but it's not the end of the ball game. In fact, it's not really even a strike. It's not, because they don't have press parties no more. Even half a party is better than none, but no party is always worse than a party. But no party isn't worse than a bad party, so their parties nowadays are not worse than their parties of yesteryear and therefore they're their equal. That's press parties, not party parties, which of course are better than ever.

Albums are not the same as parties, even if you play them at parties. But one thing's for sure:

Absolutely Live is a great party album. And what makes parties what they are? Food mostly, since fun and companionship can be had even away from parties and music can be had from the radio or TV. So with the right food to accompany it, this can be the most memorable disk of the second half-century.

THE NEW YORK TIMES • *Absolutely Live: The Doors*
by Don Heckman

Double-disk chronicles of live concerts seem to be the thing these days. And understandably so, I guess, since already-recorded material can be sold once again, this time with the added energy of an enthusiastic audience. But there's the danger, too, that less-than-super talent will have trouble surviving such repeated exposure.

I know it's going to sound like sacrilege to suggest that The Doors have overextended them-

selves with this collection, but that's precisely what has happened. Musically, the group has never been much to brag about, dependent as they are upon seemingly endless explorations of single-chord tunes. As a style, it was okay for the early days of trippy, West Coast rock, but in today's market it's beginning to sound as outdated as a Frankie Avalon surfing song.

FUSION • *Absolutely Live: The Doors*
by Lester Bangs

Like many people, I used to hate The Doors. I decided early on that they were a shuck, and having a somewhat reactionary bent, I was especially incensed that so many people idolized them when their whole nightworld was so obviously hokey. Somewhere between then and now, I began to change my tune when I realized that The Doors' music, verbose and repetitious though it might be, made perfect rock 'n' roll by its very "weaknesses." In a time when seemingly every album was packed with Significance impassable with a machete, blatantly foolish songs like "Five to One" were positively refreshing. There's a crying need these days for groups who aren't afraid of being foolish, who can take themselves less than seriously. The Doors obviously aren't and can, and now we need them more than ever.

I like this album a lot. I wouldn't pay $6.98 for it, because most of the songs sound exactly like the originals and most of the new ones are second-rate, but I still think it's a lot of fun to listen to, and next to most of the other stuff out these days, from name groups and novices alike, The Doors stand up damn well. Who else would make up lyrics like "Dead cat in a top hat/Suckin' on a young man's blood . . ."?

It takes a certain spirit to write and sing things like that, a healthy spirit of self-satire. The Doors have it, and know exactly what they're doing, and get a hearty yuk out of it, as is perfectly obvious in Morrison's between-songs raps with the audience: at one point he says, "I don't know if you realize it, but tonight you're in for

a special treat." The audience cheers in wild anticipation; he chortles, "Oh no, not that, not that!"

Mention should also be made of "Celebration of the Lizard," complete on record for the first time. But that's about all that should be made of it. It's real low comedy, typical Morrisonian undergraduate imagery, but without the support this time of a good melody and arrangement. "Not to Touch the Earth" was definitely the only part worth preserving. I get a pretty good laff out of it, but I don't want to play it again. Come to think of it, I played this whole album a lot the first three days I had it, which was a month ago, but didn't think of putting it on again until it came time to write this today.

Still, I really like this album even if I don't listen to it much, because I like The Doors and I feel like I could really throw it on any time with no strain. Manzarek and Krieger play with as much solid professional competence and occasional fire as we've come to expect from them. But Morrison is the real star. He sings that Crypt Comix imagery of his with real feeling, and even if he doesn't believe a word of it, the kids do, and I think that's fine. I'd love to be out there, singing those words and thinking about what kind of bizarre fantasies they must be getting off in all them stoned-out little noggins. Jim Morrison seems to me like an eminently sane man, one of the few left in rock with a real sense of humor, and probably a good beer-drinkin' buddy to boot. We need more like him.

JAZZ & POP · *Absolutely Live: The Doors*
by Patricia Kennealy

Despite the fact that some of the tracks here performed were in the can for as much as a year after they were recorded, and despite the fact that *Absolutely Live* is the absolutely worst album title since and including *Absolutely Free*, and despite the fact that Ray Manzarek adds insult to injury by including (in addition to his lead vocal on "Close to You") a direct cop off the Stones' "Play With Fire" on the ride section of "Break on Through, #2," and despite the fact that Jim Morrison's audience patter is a lot snottier than, say, John B. Sebastian's, despite all this, and maybe even because of all this, *Absolutely Live* is one of the absolutely finest live rock 'n' roll albums ever made, and no mistake.

Fine as everybody is—Morrison is in great voice and high spirits, Manzarek is unceasingly amazing on keyboard bass as well as on the more obvious organ, and Densmore comes across both solid and flash—it is indisputedly Robbie Krieger who is the real star of this album. Krieger, lurking insidiously in the far dark corners of the stage. Krieger, who has generally managed to be pretty badly under-recorded on previous Doors efforts. Krieger, who if he ever left the group could probably be the best studio guitarist in the world.

Yes, and in addition to Robbie Krieger, this album does contain upon its last side "The Celebration of the Lizard," that somewhat legendary leviathan of a Doors "theater piece." Now this is what I call poetry; its total effect is a truly vertiginous dazzle, and though it may not be the greatest work of poetic art in the history of Western civilization, it is possibly the most powerful piece of music and words ever recorded by any rock group, anywhere, and it alone is worth the price of the entire album.

Absolutely Live merely proves once again that The Doors are worth sixteen of Creedence any day of the week.

SEATTLE TIMES
THE DOORS STUMBLE THROUGH A CONCERT · by Victor Stredicke

A small audience at the Coliseum last night slammed the door on what was once the nation's most popular rock group.

Despite a dynamic buildup by Albert King, impressive blues singer who has been touring with The Doors on this concert swing, when Jim Morrison, lead singer, sauntered on stage he got the coldest reception this town has ever accorded a superstar.

Audience unrest flared as Morrison, in simple blue tee shirt and black pants, dawdled inexcusably between selections. There were periods of no music, no talk, no action for up to nine minutes each.

The young crowd took over.

First the shouts were for Doors favorites, like "Light My Fire," which brought the California group to the music scene in 1967. As Morrison refused to respond, a catcall suggested, " 'Sugar, Sugar' . . . anything!"

As catcalls increased, Morrison grew more remote. Ray Manzarek, organist, Robbie Krieger, guitar, and John Densmore, drums, competent musicians, were left leaderless.

West Coast Promotions, a Los Angeles firm which arranged this concert, and one which follows in Vancouver, B.C., were hoping for a revival of interest in The Doors.

This is a new wholesome show, one of the promoters explained, before the concert.

"Give the singer a chance," Morrison mumbled. "I haven't been to Seattle in two years."

The audience rebutted: "You were here last summer!"

Morrison made a tasteless pun on the Latin phrase, *tempus fugit,* and described Seattle as a 1930 version of twenty years in the future. Most understood the first joke, only half understood the second.

LOS ANGELES TIMES
SWINGIN' DOORS REALLY OPEN UP DURING CONCERT · by Lee Grant

SAN DIEGO: Right there in front of the stage she was, this girl in skintight pants and striped T-shirt, no more than sixteen.

The next instant she was on stage, hugging and kissing the thin, long-haired, full-bearded singer.

Jim Morrison stood there as the girl hugged and hung on. He kept singing, "Break on through to the other side/yeah, break on through to the other side."

From the wings, a burly bodyguard sped on stage and tore the girl off Morrison. She cried.

She was the first of a half dozen who jumped up to kiss this dynamic lead singer of The Doors.

It was Saturday night at the International Sports Arena, and it was a typical rock concert Saturday night.

There was the usual crush near the stage, no one sitting, thousands of people all trying to get as close a view of Morrison as possible.

They weren't disappointed.

He came on stage wearing flared black jeans, a blue T-shirt, and boots, and told the audience: "This whole thing started with rock 'n' roll and now it's out of control."

It was a typical Doors performance—two hours long, pulsating, sensual, and fun.

It was together. A particularly gutty vocal by Morrison and fine playing by Manzarek, one of rock music's best keyboard men.

Then came the girls. They loved him, and he loved them.

"You're out of sight," Morrison yelled to the audience, taking a sip from a perpetually filled paper cup of beer.

The singer was in top form, shouting the blues and screaming with style. But he didn't have to be.

He walked across stage, back and forth, screeching, playing with the feedback from the huge speakers and showing off.

That was enough. The kids loved it.

Another girl. She made it up, kissed Morrison on the cheek, and dove back into the audience before the guard could get to her. A loud ovation for her.

The best, however, was to be for last.

It was nearly a half hour of a Doors-arranged "history of rock 'n' roll."

There was a singing narrative and some long instrumental solos. And there was Morrison singing the music he came up with as a youngster in Los Angeles—The Kingsmen's "Louie Louie," Elvis' "Heartbreak Hotel," "Summertime," "Fever," "St. James Infirmary Blues," and his own "Light My Fire," the multimillion seller.

It was a good set and nobody had slammed The Doors.

DENVER POST
6,000 AT ROCK PERFORMANCE: It's All in the Acting to Doors' Morrison · by Jim Pagliasotti

An overflow crowd of 6,000 young theatergoers was treated to a two-hour production of The Doors Sunday night at the University of Denver Arena.

Although it was billed as a concert, the show was long in drama and rather short in music. There were moments when the theatrics seemed to be a dramatization of every parent's nightmare fantasy about rock music bands and their effect on young people.

There was this singer on stage named Jim Morrison who had been arrested for indecent exposure during a performance in Miami Beach. He didn't do anything like that in Denver, but it added to the drama, you see.

He began by leaping onto the stage, grunting out two lines of "Back Door Man," spinning and falling flat on his back (whether by accident or design, he later repeated it purposely) as if struck by all the gathered voltage in the mountain of amplifiers behind him, then rising in the red and purple light with a high-pitched, evil laugh, and singing. He never missed a beat.

And out in the darkness, the audience of young girls and young men loved every minute of it. It went on like that for two hours, and the audience clapped, shouted, and stomped feet and screamed for more. I've seen The Doors six times in the last three years and the audience reaction has been the same each time.

And I still don't know why.

"The singer, not the song" is a fitting line. The Doors without Morrison would be a fairly good trio. Robbie Krieger plays sparse, inter-esting guitar lines, Ray Manzarek is a competent organist, and John Densmore bangs out heavy, driving rhythms on drums. With Morrison, they are a lesser band but a great show.

Jim Morrison is something for the world to behold, and contemplate. He writes terribly pretentious lyrics ("Before I slip into the Big Sleep—I want to hear the scream of the butterfly" is one of the milder examples), his voice has a range of perhaps three-quarters of an octave, his phrasing isn't particularly good, and he doesn't even move well.

What he does is simply put it all out front. He is crude in the extreme, drinking beer on stage in huge gulps, belching into the mike, screaming indistinguishable lyrics while going through spastic contortions, straddling the mike, strangling it in a death grip, falling to the floor in agony-ecstasy throes of passion, then as quickly changing the tempo to a slow, whispered, intensely felt interpretation.

Above all, he is dramatic. It is truly theater, with music as its pulse. He acts out the role of rock-music star, larger than life, the collective emotion of a hypertense generation. The concert as catharsis.

The doors do a song that goes "Break on through, break on through to the other side." Most groups in rock have done just that, and all of us are trying. The Doors are stationary, hung in the frame of their theatrics, but all of us, at one time or another, must pass through The Doors to get to the other side.

"The Doors are basically a blues-oriented group with heavy dosages of rock 'n' roll, a moderate sprinkling of jazz, a minute quantity of classical influences, and some popular elements. But basically, a white blues band.

"Our music has returned to the earlier form, just using the four instruments. We felt that we had come too far in the other direction, i.e., orchestration, and wanted to get back to the basic format."

— JIM MORRISON

7

L.A. WOMAN

April, 1971

CREEM • L.A. WOMAN: The Doors
by Rob Houghton

Warm-blooded animals seem to loathe reptilian forms of life. That might have been the reason for the incredible wellsprings of disgust that washed over The Doors, who were almost universally loved, after Jim Morrison proclaimed himself to be the Lizard King. No other rock group went so dramatically from a position of admiration to sheer hatred in so short a time as did The Doors. Something about them must have just rubbed people the wrong way.

The Doors might have been treated with disdain because they were from Los Angeles, which seems to hang like a pall of smoke over all the bands that start out there. The Byrds, Love, and The Doors were all hurt in the minds of the intelligentsia, for having the crass lack of taste to actually like ol' Rip-Off City.

It might have been Jim Morrison's sometimes silly apocalyptic poetic lyrics. Thousands of flower children, and their intellectual cohorts, who were trying to save the world through love, were put off by that punk in his black shirt and pants made of the leather of an unborn lamb, or whatever it was, singing about killing his father, raping his mother, throwing animals out of boats in the midst of horrible storms, walking in streets with blood up to his knees, and so on.

Their image was definitely wrong. I remember seeing them on television only once, on a rock survey show hosted by Murray the K, back in 1967. After a half hour of sitars, meadowlands, and velour caftans, The Doors came on looking like a road gang and completely ruined the effect. We used to hear strange rumors of The Doors forsaking acid for heroin. And this was at a time when Timothy Leary was still stomping the Ivy League circuit. Of course, later when all the superstars were using cocaine, and heroin, everybody was scandalized to find out that Jim Morrison had turned into a beer hound.

What kind of sex symbol can a group have, once the lead singer has grown a full beard and a beer belly? That would be like John Wayne with his toupee off, or Iggy Stooge with a partial plate. If Pabst Blue Ribbon beer was smart, they would sign up The Doors for a whole series of commercials. They could increase sales by as much as a hundred percent. Mostly by me.

L.A. Woman is the last album of The Doors' present contract with Elektra. The capitalists in the front office are no doubt thinking hard about the possibility of dumping one of the all-time headache groups. Which would make it very awkward for them if the record turns out to be a hit. "Love Her Madly," which is settling in for a long stay on AM radio, is a great boogying song. Not a fantastic piece of music, mind you, but when sandwiched between The Jackson Five and Steve Stills, it shines. "The Changeling," "Been Down So Long," and "L'America" show Jim Morrison at his most mock tough, like some kind of fifties delinquent, as played by John Cassavetes in a B movie. When too many rock musicians are overpraised as virtuosos, almost no words have ever been laid on the organ of Ray Manzarek, or the guitar of Robbie Krieger. And yet it is they who actually make The Doors. They are the ones who fill in the background to Morrison's melodramatics, and provide the primeval power to the group's sound.

"Crawling King Snake" is Morrison at his most reptilian. He just kind of slithers up to ya in a vision right out of Burroughs. "The Wasp (Texas Radio and the Big Beat)" combines Morrison's finest imagery with some of the most engrossing music that anyone has made in some time. "Cars Hiss by My Window," "L.A. Woman," and "Riders on the Storm" are some of the best songs that The Doors have ever made. They seem to be that strange breed of songs that The Doors use when they want to end an album. They are like "Light My Fire," "The End," or "When the Music's Over" but with a subtler effect, more calm, more resigned.

The Doors were a group who were forced to pay their dues after they had become a success. Even now, too many people are content to dismiss them as not being worthy of attention by serious listeners with limited time on their hands to listen to pop music. The Doors at their worst were one of the most wart-covered, pretentious bands of the sixties. But no other group had a clearer grasp of the age. Too much passes away from us too quickly these days. Are we really going to be better off if Jim Morrison becomes a single act? Are we really so affluent that we could give up one of our best bands in a swamp of indifference? What I'm trying to say is that we should hold on to those things that have value. What I'm trying to say is, let's make sure that *L.A. Woman* will not be the album that will finally close The Doors!

UNIVERSITY REVIEW · *L.A. WOMAN: The Doors*

by Bruce Harris

L.A. Woman is The Doors' new album. If it were their first album, they would no doubt be hailed as the "Most Promising New Group of 1971," though there's no telling what James Taylor and Elton John might say. But *L.A. Woman* is not The Doors' first album and whether it will be their last remains to be seen. As one might expect, the theme of the album is change, not just because The Doors have changed since then, but because they are still changing. It isn't, as I'm sure some critics will say, The Doors returning to their basic style, to the direct simplicity of their first album. It is The Doors going one step beyond everything. Never much involved in the mainstream of rock music—always more of a monument than an influence—The Doors remain aloof. Unaffected by trends and fads, they are simply making music.

 L.A. Woman is hardly perfect, but its few weak moments somehow seem right in connection with the whole. When a lyric just misses the mark, as in "Been Down So Long," for instance, it seems to convey a certain feeling as a result; an hon-

esty, a realness, a humanity. On their first self-produced album, The Doors sound more like real people than ever before. The Godlike, majestic edge has been taken from Morrison's voice, and where he used to sound superhuman, he now sounds real. His singing, never more raw and unrefined, has also never been more convincing, more natural, more human. The group, too, has opened up. Their genius for free-flowing music is now inherent in practically every cut, and as a result all the tracks are long, filled with the exquisite playing of the band. Robbie's guitar swoops and slides madly, its sleek, liquid phrases perfectly capturing mood and meaning. On keyboards, Ray Manzarek is tart, tasty, and always right, and drummer Densmore perpetually explores the rhythmic regions that only he can hear.

 Like previous Doors albums, *L.A. Woman* is preoccupied with America, viewing it as a museum of diseases. The music is tough, raw, violent, and the lyrics, catapulted by Morrison's powerful voice, are often stark and soaring.

DETROIT FREE PRESS • *L.A. Woman: The Doors*
by Bob Talbert

The Doors, Elektra: The Beatles are dead! Long live the Stones? The Doors? The shoot-out for rock's king group has begun, and if these two new albums are any indication, it's going to be a battle royal for the throne. The Stones' record is the best rock album since the Beatles' *Rubber Soul*. The Doors' is a close second. Both groups represent the ultimate in slightly angry but non-acid hard rock, that draws its life's blood from black blues and urban poetry.

Mick Jagger is superb as the Stones' symbol and leader, equaled by Jim Morrison's best recorded effort to date. The Doors' album has no weak tracks. "Riders on the Storm" is beautiful, and "Been Down So Long" is "on right." Ray Manzarek's subtle organ is super heavy. At the listening, the Stones are in the lead, by percentage points. The Stones' Andy Warhol-designed cover is a zip-off.

"There's no story really. No real narrative. Except there's a hitchhiker who . . . We don't see it, but we later assume that he stole a car and he drives into the city and it just ends there. He checks into a motel and he goes out to a nightclub or something. It just kind of ends like that."

Jim Morrison is talking about the story of his latest movie, HIGHWAY. This amorphous plot summary seems strangely interchangeable with Morrison's new image of cinema verité director. The James Douglas Morrison that I spoke to was an older man than I had expected to meet. He was a man with gray hairs mingling into his beard and hair, talking about his past of "rock star" as a convict might review his past of "criminal" with a parole officer. A sparkle of the Morrison that I had expected did at times come through, although the flashes were carefully obscured by the past tense.

"It always amazes me that people think you're two years younger than you are. I guess that's why you have to keep doing interviews. People believe old press clippings. A couple of years ago, I filled a need that some people had for a figure who represented a whole lot of things, so they created the thing. It's like seeing baby pictures or something. It's embarrassing and funny at the same time."

Morrison is not the image that he has been for so many years. He isn't wearing snakeskin or leather. He has a beer with lunch and a drink before and after. He is his own archer's arrow traveling through the time and space of oblivion with a great deal of insight as to where he's been, and an Indian's aim of where he's going. He is more anxious to talk about films than rock music, a lot of which he no longer listens to. He is also anxious to get the details of his life straight; the most recent of which were his trial on charges ranging from obscenity to plane hijacking. Along with getting straight is the realization that with age, trials, and tribulations has come a loss of naïveté.

Morrison: I wasted a lot of time and energy with the Miami trial. About a year and a half. But I guess it was a valuable experience because before the trial I had a very unrealistic school-boy attitude about the American (Did I hear a "k"?) judicial system. My eyes have been opened up a bit. There were guys down there, black guys, that would go on each day before I went on. It took about five minutes and they would get twenty or twenty-five years in jail. If I hadn't had unlimited funds to continue fighting my case, I'd be in jail right now for three years. It's just if you have money you generally don't go to jail. The trial in Miami

broke up a lot of things. It's on appeal to the Supreme Court right now.

Chorush: *Whatever happened to the other busts that you were involved in?*

Morrison: I got acquitted on everything else. We're trying to get this erased because it's not good to have something like that on your record.

Chorush: *Are you still concerned with that kind of record?*

Morrison: It's just if something really serious happens, then you have a record and it looks a lot worse.

Chorush: It looked for a while like they were out to get you. There was a federal hijacking charge also, wasn't there?

Morrison: Well, it came under a law that was created because of hijacking, but it wasn't really a hijacking. It was just a little over-exuberant kind of playing. It wasn't a threat to safety or anything. Actually we were ac-quitted because the stewardesses mistook me for someone who I was with. They were going by the seat number. They were saying that the person in such and such seat was causing all this trouble. They all identified me as being in this seat. They were just trying to hang me because I was the only one that had a well-known face. So they were trying to get me for it. I don't know: I guess it was an example of the kind of people you meet on airplanes.

The trouble with all these busts is that people I know, friends of mine, think it's funny and they like to believe it's true and they ac-cept it: people that don't like me like to believe it because I'm the reincarnation of everything they consider evil. I get hung both ways. I went through a trial there in Phoenix. I had to go back several times to get that cleared up.

Chorush: What do you think the chances are of getting off in Miami? It's just a misdemeanor now, isn't it.

Morrison: Well, it's two misdemeanors. I have to be optimistic, so I figure there's a good chance. We're going to appeal on several grounds. First of all, they never really proved anything except profanity, which we admitted all along. We were going to attempt to prove that profanity did not violate contemporary community standards in the City of Miami. To do that we were going to take the jury to see all the movies like *Woodstock* and *Hair*. *Hair* was playing in town at that time. And they had nudity on stage every night and they were allowing young people to go in at any age. And all of the books that were available in even junior high school libraries with four-let-ter words. The judge refused to allow any in-vestigation along those lines and limited it to criminal actions. They brought out thirteen wit-nesses. Every witness was either a policeman who was working there that night or someone who worked for the city and happened to be there or a relative of a policeman. In fact, their biggest witness was a sixteen-year-old girl who was the niece of a police officer who got her and her date in free that night. All their testimony was very contradictory. Every one of them had a different version of what happened.

Chorush: I heard that girl called someone "a little bitch."

Morrison: I didn't hear her do it but that's what I heard. They had thousands of photographs from many different people that were there, but there was no photograph of an exposure or anything near it. The other charges I think were just put in there to make it look more serious. Simulated masturbation, oral copulation . . .

Chorush: With yourself?

Morrison: Masturbation on myself and oral copulation on the guitar player. There's a picture of that on the inside sleeve of the *13* album.

Chorush: Is that a lamb's head you're holding there?

Morrison: No, that's a real lamb. That guy, Lewis Marvin of the Moonfire, happened to be there. He travels around spreading his philosophy of nonviolence and vegetarianism. He carries this lamb around to demonstrate his principles that if you eat meat you're killing this little lamb. He gave it to me during the middle of the show. I just held it for a while. It's interesting. There was a lot of noise, a lot of commotion. It was almost deafening, but the lamb was breathing normally, almost purring like a kitten. It was completely relaxed. I guess what they say about lambs to the slaughter is true. They don't feel a thing. Anyway, the judge limited the defense's witnesses to the number of witnesses that the prosecution

brought on, which is an entirely arbitrary maneuver.

Chorush: *Did you get all those witnesses through an ad?*

Morrison: Yeah, and just through the grape-vine. But we had over three hundred people that were willing to testify that they didn't see any of those alleged incidents. What it turns out actually happened is that a journalist happened to be there or heard about this concert, about inciting to riot. The citizens became irate and began calling the police station, asking why this had been allowed to go on and why I wasn't arrested. I had gotten up and gone on to Jamaica for a holiday that had been planned there. About three or four days after the whole thing, they swore out a warrant for me. So you can see how the whole thing began.

The only thing I did was the Isle of Wight for a day and then I came right back. We could have done performances but we never knew from one day to the next when court was in session.

Chorush: *They were doing alternate days weren't they?*

Morrison: Yeah. And he changed it every day. So we never knew. I really needed the weekends to rest up. It was an ordeal.

Chorush: *Do you think they were out to get you or out to get the culture?*

Morrison: I think it was really the life-style they were going after. I don't think it was me personally. I just kind of stepped into a hornet's nest. I had no idea that the sentiment down there was so tender. The audience that was there seemed to enjoy it. I think that the people who read about it in the paper in this distorted version created a climate of hysteria. A few weeks later they had an antidecency—I mean an anti-indecency rally at the Orange Bowl with a famous fat comedian.

Chorush: *Well known for his decency.*

Morrison: Right. The President congratulated the kid that started this rally. They had them all over the country.

Chorush: *Did you find yourself excluded from the proceedings the way Manson feels?*

Morrison: Yeah, I felt like a spectator, but I wouldn't have wanted to defend myself because I would have blown it, I'm sure. It's not as easy as it looks.

Chorush: *Did you ever get to testify at all?*

Morrison: Yes. I didn't have to testify, but we decided that it might be a good thing for the jury to see what I was like because all they could do is look at me for six weeks or as long as it went. So I testified a couple of days. I don't think it meant anything one way or an-

other. They drag it out so long that after a while no one would care. I suppose that's one of the functions of a trial. They muddle it up so much that you don't know what to think anymore. That's society's way of assimilating a horrible event.

After clearing up things to the present, Morrison seems to feel more at ease about talking about the past. Someone has told me that Morrison used to be close with the Company Theater in Los Angeles until the group did *Children of the Kingdom*. This play is a study of the thoughts and backstage actions of a "rock star." The resemblance of the play's protagonist and Morrison seems to be more than just mere coincidence. The protagonist, like Morrison, tried to realize what was going on in the heads of those that came to see him. Morrison's sense of theatrics had put him in front of a Los Angeles capacity and audience asking, "What do you want? You didn't come here to hear music. What do you want? What do you REALLY want?"

"I saw half of *Children of the Kingdom* . . . I couldn't sit through the rest of it. It made me feel uneasy. Not that I don't appreciate satire, but it just hit too close to home.

"I think people go to rock concerts because they enjoy being in crowds. It gives them a feeling of power and security in a strange way. They like to rub up against hundreds of other people that are like them. It reinforces their trip.

"As a performer, then, I'm just a focus for everyone's attention, because you have to have an excuse to mob together. Otherwise it becomes a riot.

"The Doors never really had any riots. I did try and create something a few times just because I'd always heard about riots at concerts and I mean I thought we ought to have a riot. Everyone else did. So I tried to stimulate a few little riots, you know, and after a few times I realized it's such a joke. It doesn't lead anywhere. You know what, soon it got to the point where people didn't think it was a successful concert unless everybody jumped up and ran around a bit. It's a joke because it leads nowhere. I think it would be better to do a concert and just keep all that feeling submerged so that when everyone left they'd take that energy out on the streets and back home with them. Rather than just spend it uselessly in a little crowd explosion.

"No, we never had any real riots. I mean a riot's an out-of-control, violent thing. We never had too much of what I call a real riot. I think also it had something to do with the swarming theory: the idea that insect and animal species, when the population starts outstripping the food supply, the animals or insects swarm together. It's a way of communicating. Working out a solution or signaling an awareness to each other.

Signaling that there is a danger. In nature a balance is worked out and I think that somehow that's what's happening. In Los Angeles or New York and many of the big cities, you feel crowded. You feel psychologically crowded and just physically crowded. People are getting very erotic and paranoid and I guess things like rock concerts are a form of human swarming to communicate this uneasiness about overpopulation. I haven't really got it all worked out yet, but I think there's something in it.

"I think that more than writing music and as a singer, that my greatest talent is that I had an instinctive knack of self-image propagation. I was very good at manipulating publicity with a few little phrases like 'erotic politics.' Having grown up on television and mass magazines, I knew instinctively what people would catch on to. So I dropped those little jewels here and there—seemingly very innocently—of course just calling signals.

"I think The Doors were very timely. The music and ideas were very timely. They seem naïve now, but a couple of years ago people were into some very weird things. There was a high energy level and you could say things like we did and almost half-ass believe them. Whereas now it seems very naïve. I think it was a combination of good musicianship and timeliness. And we may have been one of the first groups to come along who were openly self-conscious of being performers, and it was reflected in our career as it was happening.

"It's not that we were trend conscious or anything like that. We were doing exactly what we would have been doing anyway. It came at the right time and we could get away with expressing sentiments like that. I'm sure we would have done the same thing anyhow. For example, the first album is not really socially conscious. It's

just very universal personal statements. Each album got a little more socially aware of the whole landscape. Perhaps to the detriment of the music.

"As we traveled around and played to large groups of people, some of the words couldn't help reflecting the things I ran into. That was mainly it. It wasn't any conscious program. Probably the things we record now will get back to the blues. That's what we do best. We may even do a couple of old blues songs. Just your basic blues.

"It'll be good blues. It won't be like a guy with a guitar playing the blues. It will be electric blues, I hope. You never know when you start an

album. It could be entirely different. But that's what I'm going to push for. That's the music I enjoy best. It's the most fun to sing. I like jazz, too. But you don't need a singer really for jazz. Those guys ought to do some instrumentals. I've always pushed for that. They've been reluctant to do it, but I wish they would. Those guys put out a lot of music, a lot of sound for just three guys.

"I like any reaction I can get with my music. Just anything to get people to think. I mean, if you can get a whole room or a whole club full of drunk, stoned people to actually wake up and think, you're doing something. That's not what they came there for. They came to lose themselves.

"I don't know if you saw the setup we have at the office or not. We have a board upstairs. We record right there. It's not that we don't like the Elektra studios, but we felt that we do a lot better when we're rehearsing. We leave a tape running. It's a lot cheaper and faster that way, too. This will be the first record that we're actually doing without a producer. We're using the same engineer that we've used. Bruce Botnick. I don't know if he'll be called a producer or not. Probably co-producer with The Doors. In the past, the producer . . . it's not that he was a bad influence or anything, but this will be a lot different without that fifth person there. So anyway we'll be by ourselves for better or worse.

"There were a few new songs on the 'live' album. A year ago we finished *Morrison Hotel*. It's been about a year since we've been in a studio.

"A few years ago I wanted to do live performances. I was trying to get everyone to do free surprise spots at the Whiskey, but no one wanted to. Now everyone wants to, and I totally lost interest. Although I know it's a lot of fun, I just don't have the desire to get up and sing right now. I still enjoy music, but I lost a lot of interest in it."

Chorush: Are you going to go in more for doing your films?
Morrison: Yeah, I think so, but there's no hurry on that.

Chorush: A couple of things that you said in The Lords interested me, like "the appeal of cinema lies in the fear of death." Is that something you can explain?
Morrison: I think in art, but especially in films, people are trying to confirm their own existences. Somehow things seem more real if they can be photographed and you can create a semblance of life on the screen. But those little aphorisms that make up most of *The Lords*—if I could have said it any other way, I would have. They tend to be mulled over. I take a few seriously. I did most of that book when I was at the film school at UCLA. It was really a thesis on film esthetics. I wasn't able to make

films then, so, all I was able to do was think about them and write about them, and it probably reflects a lot of that. A lot of passages in it—for example about shamanism—turned out to be very prophetic several years later because I had no idea when I was writing that, that I'd be doing just that.

Chorush: At the end of The Lords, you define the lords as the people that are controlling art. Did I understand that right?
Morrison: Strangely enough, that's what I meant. Not controlling art necessarily. What that book is a lot about is the feeling of powerlessness and helplessness that people have in the face of reality. They have no real control over events or their own lives. Something is controlling them. The closest they ever get is the television set. In creating this idea of the lords, it also came to reverse itself. Now to me, the lords mean something entirely different. I couldn't really explain. It's like the opposite. Somehow the lords are a romantic race of people who have found a way to control their environment and their own lives. They're somehow different from other people.

Chorush: The New Creatures. There's a lot of creatures in everything you do. Lizards and snakes and snakeskins. That's part of your reputation. The Lizard King. How did all that come about?
Morrison: I had a book on lizards and snakes and reptiles, and the first sentence of it struck me acutely: "Reptiles are the interesting descendants of magnificent ancestors." Another thing about them is that they are a complete anachronism. If every reptile in the world were to disappear tomorrow, it wouldn't change the balance of nature one bit. They are a completely arbitrary species. I think that maybe they might, if any creature could, survive another world war or some kind of total poisoning of the planet. I think that somehow reptiles could find a way to avoid it.

Chorush: Does that fit into your own self-concept?
Morrison: Also, we must not forget that the lizard and the snake are identified with the unconscious and the forces of evil. That piece "Celebration of the Lizard" was kind of an invitation to the dark forces. It's all done tongue in cheek. I don't think people realize that. It's not to be taken serious. It's like if you play the villain in a western it doesn't mean that that's you. It's just an aspect that you keep for show. I don't really take that seriously. That's supposed to be *ironic*.

On a much more basic level, I just always loved reptiles. I grew up in the southwest and I used to catch horned toads and lizards. Of course, I still can't get too close to snakes. I mean, it's hard for me to pick up a snake and play with it. There's something deep in the human memory that responds strongly to snakes. Even if you've never seen one. I think that a snake just embodies everything that we fear. Basically their skins are just beautiful. I guess that's why they're so fashionable. I think they always have been.

Chorush: What's your reputation as a drinker?
Morrison: (Long pause) I went through a period where I drank a lot. I had a lot of pressures hanging over me that I couldn't cope with. I think also that drinking is a way to cope with living in a crowded environment and also a product of boredom. I know people drink because they're bored. I enjoy drinking. It loosens people up and stimulates conversation sometimes. It's like gambling somehow; you go out for a night of drinking and you don't know where you're going to end up the next day. It could work out good or it could be disastrous. It's like the throw of the dice.

There seem to be a lot of people shooting

smack and speed and all that now. Everybody smokes grass—I guess you don't consider that a drug anymore. Three years ago there was a wave of hallucinogenics. I don't think anyone really has the strength to sustain those kicks forever. Then you go into narcotics, of which alcohol is one. Instead of trying to think more, you try to kill thought with alcohol and heroin and downers. These are pain-killers. I think that's what people have gotten into. Alcohol for me, because it's traditional. Also, I hate scoring. I hate the kind of sleazy sexual connotations of scoring from people, so I never do that. That's why I like alcohol; you can go down to any corner store or bar and it's right across the table.

I think what happens now is that people smoke so much and so constantly that it's not a trip anymore. I think they build up a cellular tolerance for it. It just becomes part of their body chemistry. They're not really stoned.

Morrison talks on. Always conscious

about his image. Relaxed. He is fascinated by a mini-skirted girl who gets out of a car across the street, and by Zap Comix. He wants to write about his trial and wonders where he should submit his story. He drops hints about a friend of his who could be the world's greatest female vocalist. He seems nervous about

getting back to the studio. He's already two hours late. But . . .

"There is no story really. No real narrative . . . he drives into the city . . . he goes out . . . or something . . . it just kind of ends like that . . . and . . . when the music's over, turn off the lights. . . ."

8

PARIS

March 10 - July 3, 1971

LOS ANGELES TIMES
MORRISON'S LAST DAYS IN L.A.: HOPE FOR THE FUTURE · *by Dan Knapp*

Riders on the storm, Riders on the storm
Into this house we're born, Into this world we're thrown
Like a dog without a bone, An actor out on loan
Riders on the storm . . .

Lyrics by Jim Morrison. The beginning of the last number on the last album cut by The Doors. Super-rock group of four that had risen from $5-a-night gigs to $100,000-plus concert fees. Three of them, shy-as-a-rabbit lead guitarist Robbie Krieger; soft-spoken but gently ebullient drummer John Densmore, and lanky, angular, professional-looking keyboard artist Ray Manzarek, were there in the tiny Elektra Records studio. Listening to *L.A. Woman,* the album upon which "Riders on the Storm" was the last cut.

An air of coolly confident expectation suffused the room—the about-to-be-released album was solid, good, maybe even great. It might pull them back up to the pre-eminent position in rock from which they had slipped somewhat since their first two gold records, the ones that contained "Light My Fire" and "Strange Days."

The cut by itself exuded promise—powerful but subdued, as haunting as earlier Doors songs, but more subtle, more palatable musically. Like "Can't You Hear Me Knocking?" on the new Rolling Stones album, *Sticky Fingers,* with which *L.A. Woman* would be competing on the charts and at the cash register, it seemed to be evidence of what might be a new, more mature musical direction.

So even though talk of disbanding had swirled around and among them, even though Jagger-caliber lead Doors singer Jim Morrison had split for Paris indefinitely before the album had received its finishing touches, hope and nervous excitement was exploding among the three like a "smeared" note from an electric guitar held distortingly close to an amplifier.

Weeks before, at a sidewalk café on La Cienega Boulevard, he had seemed like anything but the Jekyllesque character the under and overground press had painted him to be. Excessive eating had run him to fat, but that only seemed to accentuate his good nature, his quiet, intelligent conversation.

Brown hair flowing down past his nape, his full beard almost messianic, he was as placid and peaceful in his own ultramasculine way as the gentle folk singer Joni Mitchell, who graced a nearby table. There was no evidence of the writhing, suggestive, sullen, often guttural, sometimes obscene, maybe drunk or drugged gate attraction. Only three or four too rapidly finished screwdrivers too quickly washed down with bot-tles of beer hinted at the demons that were said to drive him.

Later, in the small and cluttered studio below their office on Santa Monica Boulevard, where they had decided to cut *L.A. Woman,* even that much of the Jekyll side of Morrison's coin had vanished. "We had some disagreements," Morrison said, "with Paul Rothchild, who produced our other records, so we decided to handle this one ourselves, with Elektra distributing, of course.

"Bruce Botnick, who's been our engineer all along, will be listed as co-producer. We're recording and mixing here rather than at Elektra because we didn't want all the corporate nonsense getting in our way. We haven't been comfortable over there. Here, it's like being at home, and I think it shows in the music."

There's a killer on the road, His brain is
* squirmin' like a toad*
Take a long holiday, Let your children play
If you give this man a ride, sweet family
* will die*
Killer on the road . . .

Florida-born, once a student at UCLA's film school, Morrison was a word man as much as he was a performer. Enough of a poet-recorder-analyst and demiphilosopher for a major publishing house to print a collection of his poetry, *The Lords and the New Creatures.*

He lived in the heart of the city, albeit not in dollar hotels, but with scarcely more material possessions (despite the fact that he had to be a millionaire) than would fit into a suitcase or two.

In recent months, he had been sorting himself out, attempting to duck the demons for good, but it was almost impossible in L.A., the city he hated a lot of the time, but sang of in *L.A. Woman:* "If they say I never loved you, you'll know they are a liar." Part of the sorting was about what he was going to spend his creative energies on.

At one point he said, "The next album may just be the other guys, doin' their thing instrumentally. Heavy blues stuff." The element of blues is present in *L.A. Woman,* but Morrison's decision was, finally, to sing once again. And the singing, in turn crooningly soft and stridently fierce, was what brought to him fame and money and also the agonies attendant to both.

"All of it came down on Morrison," said one Elektra official. "The other guys in the group would just split after they'd finished a record and meditate, or play for themselves, compose. Morrison, even though the deal was that he got an equal share in the money, was the superstar. He had to bear the brunt of all the hatchet jobs, all the hype."

Part of it was brought on by Morrison himself. Molding himself in the early Elvis and Jagger tradition, his movements on stage, his suggestive and incendiary lyrics, moved audiences to frenzy. Recorded in The Doors' documentary, *Feast of Friends*, which Morrison and Manzarek (they met at UCLA's cinema school) had major hands in, even the male members of one concert audience hurled themselves through and over a phalanx of police onto the stage to be nearer their idol.

It got to a point where ministers and priests were describing Morrison's performances as "ritualistic" and "religious experiences" for young people.

As for the sexual under and overtones, "Sometimes they just happen," Morrison said, alluding to the momentum and mood of the music, among other, similarly strong, more palpable influences on his mind and body. "And sometimes," he added in characteristic honesty, "it's just part of the act."

Sentencing on a conviction for indecent exposure in Florida and a monumental $50,000 bail were still pending as he stopped to stroke a stray dog on Santa Monica Boulevard, outside The Doors' studio. Inside, the others were still perfecting mix. "Duke," "Mississippi," Morrison, and another friend were heading for a bar down the street. There, Morrison ignored the stares of a few longhair-haters, played pool, and drank more beer. At the Little Club, he switched to screwdrivers, and by the time the place closed, his head was dipping forward like that of a bull pierced by one too many pics.

One of the waitresses got in the car with him as all but "Duke" headed for his place. She was the latest in a long line of chickies who had a need to bask in his light, or just spend time in the same room with him. Far gone as he was, his mind was as coldly objective as ever. "Duke" had gone off in another car to see a dealer for some grass and something a little stronger.

"He gets his hands on any cocaine," Mor-

rison said, laughing, "that's the last we'll see 'Duke' for a few days."

The car pulled up at the Chateau Marmont, off Sunset. "I had to move here," Morrison said, "because the people at the Continental Hyatt House didn't like the idea of me swinging off the tenth floor balcony."

Inside, a quart of vodka materialized, and although Morrison passed it around, most of the clear liquid found its way into his stomach. "Duke" showed up with a lid of grass and that was smoked. The tall black drifter wearing the "Cocaine" T-shirt showed up again. Almost four in the morning now, five men and one woman in a room, an ancient movie unreeling on a TV set with the sound turned down, Mexican music blaring incongruously up from the border on a powerful radio.

"You shoulda seen him after you left," "Mississippi" said the next afternoon. "He did a Tarzan act. Got up on the roof and tried to swing into his bedroom window off the rain gutter. He lost his grip and fell two stories on his head. Only reason he didn't get killed, he bounced off the roof of the shed attached to the back of his cottage. It was outasight, man."

Girl you've gotta love your man. Girl you've gotta love your man, Take him by the hand, Make him understand. The world on you depends, Our life will never end, Gotta love your man . . .

He knew he had to leave, and he did, even before *L.A. Woman* was released and began climbing to a sales level that almost equaled the best of The Doors' nine gold albums. He left for Paris and Pamela, the girl he had not been able to live with or without for at least two years. They took an apartment together and he tried to kill his demons. He seemed to be succeeding.

"It was murder," Pamela told a friend. "It took him two months to shake off L.A. and all the madness." He was simply another writer in Paris, with nobody making demands on him. He was working on a screenplay and additional poetry. He was drinking much less. He was beginning to be happy, to find himself.

He was an immensely gifted young man working his way to broader horizons and peace, and he is dead long before his time.

MUSIC IS THE MESSAGE
Sounds

JULY 10, 1971   6p

MORRISON IS DEAD STORY

'Heart attack' on Continent rumoured

RUMOURS THAT Jim Morrison, lead singer with the Doors, had died over the weekend remained unconfirmed at press-time.

Morrison was reported by Continental sources to have died from a heart attack during a holiday around Europe. First reports which reached SOUNDS early on Monday morning suggested that Morrison, who has had severe attacks of illness over the past few years, had died in France.

Mystery

However, Clive Selwood — Doors' British representative — was unable to get any confirmation of the report. He told SOUNDS that although he had immediately telephoned Jim's manager in LA, plus Doors' offices in both London and Paris, nobody seemed to know what had definitely happened.

Plans

"Nobody has spoken to Jim since last week when he came to London for a few days before going on to Europe for a holiday," said Selwood. "He also had plans to go to Marrakesh and nobody is quite sure where he is at the moment. I don't really know what to say except that this certainly isn't the first time there have been death rumours about Jim Morrison — there were two during the Paul McCartney business between 1967 and 1969."

Doors' latest album — "La Woman" — is released in Britain this Friday.

ROGER CHAPMAN in the TALK-IN P.16

LOS ANGELES TIMES
ROCK STAR JIM MORRISON DIES · *by Tom Paegel*

Jim Morrison, twenty-seven, controversial lead singer for the popular Los Angeles-based rock group, "The Doors," died Saturday night of a heart ailment in Paris, a spokesman for the group said here Thursday.

The spokesman, Beverly Hills attorney Max Fink, said Morrison was in the French capital to write a screenplay for a movie after gathering material for several months touring North Africa.

He said Morrison was buried in a Paris cemetery Thursday, "because he really loved that city."

Morrison's was the third untimely death of a major American rock star in less than a year. Hard-rock guitarist and singer Jimi Hendrix, twenty-seven, died September 18, 1970, in London of an apparent drug overdose. Rock-blues singer Janis Joplin, twenty-seven, died October 4, 1970, in Hollywood under similar circumstances.

The Doors first gained prominence in 1967 with their wild and unpredictable performances at the Whiskey-a-Go-Go on the Sunset Strip and the release of their first album.

That album, a million-seller, contained the smash single "Light My Fire." The record established them immediately as one of the nation's top rock acts.

Ever since their first album, The Doors, and particularly Morrison, had been involved in controversy.

In the spring of 1969, Morrison was accused and found guilty of indecent exposure during a Miami concert.

The Doors, who had been in the midst of a slump, recently began to regain popularity with the release of their latest album, *L.A. Woman.*

It had been recently rumored that Morrison was leaving the group to pursue a career in motion picture production. He attended classes in cinematography at UCLA.

It was while he was at UCLA in 1966 that Morrison met organist Ray Manzarek, guitarist Robbie Krieger, and drummer John Densmore, and The Doors were organized.

Morrison, who sometimes called himself "The Lizard King," had a reputation as a heavy drinker. Last year, he was fined $600 for disturbing other passengers aboard an airlines flight. He was accused of violating several safety regulations and of excessive drinking and using loud and lewd language.

Morrison leaves his wife, Pamela, his parents, a brother and a sister.

NEWSWEEK: OBITUARY

Death Disclosed: *Jim Morrison, twenty-seven, rock superstar, the lead singer of The Doors. Though his manager fueled suspicion by keeping Morrison's death a secret for six days—until after his burial last week—there was no evidence of a drug connection as in last year's deaths of Janis Joplin and Jimi Hendrix, nor was Morrison's fifth-a-day booze habit officially a factor; police listed a heart attack as the cause after Morrison was found dead in the bathtub of his apartment in Paris, where he had been living as a writer in recent months. His trademarks in the rock culture included his arcane, keenly suggestive lyrics, sung in a throaty baritone, by turns sullen and frenzied. But with his skintight pants and lascivious style, the Florida-born admiral's son was best known as an erotic male performer in the line of succession that runs from Elvis Presley to Mick Jagger; Morrison once overdid it to the extent of being found guilty of indecent exposure at a rock concert in Miami.*

TIME: OBITUARY

Died. *Jim Morrison, twenty-seven, lead singer of The Doors and the third big rock star to die within ten months; in Paris. Although Morrison at times drank heavily, he did not have a reputation as a drug user, and he died of heart attack. The son of an admiral, Morrison got a master's degree from UCLA before beginning to intone his long, theatrical poems to dark, eerie, thundering rock. His orgiastic performances and his command, "Come on, baby, light my fire," turned on teenyboppers by the millions, but his mood was often more apocalyptic: "Cancel my subscription to the Resurrection!," he protested against the ravaging of the earth.*

BALTIMORE MORNING SUN

ELEGY IN A PARIS GRAVEYARD · by Mike Jahn

Morrison was good at slouching. He was the best sloucher I have ever seen. Hendrix used to slink down hallways, all colors and flash, but was politeness when he spoke; Joplin used to bounce around like a feather boa in the summer wind, ebullient and outgoing.

But Morrison could drape himself against the edge of a door in a way that defies description, looking half forlorn, half threatening, and a bit sad. No colors, just a kind of dark-leather-and-rough-fabric innocence. At age twenty-seven I should not have to write the obituaries of three of my contemporaries. There has got to be something wrong with this.

James Douglas Morrison, twenty-seven, lead singer of The Doors, died in Paris on July 3. He went there in pursuit of his girlfriend, and ended up making her the beneficiary of his considerable estate, according to a spokesman for Elektra Records. He was buried in that city, in the "Poet's Corner" of a cemetery.

Doors manager Bill Siddons said he died of natural causes, relating to a respiratory illness. This is, of course, how it had to be. Drugs were out of the question. Morrison was a drinker, to put it mildly. He lived like there would be no tomorrow; getting sick and not taking care of himself is entirely feasible for him. It had to be this way.

The possibility that he would pull a Hemingway—the shotgun to the head, or its modern equivalent, the needle—was always too easy to imagine. The drinking, the fascination with death in his music, all of it pointed right to the likelihood that he would exit like Hendrix or Joplin.

When Janis died, I remember a few people speculating about who would be next.

"Morrison," one writer said.

"Never," said a record company person. "That's too obvious."

Morrison even caused trouble after his death. I spent a few hours working on something for the obit, just finished, when I received a cable from Paris. It read: Unable to confirm Morrison death and am leery of it. Seems there was no hospital, a death certificate but no doctor's signature on it; he was buried before the news of his death was released; the cemetery was said to be a national monument, and it was unlikely that an American rock 'n' roll singer would be buried there; and finally, the official word came from his manager, not from the police, embassy officials, or anyone in authority. It took a few more hours to satisfy the newspaper for which I write that he was indeed under the ground. His father, Rear Admiral George Morrison, said he believed it was true and had checked with the naval attaché in Paris who confirmed it. Where could he be? Following the track of the great and not-so-great poets and novelists from bar to bar in Paris? No, he's gone, it seems, not like Hemingway or even like Jimi Hendrix, but like anyone else. Death and goodbye, that's it.

Steve Harris, an executive of Elektra Records and a friend of Morrison's, was adamant on one point. "I don't want people to think of it as being like Hendrix or Joplin," he said. "Because of the way they died (drugs), everybody thinks of their death and not of their work. When you say the name Hemingway, people think of what he did, not of how he died. That's the way I would like it to be with Jim. He just died."

BILL SIDDONS' STATEMENT (JULY 8, 1971)

"I have just returned from Paris, where I attended the funeral of Jim Morrison. Jim was buried in a simple ceremony, with only a few friends present.

"The initial news of his death and funeral was kept quiet because those of us who knew him intimately and loved him as a person wanted to avoid all the notoriety and circus-like atmosphere that surrounded the deaths of such other rock personalities as Janis Joplin and Jimi Hendrix.

"I can say that Jim died peacefully of natural causes—he had been in Paris since March with his wife, Pam. He had seen a doctor in Paris about a respiratory problem and had complained of this problem on Saturday—the day of his death.

"I hope that Jim is remembered not only as a rock singer and poet, but as a warm human being. He was the most warm, most human, most understanding person I've known. That wasn't always the Jim Morrison people read about—but it was the Jim Morrison I knew and his close friends will remember . . ."

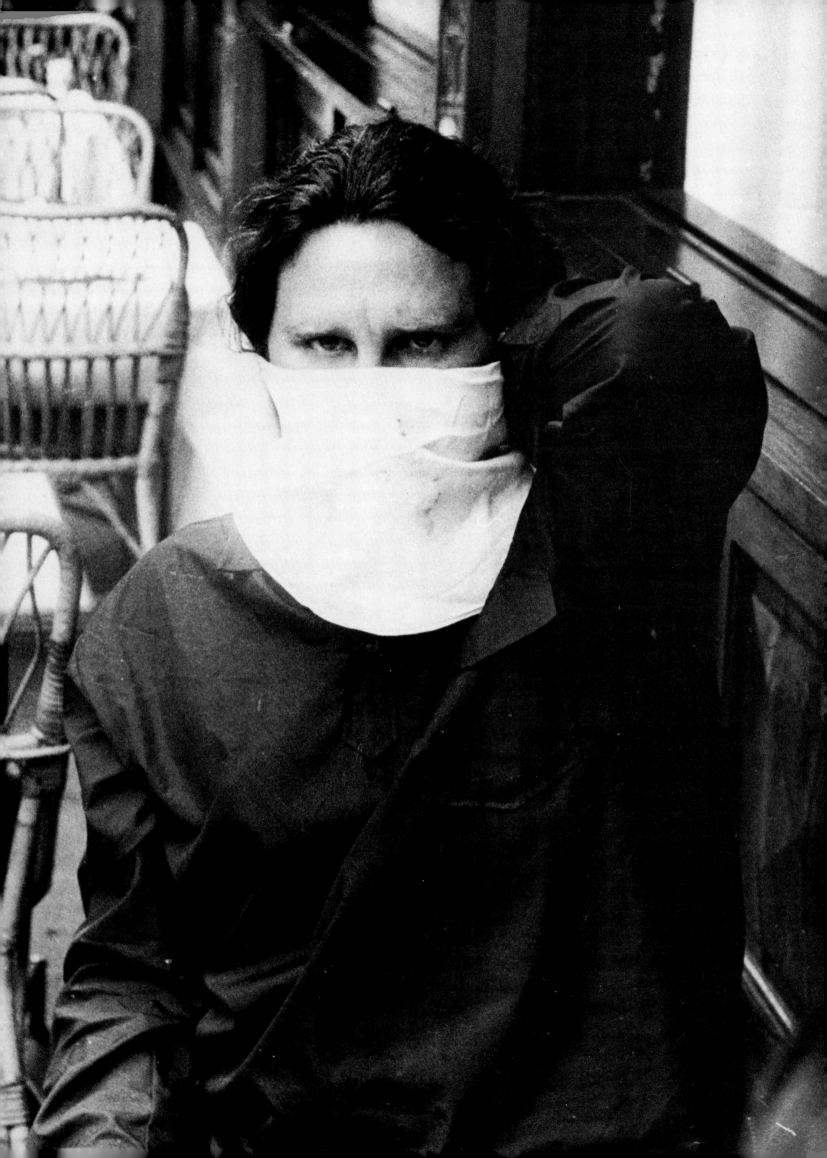

CRAWDADDY!
GOODBYES · by Tere Tereba

Every time the word of a new death in the family: rock star, friend, acquaintance reaches me, I suffer a bit of their personal agony, and die a little myself. In the case of Jim Morrison, it is more. Because Jim was not only a rock star, but also an acquaintance, and also a friend and more. The sadness of his death is overwhelming. And particularly because for the first time in a long time Jim was happy; happy in Paris, accepting himself and what he had become, what he was, and excited about the films, books, and poems he was to create. Two days before his death, a mutual friend spent some time with him in Paris, and sent this report back to me on how he was doing. I print it now as a tribute, to Jim Morrison, rock-star-idol who refused to stop growing as a human being, and as a poignant lesson in the nature of tragedy.—Editor.

On a warm Saturday night in June, I was sitting in the Café de Flore munching on a croissant, halfway listening to the conversation going on between the two young hustlers to my right when I heard a familiar voice call my name. I was surprised and delighted to see the girl with the streaming red hair was Pamela Morrison, followed by an entourage of notorious French hangers-on who quickly disappeared into the bowels of the Flore. She sat down, we exchanged greetings, and she said that she and her husband Jim had been living in Paris since March and were enjoying themselves very much. We made plans to meet the next day at her apartment.

The Morrison apartment is in the Marais on the Right Bank, one of the oldest and most beautiful sections of a city that is almost too beautiful and too grand. It is a few blocks from the Place Bastille, the Metro stops conveniently near, and there are open-air food stalls only a few paces from their door. The apartment situated in this very idyllic location is also most beautiful and grand. Jim said it was sublet and mumbled, "Can't get anything like this in L.A."

Jim looks better than he has in a while, certainly better than the Miami trial days. He claims to have quit drinking, has lost considerable weight, but the French food has taken its toll, and he still hasn't regained the licorice leather-legged look of the gaunt shadow that prowled L.A. as the "Lizard King." The days of his looking like and being the consummate rock idol are gone forever and he is the first to realize it. He sits in his spacious, elegant Paris apartment dressed in the most unlikely clothes for a rock star, a button-down-collar shirt with a V-necked sweater over it and chino trousers and desert boots. He is clean-shaven, and except for the long brown hair framing the soft, childlike face, he could be mistaken for a college senior from Middle America.

Jim proceeds to tell me how he loves Paris even though neither he nor Pamela can speak French, and that he is devoting his time to his serious pursuit of writing. Pam interjects that "he wants to be immortalized" and it does seem logical that a writer could achieve that state easier than a rock idol. Jim showed me a hand-written book that he has been working on in Paris and said it is nearly finished and will soon be ready for publication.

We decided that we wanted to go to dinner and I suggested La Coupole (the famous hangout of the Fitzgeralds and Hemingway, etc., during that long-gone literary heyday, which is now the gathering spot of the flotsam and jetsam of the international artistic society, with Jean-Paul Sartre the only remnant of its once glorious past). Jim and Pam had never been there. On the way over to the Left Bank, Jim muttered something about "how they threw the blueprint away after they made this city" and told me about the month they spent traveling in Morocco, where they were jived out of a hundred dollars immediately upon their arrival by an English-speaking Arab who said he would find them the "best and cheapest hash." Pam had her trusty Super-8 movie camera with her in Morocco, and they agreed they got some fabulous footage. Jim said that he was going to incorporate his North African adventures into something that he was planning to write. "One of the reasons I like Paris so much is that it's so centrally located, not very far from anywhere, not like L.A. We also went to Corsica, but it rained every day we were there except one and it got to be sorta boring. We are going to London for a few days next week, too."

La Coupole. La Coupole with the works of Picasso, Klee, Modigliani, and a hundred other famous artists adorning the pillars that hold up the ceiling. Art Deco heaven. Where Scott and Zelda once held court, Jim and Pam entered unrecognized. This is where pretender-princes, models, and photographers now reign, no attention here for a former rock-god, now apprentice writer, and his lady. But Jim feels the vibes of the Coupole's past and asks me more about its history. He decides, "It's really great here but I can't help thinking about how it reminds me of Ratner's in the Village."

Over dinner Jim speaks of how The Doors are trying to rehearse without him and that he has just been offered the lead in *Catch My Soul* with Tina Turner, Joe Frazier, and Melanie in L.A., and also a part with Robert Mitchum in the allegorical story of an Alaskan bear hunt in Norman Mailer's *Why Are We in Vietnam?* "I'm turning down the play, and

I don't think I'll do the movie because it will take up too much time when I could be writing. There's really an odd assortment of freaks here, it's amazing how crowded this place is. What I am going to do though is have a screening here for some people of my three films—first a documentary of a Doors concert made by some slick, professional film-makers, then another Doors documentary, a much more human, violent look made by the friends I work on films with, sort of how a similar event, a concert can be seen in different contrasting ways, and last I will show my film *Highway*. *S'il vous plait,* may we have some chocolate mousse for the ladies, please?"

We finally got back over to the apartment on the Right Bank after passing on the way a student riot in the Saint-Michel district. The riots go on every weekend like clockwork, and Jim and Pam said that they had been caught in the middle of one a few weeks before. They both agreed that the riot morbidly fascinated them, then decided against stopping in the riot area. I said goodbye after a most enjoyable day with them and said I was returning, happily, to the States in a few days. Jim was amazed that I was so glad to be going back, saying, "I won't be back in L.A. until September at the earliest." It looks like the "Lizard King" has reformed and is seriously attempting to be an American writer in Paris in the romantic tradition of the expatriates of the 20s. . . .

200 • PARIS • 1971

THE MIAMI HERALD
MORRISON AND MIAMI: BEGINNING OF THE END · *by Lawrence Mahoney*

Florida was as much of a home state as Jim Morrison could claim.

Born into a transient Navy family at Cape Canaveral, he lived as an infant at Pensacola. His family's military home of record was always listed at Clearwater. He returned to the state after years of absence to study at St. Petersburg Junior College. From there, he moved to Tallahassee and Florida State University before taking off for California and acid-rock stardom.

It was in Miami's Dinner Key Auditorium March 1, 1969, that James Douglas Morrison, in a drunken, frenzied performance before 12,000 young people, skyrocketed into the consciousnesses of American parents and other persons of other generations.

The Florida boy had come home. His homecoming performance stopped just short of a riot in the sweaty vastness of the bayside auditorium. In the following week, the matter escalated into a national clamor for Jim Morrison's scalp and into a Miami-born Teenage Crusade for Decency that half-filled the Orange Bowl.

Jim Morrison, the man, was obscured by his sudden fame among the young people of America. He was something of a media freak, and getting to the real man was always difficult during the years of fame and controversy.

Richard Goldstein, in his book *The Poetry of Rock,* said that Morrison "looks every inch the street punk gone to heaven and reincarnated as a choir boy." I believe that the enigma that was Jim Morrison can best be explained by looking at his early life in Florida, the state that wanted to send him to jail.

After the Dinner Key—Decency furor was in full cry, the "King of Orgasmic Rock" told a *Herald* writer in Los Angeles about his feelings for the state.

"I did live in Florida at a very formative period in my life," Morrison said. "I always loved the landscape most of all. I used to hitchhike from Tallahassee to Clearwater almost every weekend. I had some friends who lived near there. I got to know the landscape pretty well. To me, it was a strange, exotic, exciting place . . ."

Jim Morrison was the son of a Georgia-born Navy flier, an Annapolis graduate who, as a rear admiral, was commanding squadrons of aircraft carriers in the Pacific while his son was riding a show business, youth cult tidal wave.

Morrison and I were contemporaries at Florida State University in 1963 and 1964. Although we lived only a half-block apart in the student ghetto between the Capitol and the university gates, we never met. Morrison was studying drama, his best friends were art students, and he

spent much of his time around the musty stage of the Conradi Theater.

In 1969, at the peak of the national Decency Crusade, I went back to Tallahassee to try to find something about his pre-fame self. I found a lot of people who remembered Jim; many were more than a little proud that an FSU boy had made it so big so soon.

A girl named Bonnie Johnson told me most about Morrison, who spent five trimesters at FSU. She remembered, in particular, a costume party, a rarity in Tallahassee.

"He came as a harlequin, a court jester, I think. It was a very elaborate costume. There was a girl with him. Jim never said a word to anybody but the girl."

From FSU, Morrison went west for opportunity, enrolling at the University of California at Los Angeles. After receiving a B.A. degree in fine arts there, the admiral's son drifted to Santa Monica. He and three other young musicians founded The Doors at a sleazy club on Sunset Strip.

From there, with music and lyrics such as

"Light My Fire" and an erotic and often raw-sexual stage-style, he became Jim Morrison, rock star.

His fame had preceded Morrison to Miami when he came here in March of 1969 for his controversial performance.

It was a very heavy experience, complete with fights on stage, thousands of gate-crashers, a police tactical squad waiting in Bayfront Park for expected big trouble, which never came but which was near throughout the forty-five-minute performance.

Morrison came on stage drunk. He and his agents had been fighting with the Miami promoter Kenneth Collier about the gate and Morrison's cut of the ticket money. There was hardly room to breathe in the auditorium. Dozens of young men climbed to the rafters above the stage.

Warming up, Morrison shouted into the microphone: "Anybody here from Tallahassee?" There were whoops of affirmation.

"Well, I lived there once," he said. "I lived there until I got smart and went to California."

After that, things got rough. People were thrown from the stage.

"There are no laws! There are no rules! Grab your friend and love him!" Morrison screamed into the microphone. He said the forbidden words that would bring the law down hard on him and spawn the Decency Crusade. He unzipped his pants. The concert, if that is the correct term, was abruptly canceled by Collier and his lieutenants.

After Dinner Key, The Doors went into a decline. Their music got bad reviews.

Morrison turned more to his poetry. He had a great gift for words. He liked to quote William Blake. "If the doors of perception were cleansed, man would see things as they are, infinite."

His public appearances became rare. He performed at the Isle of Wight Rock Festival in 1970, and a writer who saw him backstage said, "He was like a ghost, man, walking around backstage with a can of beer in his hand."

Morrison, a royal figure of the drug-oriented counterculture, was not a man for narcotics himself. He drank heavily and dismissed LSD as "a new kind of wine."

So Jim Morrison, who called Florida his home, is dead and buried in France at twenty-seven. His life ended, the Paris police say, in a bathtub. The end of an American enigma.

RECORD WORLD
Jac Holzman Statement

Jac Holzman, President of Elektra, has issued the following statement:

Jim Morrison was an artist of stellar magnitude who was able to retain a bemused and detached perspective on his aura, his art, and his stardom. His exciting qualities as a performer and writer are universally known to the fascinated public for whom Jim was always news.

Jim admired those people who stretched their lives to the fullest, who lived out on the edge of experience. He possessed special insights into people, their lives and into the dark corners of human existence.

But beyond his public image, he was a friend to many, and those of us at Elektra who worked with him and The Doors so closely over the past five years will remember him as one of the kindest and most thoughtful people we have known.

He is already missed.

"In the beginning we were creating our music, ourselves, every night
. . . starting with a few outlines, maybe a few words for a song. Sometimes
we worked out in Venice, looking at the surf. We were together a lot and it
was good times for all of us. Acid, sun, friends, the ocean, and poetry and
music."

—JIM MORRISON (1943–1971)

ACKNOWLEDGMENTS

Special thanks go to: Ray and Dorothy Manzarek, Robbie and Lynn Krieger, and John Densmore. Also to The Doors' lawyers, Liz Weller and Frank Gruber, and The Doors' business manager, Jerry Swartz, for their expertise in creating and closing agreements with the photographers and writers whose works were required for this book.

My business managers, Floyd Peluce and Patty Wicker, have managed to keep my life in order, freeing me to concentrate on this book. Some associates are just more special than others. Thanks, Patty and Floyd, for being so special. Also thanks to Marty Fox for old and good reasons.

My family—my mother, father, brothers, and sisters—continued to support my work on this band I love so much. Alexandra Taylor-Abrams listened to the same stories over and over again, giving me her fresh reactions. She often inspired me to continue my effort to bring more Doors to more people.

My pal, Ben Edmonds, edited most of the writing and press and believed in the project from my initial conceptualization. He also made the material appear manageable (a good trick with sixty some pounds of content), and he continued delivering edited bundles to me long after I wished he would stop. I thank him now for his persistence and professionalism.

Paul Ferrara's photographs are among the finest I've seen of The Doors (and I've seen thousands). For his ready camera and excellent eye and, more recently, for his fairness . . . God bless Paul Ferrara.

An old and dear friend, Todd Gray, provided invaluable aid in reprocessing hundreds of old negatives and delivering, seemingly by magic, improved top-quality prints. Todd spent days matching up color prints with their original slides, and printed and reprinted photos with a Zen-like patience. He is also keeper of The Doors' photo library.

For his determination, I also thank Eric Rudolph, who hunted down writers and photographers missing in action.

Jacqui Nicholson and my friend Anne Barhydt handled the massive job of obtaining the releases for the articles I deemed necessary, a laborious task well performed.

Jim Landis, my editor, believed in the initial concept for this book and that The Doors merited such a special compilation and rich presentation. For his vision and for his patience, a special heartfelt thanks. For like reasons, I'm indebted to my literary agent, John Brockman.

For patience and beyond, I'd like to thank Deborah Karl.

John Schneider, Richie Wright, and Ilona, loyal Doors' fans, contributed their scrapbooks and trusted me with their precious materials. Salli Stevenson and Lizze James graciously struck fair bargains for their informative interviews with Jim Morrison so they could be used here. *Circus* magazine publisher Gerald Rothberg trusted me with his mint-condition *Circus/Hullabaloo* library and allowed us to pick and choose at will. Paul Williams of *Crawdaddy!* fame permitted us to reprint the marvelous early coverage that his publication gave The Doors.

There are many others to whom I am grateful: Phil Elwood, Digby Diehl, Blair Jackson, Kurt Loder, Connie Kramer and Dave DiMartino, Alan Lanier, Jim Ladd, Jim Carroll, Richard Meltzer, Henry Diltz, Michael Montford, Klaus Schnitzer, Jim Marshall, Tim Page, Keith Holzman, Mel Posner, George Steele, Bruce Botnick, Paul Rothchild, Iggy Pop, Hank Zevallos, Marsha Gleeman, Andy Kent, Barry Plummer, Harvey Kubernick, and Jerry Hopkins. Also: Joel Brodsky, David Sygal, Bob Matheau, David Fricke, Richard Hogan, Fred Powledge, Mark Norton, Harvey Zupke, Patrick Goldstein, Bill Siddons, Neal Preston, Michael McClure, and Richard Dewhurst.

And Dr. Murray Zucker and John Randell for reasons they are probably better aware of than I.

Lastly—and again—the Manzarek family, Ray, Dorothy, and Pablo, whose trust and faith in me has once more given me strength to see a project through. Whenever I wanted to give up, the thought of letting them down would keep me going. For sharing my excitement, trusting my vision implicitly, giving me their love unconditionally, and for so much more, I am eternally indebted.

And of course The Doors fans, whose existence is the cause of this book and the ultimate reason for its compilation and release.

—*Danny Sugerman*

PHOTO CREDITS · B/W

ABOUT THE AUTHOR:

Danny Sugerman, born in Los Angeles, California, in 1956, attended his first Doors concert when he was twelve. Suitably impressed, he was determined to get as close to the band as he could. He did, haunting their L.A. office and rehearsals until he was asked to answer the band's fan mail and maintain their official scrapbook. Jim Morrison encouraged his young employee to become a writer and this led to his career as a free-lance rock critic. At one point he was writing for more than a dozen periodicals here and abroad. He was then fourteen years old. He continued to work for The Doors, finally becoming their press agent and management associate.

Today Sugerman has close ties with the music business, running a management/public relations firm in L.A. He remains an intimate of the surviving Doors, particularly Ray Manzarek with whom he has worked since the disbanding of The Doors in the early seventies.

Sugerman is currently working on his third book and his first novel. It is a fictionalized autobiography of his rock and roll years.